AUDIT SAMPLING

AN INTRODUCTION

Fifth Edition

DAN M. GUY
Sante Fe, New Mexico

D. R. CARMICHAEL
Baruch College of the City University of New York

RAY WHITTINGTON
DePaul University

JOHN WILEY & SONS, INC.

ACQUISITIONS EDITOR	Mark Bonadeo
ASSISTANT EDITOR	Ed Brislin
MARKETING MANAGER	Clancy Marshall
SENIOR PRODUCTION EDITOR	Norine M. Pigliucci
SENIOR DESIGNER	Kevin Murphy
PRODUCTION MANAGEMENT SERVICES	Argosy

This book is printed on acid-free paper.

To order books please call 1(800) 225-5945

Library of Congress Cataloging in Publication Data

Guy, Dan M.
   Audit sampling: an introduction/Dan M. Guy, D.R. Carmichael, Ray Whittington. —5th ed.
     p.   cm.
   Includes bibliographical references and index.

   ISBN 0-471-37590-X (pbk.: alk. paper)
     1. Auditing—Statistical methods. 2. Sampling (Statistics) I. Carmichael, D.R.(Douglas R.) 1941-II. Whittington, Ray, 1948-III. Title.

   HF5667 G856 2001
   657'.45'015195—dc21   2001045653

10 9 8 7 6 5 4 3 2 1

ABOUT THE AUTHORS

Dan M. Guy, Ph.D., CPA, lives in Santa Fe, New Mexico, where he is a writer and consultant in litigation services. He completed an 18-year career with the AICPA in New York City in January 1998, where he had overall responsibility for, among other things, the Auditing Standards Board and the Accounting and Review Services Committee. Dr. Guy was Vice President, Auditing, at the AICPA from 1983 until 1996, when he became Vice President, Professional Standards and Services. Dr. Guy has written numerous books on auditing, sampling, and compilation and review. He has represented the profession on numerous occasions before Congress, various regulatory agencies, and at the international level. Prior to joining the AICPA, Dr. Guy was a professor of accounting at Texas Tech University and a visiting professor at the University of Texas at Austin. He was in public practice with KPMG and Arthur Andersen. In 1998, he received the John J. McCloy Award for outstanding contributions to audit quality in the U.S. The award was presented by the Public Oversight Board that monitors the SEC Practice Section of the AICPA's Division for CPA Firms.

D. R. Carmichael, Ph.D., CPA, CFE, is the Wollman Distinguished Professor of Accountancy in the Stan Ross Department of Accountancy of the Zicklin School of Business at Bernard M. Baruch College, City University of New York. Until 1983, he was the Vice President, Auditing, at the AICPA, where he directly participated in the development of accounting and auditing standards. Dr. Carmichael has written numerous books and articles on accounting and auditing. He acts as a consultant on accounting, auditing, and control matters to CPA firms, attorneys, government agencies, and financial institutions. Dr. Carmichael has served as a consultant to the AICPA, the Securities and Exchange Commission (SEC), the General Accounting Office (GAO), the Federal Deposit Insurance Corporation (FDIC), and other federal and state government agencies. He has also investigated numerous cases involving allegations of fraudulent financial reporting and provided expert witness testimony on those matters.

Ray Whittington, Ph.D., CPA, CIA, CMA, is the director of the School of Accountancy at DePaul University. From 1989 through 1991, Dr. Whittington was the director of auditing research for the AICPA, and he previously was on the audit staff of KPMG. He also was the director of the School of Accountancy at San Diego State University. Dr. Whittington is a member of the Auditing Standards Board and was a member of the Accounting and Review Services Committee of the AICPA, and has written numerous articles published in *Abacus, The Accounting Review, the Journal of Accounting Research, Auditing: A Journal of Practice and Theory, The CPA Journal, The Journal of Accountancy, Management Accounting, The Practical Accountant, Financial Executive,* and other professional journals. He is also a coauthor of several textbooks and professional publications.

PREFACE

The fifth edition of *Audit Sampling* has been updated to reflect the rapidly changing audit environment. It has been edited to reflect the guidance contained in the newly issued AICPA Auditing Guide, entitled *Audit Sampling*. It also contains increased coverage of the determination of materiality and tolerable misstatement necessary to the performance of substantive tests using audit sampling.

Like the previous edition, this text is written from the standpoint of external auditors. However, much of the discussion is equally useful to internal auditors. The material can be easily understood by the entry-level auditing student, is useful as a supplement to a basic auditing text, and can be covered in 10 to 15 classroom hours. It can also be used in an advanced or a graduate auditing course (i.e., a second auditing course).

The textbook is particularly appropriate for an advanced auditing course, where coverage is often given to topics such as SEC reporting, computer auditing, audit risk and materiality, and audit reporting. It is also beneficial to practitioners who need guidance on audit sampling for their firms. Much of the material was originally developed and extensively tested for continuing professional education (CPE) training courses. The material was written for individuals who have a basic knowledge of business statistics (i.e., one undergraduate course).

Educational materials about audit sampling vary in depth of coverage from two chapters in a basic auditing text to lengthy, technical books on the subject. The former treatment is designed to be a very brief introduction to the subject, and the latter is designed to be a technical reference. This book occupies a middle ground between the introduction and the highly technical presentation. It is designed to reduce the gap between textbooks that give only introductory coverage to audit sampling and the basic level of professional knowledge that is required to cope with audit sampling applications in practice.

ORGANIZATION OF THE TEXT

The organization of the book is as follows. Chapter 1 explains the essential aspects of audit sampling and presents an overview of statistical sampling in auditing. Throughout the book, sampling is planted firmly in an auditing context, not as an auxiliary subject. Chapter 2 describes sample selection for both statistical and nonstatistical sampling. Chapter 3, entitled "Attribute Sampling," discusses fixed-sample-size, sequential, and discovery sampling. The purpose of Chapter 4 is to review fundamental variable sampling concepts and to illustrate unstratified mean per unit, stratified mean per unit, and difference estimation; ratio estimation is also discussed briefly. Chapter 5 deals with variable sampling in an audit decision framework and explains the audit risk model. This chapter also contains a supplementary topic entitled "Using Audit Sampling for Compliance Auditing." Chapter 6 explains probability-proportional-to-size (or dollar unit) sampling. Finally, Chapter 7 concludes with a description of a formal approach to nonstatistical sampling. All chapters are preceded by learning objectives and are followed by a glossary of key terms used in the chapter. The appendices contain calculation worksheets, a list of equations, a copy of Statement on Auditing Standards (SAS) No. 39, *Auditing Sampling*, and the interpretations of SAS No. 39.

In teaching this material in an advanced undergraduate auditing course meeting 90 minutes per class, we have found the following schedule desirable.

Class Meeting No.	Topic	Chapter Assignment
1	Review of Audit Sampling	Chapters 1–2
2	Attribute Sampling Review	Chapter 3
3	Variable Sampling: Accounting Estimation	Chapter 4
4	Empress Cosmetique Case	—
5	Variable Sampling: Audit Hypothesis Testing	Chapter 5
6	Audit Hypothesis Problems and Cases	—
7	Using Audit Sampling for Compliance Auditing	Supplementary Topic
8	Probability-Proportional-to-Size Sampling	Chapter 6
9	Roll Tide Case	—
10	Nonstatistical Audit Sampling	Chapter 7

This schedule requires 15 classroom hours. A shorter version of the material can be presented by starting with Chapter 3, or by reducing coverage of Chapters 4, 5, and 6 to one period each.

PROBLEM MATERIALS

The end-of-chapter problem materials consist of review questions, multiple-choice questions from professional examinations, and cases. The review questions are closely related to the material in the chapter and provide a convenient means of determining whether students have grasped the major concepts and details contained in the chapter. The multiple-choice questions were selected from Certified Public Accountant and Certified Internal Auditor examinations. They are used with the permission of the American Institute of Certified Public Accountants and the Institute of Internal Auditors, Inc. Most chapters have case studies, fashioned after real-world auditing applications, to be solved. A number of new cases have been added to this fifth edition.

Spreadsheet data sets are available for certain cases on the textbook's Web site at www.wiley.com/college/guy. There cases are identified with the following logo:

SUPPLEMENTARY MATERIALS

An Instructor's Resource Manual presents answers to all end-of-chapter questions and cases, additional multiple-choice questions, and transparency masters. To assist in the presentation of the materials, we have prepared detailed Teaching Notes that are available to adopters of the textbook.

ACKNOWLEDGMENTS

Our appreciation and thanks are extended to the following individuals. Doyle Z. Williams (University of Arkansas) contributed the "Empress Cosmetique" case in Chapter 4. We benefited from the statistical sampling material and training course in audit sampling developed by Ernst & Young LLP, and we thank them for their willingness to share their materials and to contribute to educational institutions. We are also grateful to the American Institute of Certified Public Accountants and the Institute of Internal Auditors, Inc., for permission to use selected CPA and CIA Examination questions and problems.

Notwithstanding the involvement and contributions of others, responsibility for any deficiencies in this book remains solely our own.

Dan M. Guy
D. R. Carmichael
Ray Whittington

CONTENTS

4   USING VARIABLE SAMPLING FOR ACCOUNTING ESTIMATION   91

5 USING VARIABLE SAMPLING FOR AUDIT HYPOTHESIS TESTING   143

6 PROBABILITY-PROPORTIONAL-TO-SIZE SAMPLING   193

7   NONSTATISTICAL AUDIT SAMPLING

219

1 OVERVIEW OF AUDIT SAMPLING

LEARNING OBJECTIVES

After a careful study and discussion of this chapter, you will be able to:

1. Define audit sampling and distinguish statistical and nonstatistical sampling.
2. List and define three types of attribute sampling plans.
3. List and define three types of variable sampling plans.
4. Cite the important AICPA developments in statistical sampling.
5. Discuss the advantages and disadvantages of statistical sampling relative to nonstatistical sampling.
6. Define nonsampling and sampling error.
7. Identify areas of professional judgment inherent in using statistical sampling.
8. List and describe characteristics of application areas where statistical sampling may be efficient and effective.
9. Relate statistical sampling to generally accepted auditing standards.

Audit sampling, according to Statement on Auditing Standards (SAS) No. 39 (AU 350.01),[1] is defined as follows:

Audit sampling is the application of an audit procedure to less than 100 percent of the items within an account balance or class of transactions for the purpose of evaluating some characteristic of the balance or class.

Many auditing procedures are not susceptible to application by sampling. For example, inquiry, observation, most analytical procedures, and general procedures such as reading minutes and contracts and scanning accounting records for unusual items, do not involve sampling. Also, as is explained in more detail in Chapter 7, sampling is not involved when the auditor applies a procedure *only* to the significant items in an account balance.

NONSTATISTICAL AND STATISTICAL AUDIT SAMPLING

When an auditor uses audit sampling, the same basic requirements apply whether the approach to sampling is statistical or nonstatistical. SAS No. 39 (AU 350.03) states:

There are two general approaches to audit sampling: nonstatistical and statistical. Both approaches require that the auditor use professional judgment in planning, performing, and evaluating a sample.... The guidance in this section applies equally to nonstatistical and statistical sampling.

Historically, **nonstatistical sampling** was called judgment sampling, but as the previously quoted passage states, both approaches require judgment.

Whenever an auditor uses audit sampling (statistical or nonstatistical), the following basic requirements apply:

- *Planning.* When planning an audit sample, the auditor should consider the relationship of the sample to the relevant specific audit or internal control objective and consider certain other factors that influence sample size.
- *Selection.* Sample items should be selected so that the sample can be expected to be *representative* of the population. All items in the population should have an opportunity to be selected. (The methods that meet this requirement for representative selection are explained in Chapter 2.)
- *Evaluation.* The auditor should *project* the results of the sample to the items from which the sample was selected and consider the sampling risk. The auditor should also consider the qualitative aspects of the sample results.

These basic requirements are necessarily an integral part of statistical sampling. Their application to nonstatistical sampling is relatively recent in auditing practice.

---

[1]SAS No. 39, *Auditing Sampling,* is reproduced in Appendix C.

	Example Audit Application	Sample Selection	Sample Evaluations
Representative (nonstatistical) sample	Fifty sales invoices processed during year	Random or haphazard	Judgmental
Statistical sample	Sixty sales invoices processed during first 10 months of year	Random	Mathematical

FIGURE 1.1   **Distinction Between Types of Audit Sampling**

The rationale of SAS No. 39 for imposing these basic requirements on all audit samples is that there is an underlying logic for sampling that holds true whether the sampling approach is statistical or nonstatistical.

The essential features of **statistical sampling** are:

- The sample items should have a known probability of selection—for example, random selection.
- The sample results should be evaluated mathematically—that is, in accordance with probability theory.

Just because one of these requirements is met does not mean that the application is statistical. For example, practitioners and others will sometimes state that they are using statistical sampling solely because a random number method is employed to select the sample. However, this is not statistical sampling; no attempt has been made to evaluate mathematically sample findings (requirement no. 2).

A **block sample** is a good illustration of a selection method that generally is unacceptable for audit sampling. A block sample includes all items in a selected time period. An example is the selection by the auditor of all checks issued for the months of March and June to test cash disbursements for the year. This sample includes only two sample items out of 12 because the sampling unit is a month rather than an individual transaction. A sample with so few items is generally not adequate to reach a reasonable audit conclusion about cash disbursements for the entire year.

Figure 1.1 illustrates the two types of audit sampling: nonstatistical and statistical. It also shows that representative sampling, whereby the sample items are randomly or haphazardly[2] selected from the population, is not equivalent to statistical sampling if the sample is not mathematically evaluated. Sampling concepts such as representative sampling are sometimes confused with statistical sampling. Figure 1.1 clearly shows that a statistical sample has to be *selected randomly* and *evaluated mathematically.* Chapter 7 describes the use of nonstatistical sampling in auditing.

---

[2]Haphazard selection is explained in Chapter 2. Essentially, it means selecting items without conscious bias, but not using a formal random-based selection method.

TYPES OF STATISTICAL SAMPLING PLANS

There are three broad categories of statistical sampling: attribute, variable, and probability-proportional-to-size sampling. Attribute sampling is used primarily in tests of controls. In contrast, variable sampling and probability-proportional-to-size sampling are most frequently used to test the monetary value of account balances.

Attribute Sampling Plans

"Attribute sampling" is used in practice to refer to three different sampling plans that are generally used by auditors to test the operating effectiveness of controls by estimating the rate of deviation from performance. These sampling plans include:

1. **Attribute sampling** (or fixed-sample-size attribute sampling) is a sampling plan that is used to estimate the rate (percentage) of occurrence of a specific quality (attribute) in a population. It answers the question, "How many?" An attribute sampling plan might be used to estimate the number of invoices paid twice. Attribute sampling would help the auditor answer the question, "How often?" The auditor using attribute sampling might conclude: "There is only a 5 percent risk that the true rate of double payment in the population exceeds 6 percent."

2. **Sequential (stop-or-go) sampling** is a sampling plan that helps prevent oversampling (for attributes) by permitting the auditor to halt an audit test at the earliest possible moment. It is used when the auditor believes that relatively few deviations will be found in the sampling population.

3. **Discovery sampling** is a sampling plan that is appropriate when the expected occurrence rate is extremely low (near zero). Discovery sampling is used when the auditor desires a specified chance of observing at least one example of an occurrence (e.g., payroll padding) if the true proportion of occurrences is greater than specified. In a discovery sampling plan the auditor might conclude: "Since I did not observe an occurrence in the sample, there is only a 5 percent risk that payroll padding exists in the population at a rate greater than 2 percent."

Variable Sampling Plans

In contrast to attribute sampling, **variable sampling** (or quantitative sampling) is employed when the auditor wishes to estimate (or project) a quantity. For example, if students wanted to employ a sample to estimate the total dollar amount of money in their auditing class for a given day, a variable sampling plan could be used. On the other hand, if students wished to estimate the percentage of people in their auditing class 6-feet tall or over, the appropriate approach would be an attribute sampling plan. The auditor typically uses variable sampling in performing **substantive tests** to estimate the monetary misstatement in an account balance.

Like the term "attribute sampling," "variable sampling" is used in practice to refer to a number of different types of quantitative sampling plans. The primary plans discussed in this book are described below.

1. **Unstratified mean-per-unit** is a statistical plan whereby a sample mean is calculated and projected as an estimated total. For example, if students use unstratified mean-per-unit to estimate the dollar amount of money in their auditing class, the results might be: Ten students out of a class of 78 students are selected. They have a total of $150 that yields a mean of $15 per student. The mean of $15 times 78 produces an estimated total for the class of $1,170.

2. **Stratified mean-per-unit** is a statistical plan in which the population is divided into different groups (strata) and samples are drawn from the various groups. Stratified mean-per-unit sampling is used to produce a smaller (more efficient) overall sample size relative to unstratified mean-per-unit. In the auditing classroom illustration, to apply stratified mean-per-unit the auditing students might be divided into two groups—students who work part-time and students who are not presently employed.

3. **Difference estimation** is a statistical plan used to estimate the total difference between audited values and book (unaudited) values based on differences obtained from sample observations. The estimated population difference (sample mean difference times population size) is added or subtracted from the total book value to produce an estimate of the true population total. Difference estimation cannot be applied to the auditing classroom illustration. To apply difference estimation, a book value and an audit value must exist for each student. This is discussed in detail in Chapter 4, and a similar estimation method—ratio estimation—is introduced and discussed briefly.

In addition to the three variable sampling plans defined above, probability-proportional-to-size sampling is discussed in Chapter 6. It is a hybrid plan combining characteristics of attribute and variable sampling. Unstratified mean-per-unit, stratified mean-per-unit, and difference estimation sampling are often distinguished from probability-proportional-to-size sampling by calling them "classical variable sampling plans." They are called classical plans because they are based on normal distribution theory.

HISTORICAL DEVELOPMENTS OF STATISTICAL SAMPLING IN AUDITING

In 1962, the first official American Institute of Certified Public Accountants (AICPA) literature on statistical sampling was published (*Journal of Accountancy,* February 1962, pp. 60–62) by the Subcommittee on Statistical Sampling, a subcommittee of the Auditing Standards Board that no longer exists. The subcommittee concluded that statistical sampling is permitted under generally accepted auditing standards. Also, the report stressed that statistical sampling does not eliminate judgment. Some practitioners are wary about using statistical sampling in auditing because of an erroneous belief that its use encroaches on professional judgment. In this book, we demonstrate that statistical sampling actually sharpens the professional judgment of auditors and enhances understanding of the audit process.

"Statements on Auditing Procedure," SAP No. 33, published in 1963, indicated that a practitioner might consider using statistical sampling in certain circumstances.[3] However, the circumstances were not defined.

In determining the *extent* of a particular audit test and the method of selecting items to be examined, the auditor *might* consider using statistical sampling techniques which have been found to be advantageous in certain instances. The use of statistical sampling *does not reduce* the use of judgment by the auditor but provides certain statistical measurements as to the results of audit tests, which measurements may not otherwise be available (emphasis supplied).[4]

SAP No. 36, "Revision of Extensions of Auditing Procedures Relating to Inventories," published in 1966, indicates that clients are not required to take a 100 percent inventory if they use a valid and reliable statistical model.[5] The auditor, of course, has a responsibility to review the application to ascertain if it is, in fact, valid and reliable. The ramifications of SAP No. 36 are discussed in Chapter 4 in connection with the Empress Cosmetique case.

From 1967 to 1974, the AICPA published the professional educational series entitled *An Auditor's Approach to Statistical Sampling.* The following volumes were published.[6]

Volume 1   *An Introduction to Statistical Concepts and Estimation of Dollar Values* (1967)

Volume 2   *Sampling for Attributes: Estimation and Discovery* (1974)

Volume 3   *Stratified Random Sampling* (1968)

Volume 5   *Ratio and Difference Estimation* (1972)

Volume 6   *Field Manual for Statistical Sampling* (1974)

In 1972, SAP No. 54, "The Auditor's Study and Evaluation of Accounting Control," was issued with an appendix on the use of statistical sampling in audit tests. The appendix explained the relationship of statistical terms to established auditing concepts such as materiality and risk, and provided guidance on the incorporation of statistical sampling in planning and applying audit procedures. Although use of statistical sampling was clearly permitted, it was not required.

---

[3]Statements on auditing procedure are now referred to as statements on auditing standards (SAS).

[4]AICPA Professional Standards, Volume 1 (Chicago: Commerce Clearing House, Inc., 1978), AU 330.14. (This section has been superseded but is quoted because of its historical interest.)

[5]AU 331.11. SAP No. 36 also was codified in SAS No. 1.

[6]Volumes 2 and 4 in the series are combined in the updated revision of Volume 2.

In 1975, the AICPA published Auditing Research Monograph No. 2, *Behavior of Major Statistical Estimators in Sampling Accounting Populations,* by John Neter and James K. Loebbecke. Auditing Research Monograph No. 2 discusses variable sampling as applied to accounting populations. It contains several policy overtones that are important to students of auditing and practitioners.

Statistical Auditing, an AICPA practitioner's handbook, was published in 1978. It was designed to extend the series *An Auditor's Approach to Statistical Sampling* and to serve as a comprehensive reference book for practitioners. The professional education series introduces basic statistical concepts, and *Statistical Auditing* helps practicing accountants and auditors implement statistical sampling in audit engagements.

In 1981, SAS No. 39 (AU 350), "Audit Sampling," moved statistical sampling from the subordinate status of an appendix to the body of a statement, and equated statistical and nonstatistical sampling in a common approach. Basically, the SAS says that there is an underlying rationale for sampling in auditing that is applicable whether the sampling is statistical or nonstatistical.[7]

In 1983, the AICPA issued an Auditing Guide titled *Audit Sampling* to provide auditors with additional guidance in complying with the requirements of SAS No. 39. In 1997 and 2001, the guide was revised.

Several Statements on Auditing Standards issued after SAS No. 39 also have implications for audit sampling. SAS No. 47 (AU 312), "Materiality and Audit Risk," which was issued in 1983, provides guidance for the auditor's consideration of audit risk and materiality when planning and performing a financial statement audit. Audit risk and materiality are important to determining the extent of auditing procedures, including those that involve the use of audit sampling. In addition, SAS No. 55 (AU 319), "Consideration of the Internal Control in a Financial Statement Audit," was issued in 1988 and amended by SAS No. 78 in 1995 and by SAS No. 94 in 2001. This statement, and a related Audit and Accounting Guide of the same title, provide guidance for the auditor in obtaining an understanding of an entity's internal control and assessing control risk. These two pronouncements describe the manner in which the auditor designs, performs, and evaluates **tests of controls,** including those that involve audit sampling.

WHAT ARE THE ADVANTAGES OF STATISTICAL SAMPLING?[8]

Statistical sampling:

1. Allows auditors to calculate sample reliability and the risk of reliance on the sample. (Conceptually, this is the *sole* distinction between statistical sampling and nonstatistical sampling.)

---

[7]See Appendix C.

[8]It should be noted that many of these advantages are shared by structured nonstatistical sampling plans as described in Chapter 7.

2. Permits auditors to optimize the sample size given the mathematically measured risk they are willing to accept. In this way, both overauditing and underauditing can be avoided.

3. Enables auditors to make objective statements about the sampled population on the basis of the sample. In other words, the sample findings can be projected to the population, and sampling risk can be explicitly considered by using accepted mathematical calculations.

Auditors who have used statistical sampling report the following benefits:

- They tend to develop better working paper documentation.
- They believe that their audit work is more objective and defensible.
- They save time by eliminating tests of controls that have no influence on substantive audit procedures.
- They are more capable of rendering suggestions to clients.
- They have greater confidence about the audit opinion.

Many audit tests do not involve sampling, such as footing of journals, scanning records, searching for unusual relationships, and inquiring of client personnel. Also, in some instances, the cost of performing statistical sampling, including the cost of training the professional staff, may exceed the benefits derived. An auditor should remember that statistical sampling is a tool that is useful in some but not all situations. Whether statistical sampling should be used is a question that depends primarily on audit judgment and audit objectives, giving consideration to differential costs and cost trade-offs (i.e., opportunities for cost reduction in other aspects of the audit).

THE RISK OF SAMPLING

Traditionally, the basis for determining the extent of testing has been the degree of reliability (assurance) that the auditor requires about the financial information recorded in the accounts. The auditor always has some idea, on a judgment basis, of what this degree of assurance is. In statistical sampling applications, the auditor must use judgment in selecting a desired level of reliability, but he or she should be able to mathematically determine the *extent of testing* that is necessary to achieve the desired reliability. Figure 1.2 indicates the degree of reliability that can normally be achieved in terms of the extent of testing. The Y axis reflects the reliability achieved; the X axis reflects the extent of testing (sample size).

Complete confidence can only be approached with a complete examination, but the curve shows that a small test can achieve a relatively high degree of reliability and that, beyond a certain point, additional testing improves reliability by only a very small amount. This fact is the basic justification for testing in audits. The risk of sampling is the complement of reliability; that is, one minus reliability is risk. The auditor, knowing that some risk is always involved when a test instead of a com-

FIGURE 1.2   Relationship Between Extent of Testing and Reliability

plete examination is made, has always consciously or unconsciously been aware of the characteristics of this curve. With the use of statistical sampling techniques the auditor can, in a given situation, mathematically determine the extent of testing necessary to provide a desired degree of reliability. Conversely, the auditor, by using statistical sampling, can determine the degree of risk associated with the extent of testing. The risk of sampling also is present for a nonstatistical sample, and the auditor has to hold this risk to a relatively low level. However, a nonstatistical sample does not permit objective measurement of sampling risk.

WHAT ARE SAMPLING AND NONSAMPLING ERRORS?

Two concepts that are very important in any audit sampling application are sampling error and nonsampling error. A **sampling error** occurs when the auditor makes an erroneous conclusion because he or she did not audit the complete population. The risk of sampling creates the possibility of sampling error. If all items rather than a sample were examined, there would be no sampling error.

There is also nonsampling risk that is caused by mistakes in auditor judgment. A **nonsampling error** occurs when the auditor makes an erroneous conclusion for any reason not related to the size of the sample. Examples of nonsampling error are as follows:

- Selection from a population that is not appropriate for the objective of the test.
- Failure to adequately define deviations or misstatements, causing an auditor not to recognize one that exists in the sample.
- Failure to identify a deviation or misstatement that has been adequately defined.
- Failure to draw a **random sample** (or a sample that can be expected to be **representative**).
- Failure to evaluate findings properly.

A sampling error occurs when a sample indicates characteristics that are not the actual (true) characteristics of the population. Conceptually, sampling error represents the difference between findings based on sample results versus findings based on examination of all the population items. Nonsampling errors are human errors and can be reduced, deleted, or prevented. Sampling errors are due entirely to chance. They are inherent in any sampling process, statistical or otherwise. Sampling error can be precisely measured and, hence, controlled when statistical sampling is used.

The risk of nonsampling errors can be reduced to a very low level by proper engagement planning, supervision, and review. Control of sampling error is discussed in detail later. The control of sampling error is accomplished in statistical applications through establishing appropriate relationships among sample size, characteristics of the population being sampled, and the degree of reliance being placed on nonsampling audit procedures.

In addition to the types of nonsampling errors that arise in using statistical sampling listed earlier, there are other nonsampling errors that are inherent in the auditing process. A selected audit procedure may not be effective in identifying an internal control deviation or a monetary misstatement. For example, an auditor may examine vouchers to determine if they were properly approved before cash was disbursed. If the only evidence of approval is the controller's signature on a voucher, there is a risk that the disbursement was not approved, even though the signature appears. Reliance on the controller's signature entails additional risk that cannot be statistically controlled. Consequently, audit risk can never be reduced below nonsampling risk, even if 100 percent of the items are audited.

In auditing, sampling risk and nonsampling risk have been defined in terms related to audit objectives and conclusions. According to SAS No. 39 (AU 350.10 and .11):

> *Sampling risk* arises from the possibility that, when a test of controls or a substantive test is restricted to a sample, the auditor's conclusions may be different from the conclusions he or she would reach if the test were applied in the same way to all items in the account balance or class of transactions.

> *Nonsampling risk* includes all aspects of audit risk that are not due to sampling. An auditor may apply a procedure to all transactions or balances and still fail to detect a material misstatement or a material internal control weakness. Nonsampling risk includes the possibility of selecting audit procedures that are not appropriate to achieve the specific objective.

The specific types of sampling risk associated with tests of controls and substantive tests are explained in Chapters 3 and 4.

STATISTICAL SAMPLING AND PROFESSIONAL JUDGMENT

Statistical sampling does not eliminate professional judgment. For example, the auditor has to decide whether to use nonstatistical or statistical sampling (assuming, of course, that he or she elects to sample in the first place). There are also areas in a statistical sampling plan where judgment must be exercised and quantified. Some of them are:

Population Definition. The auditor must decide what population is appropriate for the particular audit objective. For example, if the auditor is testing for the completeness of the items in an account, the appropriate population would not be the population of recorded items.

Population Characteristics. The auditor must describe the population in terms of its size and the characteristics of audit significance to the auditor.

Deviation or Misstatement Definition. For tests of controls, the auditor must define what constitutes a deviation from performance of the control. A misstatement of the account being audited must be specifically defined when the auditor is performing a substantive test.

Sampling Plan. The auditor must determine the type of sampling plan to be used (e.g., an attribute sampling plan or a variable sampling plan).

Selection Method. The auditor must decide which sampling selection process is to be used (e.g., computer generator, random number table selection, or systematic selection).

Evaluation of Results. Statistical sampling findings must be evaluated both *quantitatively* and *qualitatively*. The primary input into the auditor's qualitative evaluation is his or her professional judgment and experience, not statistical sampling.

RELATIONSHIP OF STATISTICAL SAMPLING TO AUDITING STANDARDS

The 10 generally accepted auditing standards are authoritative guides for measuring the quality of audit performance. The first sentence in the scope paragraph of the unqualified audit report indicates that the audit was performed in accordance with generally accepted auditing standards. In this section we view the 10 standards in a statistical sampling context.

General Standards

1. The audit is to be performed by a person or persons having adequate technical training and proficiency as an auditor.
2. In all matters relating to the assignment, an independence in mental attitude is to be maintained by the auditor or auditors.
3. Due professional care is to be exercised in the planning and performance of the audit and the preparation of the report.

Standards of Field Work

1. The work is to be adequately planned, and assistants, if any, are to be properly supervised.
2. A sufficient understanding of internal control is to be obtained to plan the audit and to determine the nature, timing, and extent of tests to be performed.
3. Sufficient competent evidential matter is to be obtained through inspection, observation, inquiries, and confirmations to afford a reasonable basis for an opinion regarding the financial statements under audit.

Standards of Reporting

1. The report shall state whether the financial statements are presented in accordance with generally accepted accounting principles.
2. The report shall identify those circumstances in which such principles have not been consistently observed in the current period in relation to the preceding period.
3. Informative disclosures in the financial statements are to be regarded as reasonably adequate unless otherwise stated in the report.
4. The report shall contain either an expression of opinion regarding the financial statements, taken as a whole, or an assertion to the effect that an opinion cannot be expressed. When an overall opinion cannot be expressed, the reasons therefore should be stated. In all cases where an auditor's name is associated with financial statements, the report should contain a clear-cut indication of the character of the auditor's work, if any, and the degree of responsibility the auditor is taking.

In viewing the 10 standards from a statistical sampling perspective, general standard no. 1 and all three field work standards take on special meaning. For instance, auditors, if they elect to use statistical sampling, should have adequate knowledge and training in the sampling plan they use (e.g., attribute or variable). The practicing CPA also should be given on-the-job training in addition to formal training in the statistical sampling area. The CPA should read and study current sampling literature to understand the limitations and pitfalls of statistical sampling. It is also desirable that the partner reviewing an application of statistical sampling be knowledgeable and proficient in the area of attribute or variable sampling.

The field work auditing standards have new meaning when they are considered in a statistical sampling context. Figure 1.3 depicts the special meaning the field work standards have when statistical sampling is applied to important areas in an audit engagement.

Standards of Field Work	Audit Tasks	Statistical Sampling Tasks
The work should be adequately planned, and assistants, if any, should be properly supervised.	Plan work. Supervise assistants. Review work.	Define population and deviations or misstatements. Specify decision criteria in terms of risk and precision (tolerable rate or tolerable misstatement). Evaluate results both quantitatively and qualitatively.
A sufficient understanding of internal control is to be obtained to plan the audit and to determine the nature, timing, and extent of tests to be performed.	Obtain an understanding of internal control sufficient to plan the audit. Document the internal control system. Perform detailed tests of controls. Determine extent of substantive tests based on assessed level of control risk.	Determine the attributes to be tested to support the auditor's planned assessed level of control risk. Select appropriate attribute sampling plan. Vary substantive sample size directly with the assessed level of control risk.
Sufficient competent evidential matter should be obtained through inspection, observation, inquiries, and confirmations to afford a reasonable basis for an opinion regarding the financial statements under audit.	Obtain evidential matter by substantive tests. Evidence should be: 1. Relevant 2. Sufficient 3. Competent Evidence must establish a reasonable basis for opinion.	Sample for variables. Specify risk level and precision limits (tolerable misstatement). Determine extent of audit tests. Evaluate sample results mathematically.

FIGURE 1.3   Relationship of Statistical Sampling to Field Work Auditing Standards

CHAPTER ORGANIZATION

The order of presentation of the topics discussed in the chapters that follow is:

Each chapter is preceded by learning objectives to aid in identifying the important material in the chapter and facilitate studying for examinations. Each chapter is also followed by a glossary of new terms, review questions, and case problems (for selected chapters).

GLOSSARY

Attribute sampling   A statistical plan used to statistically estimate the actual and the upper precision limit of the occurrence rate of the attribute.

Audit sampling   The application of an audit procedure to less than 100 percent of the items within an account balance or class of transactions for the purpose of evaluating some characteristic of the balance or class.

Block sample   A sample including all items in a selected time period, numerical sequence, or alphabetical sequence: for example, selecting 50 checks in sequence for testing or testing one entire week. (Unless a large number of blocks are selected, it is not acceptable to project the results of a block sample to the entire population.)

Difference estimation   A statistical plan used to estimate the total difference between audited and book values based on differences obtained from sample observations. The estimated population difference $\hat{D}$ is added/subtracted to the footed book value to yield a point estimate of the population total.

Discovery sampling   A special case of attribute sampling that is used to determine a specified probability of finding at least one example of an occurrence (attribute) in a population. Also referred to as *exploratory sampling*.

Nonsampling error   An error not related to the size of the sample. For example, nonsampling errors include failing to recognize a misstatement in an item tested and performing an inappropriate audit test.

Nonstatistical sample   A sampling plan that is evaluated judgmentally rather than mathematically.

Random sample   A sample that can be evaluated statistically because each item in the population has a known probability of being selected.

Representative sample   An audit sample that is selected either randomly or by the haphazard selection method (see Chapter 2).

Sampling error   The chance that a representative sample will lead to the wrong conclusion or an inaccurate projection. Sampling error is inherent in any sampling process, nonstatistical or statistical, where less than 100 percent of the items are examined. Sampling error results when a nonrepresentative sample characteristic is extrapolated to a population.

Sequential sampling   A type of attribute sampling that permits sampling to halt if a certain number (including zero) of occurrences are observed. The sampling units are examined in groups until the cumulative evidence is sufficient to achieve a defined precision and reliability. Also referred to as *stop-or-go sampling*.

Statistical sampling   A sampling plan applied in such a manner that the laws of probability can be used to make statements about a population. Statistical sampling is the whole process by which the size of a sample is determined, items are selected and examined, and results are evaluated.

Stratified mean-per-unit   A statistical plan in which the population is divided into strata and samples are drawn from the various strata. Stratification, properly applied, reduces the sample size relative to unstratified mean-per-unit.

Substantive tests   Tests of details of account balances and analytical procedures. Substantive tests are sometimes referred to as "test of bona fides" and "year-end tests." Audit sampling may be used for substantive tests of details to estimate the amount of misstatement of the account balance.

Tests of controls   Tests that are used to determine the design and operating effectiveness of controls.

Unstratified mean-per-unit   A statistical plan whereby a sample mean is calculated and projected as an estimated total. Also referred to as *simple extension*. Unstratified simple extension tends to produce inefficient sample sizes relative to stratified simple extension.

Variable sampling   A statistical plan used to project a quantitative characteristic, such as a dollar amount. Variable sampling includes unstratified mean-per-unit, stratified mean-per-unit, and difference estimation.

REVIEW QUESTIONS

1-1. Indicate whether each of the following is true (T) or false (F).

    a. If an auditor selects a sample randomly, he or she is using statistical sampling.

    b. Two broad classes of statistical sampling plans are attribute sampling and discovery sampling.

    c. SASs require the use of statistical sampling in selected situations.

    d. Nonstatistical sampling permits objective determination of sample risk.

     e. The failure to define the nature of an audit error is an example of a sampling error.

     f. Statistical sampling requires that selected audit judgments be quantified but not eliminated.

     g. If an auditor examines 100 percent of the items in a population, uncertainty is not eliminated.

1-2. Two requirements must be met for a sampling application to qualify as a statistical sample. What are these two requirements?

1-3. List three types of attribute sampling plans.

1-4. List three types of variable sampling plans.

1-5. List four audit areas where attribute sampling might be used for tests of controls.

1-6. List four areas where variable sampling might be used for substantive testing.

1-7. How can nonsampling error be controlled?

1-8. Cite four advantages of statistical sampling relative to nonstatistical sampling.

1-9. Statistical sampling does not eliminate professional judgment. Identify four areas involving professional judgment that are inherent in a statistical sampling application.

1-10. "Audit risk" cannot be eliminated even if the total population is audited. Why?

1-11. Which of the 10 generally accepted auditing standards are primarily affected by the use of statistical sampling in an audit engagement?

MULTIPLE-CHOICE QUESTIONS FROM PROFESSIONAL EXAMINATIONS

1-12. Which of the following statistical sampling plans does *not* use a fixed sample size for tests of controls?

     a. Mean-per-unit sampling.

     b. Sequential sampling.

     c. Probability-proportional-to-size sampling.

     d. Variable sampling.

1-13. Auditors who prefer statistical sampling to nonstatistical sampling may do so because statistical sampling helps the auditor:

     a. Measure the sufficiency of the evidential matter obtained.

     b. Eliminate subjectivity in the evaluation of sampling results.

     c. Reduce the level of tolerable misstatement to a relatively low amount.

     d. Minimize the failure to detect a material misstatement due to nonsampling risk.

1-14. Which of the following is an element of sampling risk?

    a. Choosing an audit procedure that is inconsistent with the audit objective.

    b. Choosing a sample size that is too small to achieve the sampling objective.

    c. Failing to detect an error on a document that has been inspected by the auditor.

    d. Failing to perform audit procedures that are required by the sampling plan.

1-15. The primary reason for an auditor to use statistical sampling is to:

    a. Obtain a smaller sample than would be required by nonstatistical sampling techniques.

    b. Obtain a sample more representative of the population than would be obtained by nonstatistical sampling techniques.

    c. Allow the auditor to quantify and control the risk of making an incorrect decision based on sample evidence.

    d. Meet requirements of professional standards.

1-16. There are many kinds of statistical estimates that an auditor may find useful, but basically every accounting estimate is of either a quantity or a deviation rate. The statistical terms that roughly correspond to "quantities" and "deviation rate," respectively, are:

    a. Attributes and variables.

    b. Variables and attributes.

    c. Constants and attributes.

    d. Constants and variables.

1-17. A sampling method that can be used to estimate the dollar misstatement of an account balance but is not based on normal-curve mathematics is:

    a. Discovery sampling.

    b. Mean-per-unit (MPU) sampling.

    c. Attribute sampling.

    d. Probability-proportional-to-size sampling.

1-18. To test the accounts receivable file to compute an estimated dollar total, the auditor could use any one of the following sampling techniques except:

    a. Difference estimation.

    b. Unstratified mean-per-unit estimation.

    c. Ratio estimation.

    d. Attribute estimation.

1-19. Each time an auditor draws a conclusion based on evidence drawn from a sample, an additional risk, sampling risk, is introduced. An example of sampling risk is:

    a. Projecting the results of sampling beyond the population tested.

    b. Using an improper audit procedure with a sample.

    c. Incorrectly applying an audit procedure to sample data.

    d. Drawing an erroneous conclusion from sample data.

1-20. Management is legally required to prepare a shipping document for all movement of hazardous materials. The document must be filed with bills of lading. Management expects 100 percent compliance with the procedure. Which of the following sampling approaches would be *most* appropriate?

    a. Attribute sampling.

    b. Discovery sampling.

    c. Targeted sampling.

    d. Variable sampling.

CASE

Case 1-1   Is Sampling Involved?

(estimated time to complete: 15 minutes)

The following list contains examples of tests an auditor might perform in an audit of financial statements. For each test listed, identify whether the procedure usually involves sampling, and if it does, state whether attribute or variable sampling would typically be used.

    a. Tests of recording of shipments.

    b. Comparison of financial information with budgeted information.

    c. Tests of controls over payroll and related personnel policy systems.

    d. Obtaining written representations from management.

    e. Inspecting land and buildings.

    f. Obtaining an understanding of internal control.

    g. Tests of controls over inventory pricing.

    h. Tests of recorded payroll expense.

    i. Observing cash-handling procedures.

    j. Tests of the amount of transactions that are not supported by proper approval.

    k. Selecting one transaction to obtain an understanding of the entity's internal control.

    l. Scanning accounting records for unusual items.

    m. Interviewing client employees.

Organize your answer as follows:

Procedure	Involves Sampling? (Yes or No)	Attribute/Variable/ Not Applicable

2 SELECTING A REPRESENTATIVE SAMPLE

LEARNING OBJECTIVES

After a careful study and discussion of this chapter, you will be able to:

1. Define representative sampling, sampling with replacement, and sampling without replacement.
2. Determine how selected sample items that are not examined should be treated.
3. Use a random-number table to select a representative sample.
4. Discuss the use of a computer to generate random numbers.
5. Use systematic sampling or random systematic selection to generate sample elements.
6. Illustrate the probability-proportional-to-size selection technique.
7. Cite the advantages of stratified sample selection.
8. Describe the haphazard selection method that is permissible for a nonstatistical sample.

Chapter 1 delineates two requirements that must be met before a sampling plan can be statistical. These requirements are: (1) the sample items should have a known probability of selection, and (2) the sample results must be mathematically evaluated. This chapter explains and illustrates the first requirement.

Statistical sampling requires that a sample be selected in an unbiased way; that is, the sample must be random. Six techniques are available to aid the auditor in generating an acceptable sample. They are: random-number table selection, computer selection, systematic selection, random systematic selection, probability-proportional-to-size selection, and stratified selection. We discuss each of these selection techniques in this chapter. The selection techniques presented are used whenever it is desirable to produce a random sample, usually without regard to whether the sampling model is an attribute or a variable sampling application. In fact, the selection techniques can also be used for nonstatistical as well as statistical sampling.

DEFINITION OF RANDOM SAMPLE, POPULATION, AND SAMPLING FRAME

If the auditor wishes to measure a sampling risk when less than 100 percent of a population is examined, a **random (probability) sample** must be used. Recall from Chapter 1 that nonstatistical samples are those in which the inclusion or exclusion of individual sampling elements depends on professional judgment. Such judgment samples may indeed yield good estimates or correct decisions, but with this type of sampling technique, the auditor has no objective method for evaluating the adequacy of the sample.

Of course, because of sampling risk, an auditor may decide that a complete enumeration is desirable. Often the auditor will decide that at least part of the population should be examined 100 percent. Because of cost and time considerations, however, the decision to sample a portion of a population and to accept some sampling risk is usually made. In such situations, proper sample design is of utmost importance.

SAS No. 39 (AU 350.21) explains the matter as follows:

When planning a sample for a substantive test of details, the auditor uses his judgment to determine which items, if any, . . . should be individually examined and which items, if any, should be subject to sampling. The auditor should examine those items for which, in his judgment, acceptance of some sampling risk is not justified. . . . Any items that the auditor has decided to examine 100 percent are not part of the items subject to sampling. Other items that, in the auditor's judgment, need to be tested to fulfill the audit objective but need not be examined 100 percent, would be subject to sampling.

Auditors must exercise caution to avoid projecting sample results to a population if all population items did not have a chance of being included in the sample. In other words, it is improper to conclude that all vouchers for cash disbursements processed during the year are properly supported if the sample was selected only from vouchers processed in July. Similarly, it would be improper to conclude that all sales were properly recorded if the sample were selected only from charge sales and excluded cash sales.

A *simple random sample* may be defined as a sample that is selected in such a way that every element in the population has an equal chance of being selected. The **population** is the universe or field about which the auditor desires certain information. The population the auditor wishes to generalize about must be defined in advance. When defining a population, the auditor should adhere to two stipulations:

- The population should be relevant to the audit objectives.
- The population definition should enable anyone to tell whether or not an item belongs to the population.

The following examples illustrate population definition.

Population Definition	*Items Included*
All accounts receivable as of year end	Accounts with zero balances, positive balances, and negative (credit) balances
All accounts receivable appearing in the year-end trial balance	Accounts with positive or negative balances
All checks written for the year	All checks, including voided and unrecorded checks

In addition to very carefully defining the population, the auditor must define the sampling frame in advance. The **sampling frame** is a listing or other physical representation of the individual items in the population. For example, in testing physical inventory there are three possible sampling frames: (1) an inventory listing, (2) the perpetual inventory records, or (3) the physical items of inventory. The major requirement in selecting a sampling frame is to make certain that the frame is a complete representation of all the items in the sampled population. However, frames may contain units that do not belong to the population. For example, a listing of accounts receivable may contain zero and credit balance accounts, even if the auditor is interested in only the positive balances. If a zero balance or credit balance account is selected, it is excluded from the sample and another item is drawn.

SAMPLING WITH OR WITHOUT REPLACEMENT

Sampling with replacement is a sample selection method that permits a selected sample item to be returned to the population and reselected. In other words, the same item may be included in the sample more than once.

Sampling without replacement is a technique whereby once an item is selected, it is removed from the population and cannot be selected again. The item can be included only once in a sample selection.

To illustrate sampling with or without replacement, let us assume that we have a goldfish bowl that contains 100 marbles numbered from 1 to 100. If sampling with replacement is employed in drawing a random sample of 20 marbles, marble 54 may be selected as the first sample item and, again, as say, the eighteenth sample item. If it is, marble 54 is included twice in the total sample of 20. On the other hand, if we are sampling without replacement, marble 54, once selected, is removed from the goldfish bowl and cannot be reselected.

Because of logic and sample efficiency (smaller sample size), sampling without replacement is more applicable to accounting and audit sampling problems. *Consequently, throughout this book sampling without replacement is assumed unless otherwise stated.*

UNEXAMINED SAMPLE ITEMS

Auditors should not substitute one sample item for another; substitution is not permissible. However, if the item is not considered to be part of the population (say, a voided check), a replacement item may be selected at random. In this respect, the auditor should distinguish between legitimately voided or unused documents and missing supporting documentation. According to SAS No. 39 (AU 350.40):

Auditing procedures that are appropriate to achieve the objective of the test of controls should be applied to each sample item. If the auditor is not able to apply the planned audit procedures or appropriate alternative procedures to selected items, he or she should consider the reasons for this limitation and he should ordinarily consider those selected items to be deviations from the controls for the purpose of evaluating the sample.

For substantive testing, SAS No. 39 (AU 350.25) states:

The auditor's treatment of unexamined items will depend on their effect on his evaluation of the sample. If the auditor's evaluation of the sample results would not be altered by considering those unexamined items to be misstated, it is not necessary to examine the items. However, if considering those unexamined items to be misstated would lead to a conclusion that the balance or class contains material misstatement, the auditor should consider alternative procedures that would provide him with sufficient evidence to form a conclusion. The auditor should also consider whether the reasons for his inability to examine the items have implications in relation to his planned assessed level of control risk or his degree of reliance on management representations.

RANDOM-NUMBER TABLES

A random, as opposed to an arbitrary or judgmental, selection of the sample offers the best chance that the sample will be unbiased. A **random-number table** is one device for helping to achieve randomness. Such a table is composed of randomly generated digits 0 through 9. Each digit should appear in the table approximately the same number of times, and the order in which they appear is random. Columns in the table are purely arbitrary and otherwise meaningless. Columns do, however, make random-number tables easier to read.

In using a random-number table to determine which population items will be included in a sample, once an item has been randomly selected to be part of the sample, it cannot be ignored or excluded for any reason. Selected random numbers should be documented in audit work papers by identifying each of the following:

1. *Correspondence*—defines the relationship between population sampled and random-number table.
2. *Route*—specifies selection path. The auditor may go up or down the columns—left or right. Any route desired can be selected as long as it is consistently followed until all required numbers are drawn.
3. *Starting point*—identifies row, column, digit starting position, as well as source (book) and page number of selection route.
4. *Stopping point*—facilitates adding new sample items, if needed.

To establish correspondence, each population item must have a unique number in the random-number table. It must be possible to read the random-number table and arrive at the proper sample element. To illustrate, assume that an auditor is examining a population of sales invoices numbered from 1 to 750. To establish correspondence, it is necessary to use a three-digit number scheme in the random-number table.

In selecting a route to identify sample elements, the only stipulation is to document the route definition in the audit work papers so that a reviewer could, if necessary, reproduce the exact sample selection. Another point to remember is that the route used should not be cumbersome or complex. A complex route definition increases the probability of human error (nonsampling error).

To determine a starting point, the random-number table that consists of many pages may be opened at random and the **random-stab method** used to define row, column, and digit starting position. In the unlikely event an entire random-number table is exhausted in meeting the needs of a large sample, the table should not be used again. In that instance, a large random-number table should be used. Auditors are not likely to encounter this problem, however.

USING A RANDOM-NUMBER TABLE

Figure 2.1 is an illustrative page from a random-number table. It is included to show the efficient use of a table of this kind. Figure 2.1 should not be used in actual practice, since it is only one page from a table that contains 3000 rows of random numbers. Note that the figure contains 45 rows and 10 columns.

To demonstrate the use of the table in Figure 2.1, we present a series of four illustrations. Assume a route definition as follows: Read down the column to the

Table of Random Numbers

	(01)	*(02)*	*(03)*	*(04)*	*(05)*	*(06)*	*(07)*	*(08)*	*(09)*	*(10)*
(0001)	9492	4562	4180	5525	7255	1297	9296	1283	6011	0350
(0002)	1557	0392	8989	6898	1072	6013	0020	8582	5059	9324
(0003)	0714	5947	2420	6210	3824	2743	4217	3707	5894	0040
(0004)	0558	8266	4990	8954	7455	6309	9543	1148	0835	0808
(0005)	1458	8725	3750	3138	2499	6017	7744	0485	3010	9606
(0006)	5169	6981	4319	3369	9424	4117	7632	5457	0608	4741
(0007)	0328	5213	1017	5248	8622	6454	8120	4585	3295	0840
(0008)	2462	2055	9782	4213	3452	9940	8859	1000	6260	2851
(0009)	8408	8697	3982	8228	7668	8139	3736	4889	7283	7706
(0010)	1818	5041	9706	4646	3992	4110	4091	7619	1053	4020
(0011)	1771	8614	8593	0930	2095	5005	6387	4002	7498	0066
(0012)	7050	1437	6847	4679	9059	4139	6602	6817	9972	5360
(0013)	5875	2094	0495	3213	5694	5513	3547	9035	7588	5994
(0014)	2473	2087	4618	1507	4471	9542	7565	2371	3981	0812
(0015)	1976	1639	4956	9011	8221	4840	4513	5263	8837	5868
(0016)	4006	4029	7270	8027	7476	7690	6362	1251	9277	5833
(0017)	2149	8162	0667	0825	7353	4645	3273	1181	8526	1176
(0018)	1669	7011	6548	5851	8278	9006	8176	1268	7113	4548
(0019)	7436	5041	4087	1647	7205	3977	4257	9008	3067	7206
(0020)	2178	3632	5745	2228	1780	6043	9296	4469	8108	5005
(0021)	1964	3043	3134	8923	1019	8560	5871	7971	2233	7960
(0022)	5859	7120	9682	0173	2413	8490	6162	1220	3710	5270
(0023)	2352	1929	5985	3303	9590	6974	5811	4264	0248	4295
(0024)	9267	0156	9112	2783	2026	0493	9544	8065	4916	3835
(0025)	4787	0119	1261	5197	0156	2385	9957	0990	6681	2323
(0026)	5550	0699	8080	1152	6002	2532	3075	2777	8671	4068
(0027)	7281	9442	4941	1041	0569	4354	8000	3158	9142	5498
(0028)	1322	7212	3286	2886	9739	5012	0360	5800	9745	8640
(0029)	5176	2259	2774	3641	3553	2475	1974	4578	3388	6656
(0030)	2292	1664	1237	2518	0081	8788	8170	5519	0467	4646
(0031)	6935	8265	3393	4268	4429	1443	4670	4177	7872	9298
(0032)	8538	5393	8093	7835	0484	2550	0827	3112	1065	0246
(0033)	4351	0691	0592	2256	4881	4776	4992	2919	3046	3246
(0034)	6337	8219	9134	9611	8961	4277	6288	2818	1603	4084
(0035)	2257	1980	5269	9615	8628	4715	6366	1542	7267	8917
(0036)	8319	9526	0819	0238	7504	1499	8507	9767	1345	7509
(0037)	1717	8853	2651	9327	7244	0428	6583	2862	1452	8061
(0038)	6519	9348	1026	4190	4210	6231	0732	7000	9553	6125
(0039)	1728	2608	6422	6711	1348	6163	4289	6621	0736	4771
(0040)	5788	5724	5388	5218	8929	3299	0945	6760	8258	5305
(0041)	7495	0547	0226	1188	1270	0689	5048	7689	9477	2210

	(01)	*(02)*	*(03)*	*(04)*	*(05)*	*(06)*	*(07)*	*(08)*	*(09)*	*(10)*
				Table of Random Numbers						
(0042)	1519	1689	9573	7207	4188	1155	1366	1517	1943	2399
(0043)	0493	2858	2812	7122	4852	7317	6895	3666	5095	7681
(0044)	7235	8838	6680	7231	3713	9231	8510	6206	8596	3657
(0045)	2240	8303	9164	9119	3531	8567	9007	6877	5646	6305

Source: From *Handbook of Sampling for Auditing and Accounting,* Second Edition by Herbert Arkin, Copyright © 1974 by McGraw-Hill Book Company, Inc. Used by permission of McGraw-Hill Book Company, Inc.

FIGURE 2.1   Illustrative Page from a Random-Number Table (Continued)

bottom of the table. After reaching the bottom of the page, start with the next column by using the same digit starting position.

Illustration No. 1

Select a sample of four items[1] from prenumbered canceled checks numbered from 1 to 500. Start at row 5, column 1, digit starting position 1. Select three-digit numbers. Items selected are:

145 (sample item no. 1)

516 (discard because check numbers do not go beyond 500)

032 (sample item no. 2)

246 (sample item no. 3)

840 (discard)

181 (sample item no. 4)

Illustration No. 2

To minimize **discards** (i.e., unusable numbers) in Illustration No. 1, table numbers greater than 500 can be reduced by 500 to produce a sample item within the population boundary of 1 to 500. The five sample items selected are:

145 (sample item no. 1)

016 (sample item no. 2 = 516 − 500)

032 (sample item no. 3)

246 (sample item no. 4)

340 (sample item no. 5 = 840 − 500)

[1]A sample of four is used to simplify the illustration; it would not be sufficient for audit purposes.

Illustration No. 3

Select a sample of four items from a population of sales invoices numbered from 2586 to 8892. Start at row 12, column 8, digit starting position 4. (Remember columns in the table are arbitrary and simply aid in table reading.) Select four-digit numbers. Items selected are:

7997 (sample item no. 1)

5758 (sample item no. 2)

1398 (discard)

3883 (sample item no. 3)

1927 (discard)

1852 (discard)

8711 (sample item no. 4)

Illustration No. 4

Select four sales invoices numbered from 5000 to 12,000. Start a row 21, column 2, digit starting point 1. Rather than using a five-digit number, which produces a large number of discards, subtract a constant to get a population with four digits. If a constant of 3000 is used, the usable numbers selected from 2000 to 9000 are:

3043 (usable no. 1)

7120 (usable no. 2)

1929 (discard)

0156 (discard)

0119 (discard)

0699 (discard)

9442 (discard)

7212 (usable no. 3)

2259 (usable no. 4)

The above four usable sample items must be increased by 3000 to correspond with the selected population items. Thus, population items selected are:

6043 (sample item no. 1 = 3043 + 3000)

10,120 (sample item no. 2 = 7120 + 3000)

10,212 (sample item no. 3 = 7212 + 3000)

5259 (sample item no. 4 = 2259 + 3000)

Sometimes problems other than many discards arise from using a random-number table. A population may have an alphabetical prefix instead of a consecutive numbering prefix. Inventory items, for example, are often not identified by a numerical numbering system. A possible solution to such a problem is to convert the alphabetical prefix to a numerical system by numbering the items consecutively.

COMPUTER-GENERATED RANDOM NUMBERS

Computer generation of random numbers via audit software is more efficient than using a random-number table, because random-number table selection produces more discards and potential human error. Thus, when available, computers should be used to generate random numbers.

Many accounting firms have random-number generation capabilities as part of their audit software packages. Figure 2.2 illustrates the input (in italics) and output of a computer software package used to generate 30 sample items from a population.

Input Screen

```
        Enter Random-Number Generator Parameters
Generate how many random numbers  :        30
Generate random numbers from       :     142984
Up to but not including            :     283401
Enter a random-number seed         :      8351
Allow duplicate numbers (Y/N)      :        N


F1 Help                                      <Esc> Exit
```

Output Report

```
Thu June 17 2001                                  Page: 1

               Random-Number Generator
        30 Random-Numbers from 142984 up to but not
                   including 283401
        Random-Number Generator Seeded with 8351


        276739        190009        158910        235595
        276900        271393        265224        188963
        146056        262427        274717        146194
        148144        225804        176852        271614
        146519        142993        162181        196232
        198662        188424        185342        261726
        187067        217144        164154        180694
        230279        174729
                  *** End of Report ***
```

FIGURE 2.2 Illustrative Computer Software Program for Random-Number Generation

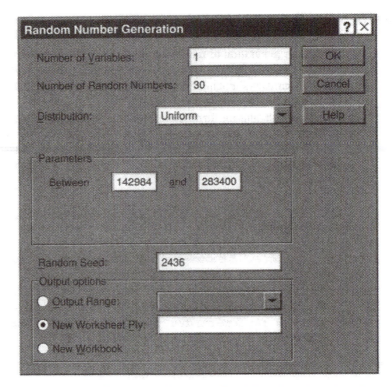

FIGURE 2.3   **Illustrative Input Screen for Microsoft Excel Random-Number Generator**

Spreadsheet programs have random-number generators as part of their data analysis tools. Figure 2.3 presents the input screen for the Microsoft Excel random-number generator that may be used to develop 30 numbers from the same population described in Figure 2.2.

SYSTEMATIC SELECTION

In **systematic sampling,** the auditor calculates a sampling interval and then selects the items for the sample based on the size of the interval. For example, if the population size N contains 1000 items and the sample size desired n is 100, the sampling interval is 10(N/n). A random start between 1 and 10 is selected as the first sample element. Afterward, every tenth item is selected.

The primary advantage of systematic sampling is ease of use. However, a major problem is that it may produce a biased sample. To guard against a biased sample, the auditor should:

1. Be satisfied that the population is in random order.

2. Use more than one random start. (One recommended approach uses five as a minimum number of starts. For illustrative purposes, we also use five.)
3. Continue sample selection until the population is exhausted.
4. Do not substitute one sample item for another (unselected) population item. (Population items that are not selected should not be substituted for sample items that are difficult to audit or locate.)
5. Use computer generation, if practical, instead of systematic sampling.

To illustrate point 2, using the sampling interval of 10 calculated above, the sampling interval is multiplied by the desired number of random starts to arrive at an adjusted sampling interval. Assuming five as the minimum number of random starts, the adjusted sampling interval is: 10 times 5 equals 50. Random numbers between 1 and 50 are selected to identify the first five sample elements. Afterward, every fiftieth item from each of the five starts is selected. To illustrate, assume that the following five random numbers between 1 and 50 were obtained from a random number table.

22   8   34   48   12

From lowest to highest these are arrayed as:

First five samples	8	12	22	34	48
Sampling interval	+ 50	+ 50	+ 50	+ 50	+ 50
6–10 samples	58	62	72	84	98
Sampling interval	+ 50	+ 50	+ 50	+ 50	+ 50
11–15 samples	108	112	122	134	148
	+ 50	+ 50	....		+ 50
	n_{16}	n_{17}	....		n_{100}

☐ = sample elements

Point 3 (continue sample selection until the population is exhausted) guards against a **biased selection** by requiring that sample selection continue until the last sample selected plus the sampling interval exceeds the last item in the population. If the auditor stops sampling when he or she reaches the desired sample size without sampling from the tail end of the population, the sample findings may not be representative.

When applying systematic sampling, the sample will usually not be evenly divisible into the population as in the above examples. In these cases, the size of the skip interval should be rounded down to an integer. For example, if the population contains 10,069 items and the auditor wants to select 100 items with five multiple starts, the adjusted skip interval is 500 (10,069 ÷ 100 = 100 rounded × 5 = 500).

RANDOM SYSTEMATIC SELECTION

Samples may also be selected by the random systematic method. This method, as the name implies, is a combination of the random number and the systematic method. It is more random than the systematic method and sometimes involves less time than random-number selection.

In systematic selection a fixed interval is used to choose items for the sample. In **random systematic sampling** a variable interval is used. The variable intervals will have an average equal to the fixed interval (N/n = sample interval), as in the systematic method. To determine the variable intervals to be used, random numbers between one and two times the fixed (average) sampling interval are chosen. These random numbers (intervals) are then added together to determine the items to be selected.

If we return to the example used under systematic selection, the calculated sampling interval is 10 (1000/100 = 10). For random systematic selection, 100 random numbers between 01 and 20 (2 × 10) would be selected to represent the interval to be used. Assume the following random numbers from a random-number table are selected as part of the 100: 8, 2, 14, 15, 3, and 8. The first sample item selected is 8, the second is 10 (8 + 2), the third is 24 (10 + 14), the fourth is 39 (24 + 15), the fifth is 42 (39 + 3), the sixth is 50 (42 + 8), and so forth. Of course, the auditor still needs 94 (100 − 6) more random numbers between 01 and 20 to complete the selection process.

PROBABILITY-PROPORTIONAL-TO-SIZE SELECTION

Probability-proportional-to-size sampling (also referred to as dollar unit sampling) gives units with larger recorded amounts proportionally more opportunity to be selected than units with smaller recorded amounts. A sales invoice with a $10,000 total would have ten times greater chance of being selected than an invoice with a $1000 total. To achieve this result, the probability-proportional-to-size selection technique selects random dollars from the population rather than random logical units. Thus, probability-proportional-to-size selection is a random process, because each recorded dollar in the population has an equal chance of selection. It is not, however, a random *unit* process because each transaction or account does not have an equal probability of selection. Before applying probability-proportional-to-size selection, negative amounts generally should be removed from the population.

In applying probability-proportional-to-size sampling, auditors may use a random-number table or generator to select random dollars from the population. However, auditors generally use a systematic selection approach with the following sequence of steps:

1. Calculate the sampling interval by dividing the total number of dollars in the population by the number of items in the sample.

$$Sampling\ interval = \frac{Book\ value\ of\ the\ population}{Sample\ size}$$

2. Select a random starting point from one dollar to the amount of the sampling interval. For example, a random-number table might be used to select the random starting point.
3. Starting with the first unit in the population, determine the cumulative dollar amount by summing the items one by one to the end of the population.
4. Note that the unit that the random starting dollar falls within is the first item selected. The next sample unit will be the one that contains the cumulative dollar that is equal to the sum of the random starting point and the sampling interval. The third sample unit is the one that contains the cumulative dollar that is equal to the sum of the random starting point and two sampling intervals, and so on.

To illustrate this method of selection, assume that the auditor is sampling 100 items from a population of accounts receivable totaling $500,000. The sampling interval would be calculated to be $5000 ($500,000/100). A random starting point is selected between $1 and $5000, say $1223. Then the sample will include the accounts receivable that contain every $5000 from the starting point, as illustrated below:

Account Number	*Recorded Amount*	*Cumulative Amount*
787678	$ 125	125
787679	2460	2585
787680	670	3255
787681	1200	4455
787682	2455	6910
787683	234	7144
787684	9	7153
787685	2222	9375
787686	675	10,050
787687	8544	18,594
787688	32	18,626
787689	3000	21,626
787690	$11,200	32,826

The first account to be included in the sample would be number 787679 because it contains the random starting dollar, $1223. The second account included in the sample would be the account that contains cumulative dollar 6223 (1223 + 5000), account number 787682. Account number 787687 would be selected next because it contains cumulative dollar 11,223 (6223 + 5000). Note that account number 787690 would be included twice because both the 16,223rd cumulative dollar and the 21,223rd cumulative dollar are contained within that account. In using probability-proportional-to-size sampling, it is necessary to sample with replacement.

STRATIFIED SELECTION

Stratified selection is not itself a technique for drawing sample items. However, it is useful in improving the efficiency of sample design. By stratifying a population, the auditor can give greater representation to the larger recorded amounts. In fact, stratification allows the auditor to use a smaller sample size to achieve the planned level of sampling risk.

Stratified selection is used more often for variable sampling applications than for attribute applications. For example, in an audit of accounts receivable, the accountant may judgmentally decide to stratify the population and apply different sample selection techniques to the various strata. To confirm accounts receivable, he or she might stratify and test as follows:

Stratum	*Size*	*Composition of Stratum*	*Sample Selection*
1	22	All accounts over $5000	100% examination
2	121	All accounts between $1000 and $5000	Random-number table
3	85	All accounts under $1000	Systematic selection
4	14	All accounts with credit balances	100% examination

Stratified selection has at least two major advantages from an audit perspective. It enables the auditor to relate sample selection to key and material items in the population and to use different audit techniques for each stratum. Stratification also improves the reliability of the sample and reduces the required sample size. If homogeneous items are grouped together, sample efficiency and effectiveness are increased.

Stratification is discussed and illustrated in Chapters 4 and 5. In addition, Chapter 6 considers probability-proportional-to-size sampling, which is actually a type of stratified selection. (Units with larger recorded amounts are more likely to be selected.) Because of the large sample sizes produced in variable sampling applications, *unrestricted random sampling* (when each unit has an equal chance of selection) is seldom used in audit situations.

HAPHAZARD SELECTION FOR NONSTATISTICAL SAMPLING

Naturally, any of the selection methods discussed above may also be used for nonstatistical sampling. However, there is a method that may produce a **representative sample** that is not one of the random-based methods. It is called **haphazard selection** and is described in the AICPA Auditing Procedure Study, *Audit Sampling*, as follows:

A *haphazard sample* consists of sampling units selected without any conscious bias, that is, without any special reason for including or omitting items from the sample. It does not consist of sampling units selected in a careless manner; rather, it is selected in a manner that can be expected to be representative of the population.

The key to haphazard selection is to avoid being biased by the nature, size, appearance, or location of items. For example, if the auditor selects invoices from a cabinet of drawers, the auditor should not select items only from the middle of the drawers because that would not give invoices in the first or last sections of the drawers a chance of selection.

Note that if the auditor only selects large or unusual items from the population or uses some other judgmental criterion for selection, the selection method has a conscious bias and cannot be considered a representative selection method.

With haphazard selection, there is no means of calculating the probability that a particular item will be selected for inclusion in the sample. As a result the method is not acceptable for statistical sampling. However, the fact that haphazard selection is not acceptable for a statistical plan does not mean that auditors should not use it for selecting items for nonstatistical sampling plans. The point is that the items selected using haphazard selection do not meet the statistical requirement that each item selected must have a known probability of selection.

SUMMARY

One of the most important ingredients of an effective statistical sampling application is a random sample. Without a random sample, sample results cannot be statistically evaluated.

Auditors use a variety of acceptable techniques to ensure that the sample selection process produces unbiased samples. Techniques introduced in this chapter include random-number table selection, computer selection, systematic selection, random systematic selection, probability-proportional-to-size selection, and stratified selection. Generally, auditors use sampling without replacement. However, when probability-proportional-to-size selection is employed, sampling with replacement is appropriate. Probability-proportional-to-size sampling is discussed in detail in Chapter 6. For a nonstatistical sample, an auditor may use random or haphazard selection.

GLOSSARY

Biased selection   A selection process that prevents each sample item from having an opportunity of being selected.

Correspondence   The defined relationship between the population sampled and a random-number table.

Discards   Unusable numbers generated from a random-number selection deviation. (e.g., a random-number table).

Haphazard sample   A sample selected without any conscious bias that is expected to be representative of the population.

Population   All the items in the account or group being audited. Also referred to as *universe* and *field*.

Probability-proportional-to-size sampling   A sampling technique in which each population unit has a probability of being selected that is proportional to its recorded amount. Also frequently referred to as *dollar unit sampling*.

Random-number table   A table composed of randomly generated digits 0 through 9 that can be used to generate random samples.

Random sample   A sample drawn from a population, each element of which has an equal probability of being selected; a valid statistical sample. Also commonly referred to as *probability sampling*.

Random-stab method   A technique whereby a random-number table is opened randomly and a random stab is used to determine row, column, and digit starting position.

Random systematic sampling   A systematic sample selection technique with a variable (random) rather than a fixed sampling interval.

Representative sample   A sample having essentially the same characteristics as the population. Haphazard selection or a random-based selection method can be expected to produce a sample that is representative of the population.

Route   The predefined path to be followed through a random-number table when selecting a sample.

Sampling frame   A listing or physical representation of a sampling unit. For example, for a test of cash disbursements, the individual check number could be a sampling frame.

Sampling with replacement   A sampling technique whereby any given item in the population may be included in the sample more than once.

Sampling without replacement   A sampling technique whereby an item, once included in the sample, cannot be selected again. Sampling without replacement is ordinarily used in auditing.

Stratified selection   A sampling technique applied by grouping sampling units with similar characteristics into separate strata to reduce the variability among sampling units.

Systematic sampling   A method of selecting a sample n from a population N by first selecting a random number between 1 and N/n and then selecting every N/nth item.

REVIEW QUESTIONS

2-1. Indicate whether each of the following is true (T) or false (F).

 a. Statistical sampling requires that a sample be random.

 b. Valid sampling frames may contain units that do not belong to the population as defined.

 c. Sampling with replacement is more widely used by auditors than sampling without replacement.

 d. If a population is numbered from 6000 to 12,000, a five-digit number must be used to generate a sample from a random-number table.

 e. Negative amounts should be eliminated from a population total before probability-proportional-to-size sampling is applied.

 f. A biased sample cannot be evaluated statistically.

 g. More than one random start should be used if systematic sample selection is employed.

 h. Random systematic selection is preferred relative to systematic selection with one random start.

 i. Computer generation is generally a less efficient method used to generate random numbers relative to a random-number table.

 j. Random sampling techniques can be used for nonstatistical samples.

 k. Haphazard selection cannot be used in statistical sampling.

2-2. Identify six sampling techniques that are useful in generating a random sample.

2-3. What other term(s) may be used for "random sample"? for "population"?

2-4. What two rules should be followed when a population is being defined?

2-5. To ascertain whether all shipments have been billed, what sampling frame should be used?

2-6. Identify the four items that should be documented in audit work papers if a random-number table is used to generate a random sample.

2-7. What rule should an auditor adhere to in specifying a route to follow in a random-number table?

2-8. How does the auditor determine the starting point in a random-number table?

2-9. For each of the following situations, identify an effective method to select a random sample by using a random-number table. Also, identify the discard range for each situation.

 a. Prenumbered disbursement vouchers numbered from 100 to 4892.

 b. Sales invoices numbered from 4562 to 13,482.

 c. Inventory listed on 52 pages, each with a maximum of 48 lines per page.

2-10. Identify the first ten random numbers for a population numbered 101 to 841. Use the illustrative page from a random-number table in Figure 2.1. The starting point is row 10, column 4, digit starting position 2. The route is down the table reading from left to right.

2-11. Why is computer generation generally more efficient than using a random-number table?

2-12. What is the major distinction between systematic selection and random systematic selection?

2-13. A number of precautions must be taken when using systematic sampling to produce a random sample. What are they?

2-14. For a population numbered from 1 to 1,000 and a sample size of 50, what is the sampling interval for only one start? for two multiple starts? for six multiple starts?

2-15. If $N = 2000$, $n = 50$, and the sampling interval with one start $= 40$, what are the first four sample items using a random-number start from 1 to 40 of 26?

2-16. Sales invoices of Muleshoe, Inc., are numbered from 1 to 15,000. The auditor has determined that 100 sample items are needed and that systematic sampling with five multiple starts will be used.

   a. What is the sampling interval for only one random start?

   b. What is the adjusted sampling interval (for five multiple starts)?

   c. How many items would be selected from a random-number table? What is the selection range?

   d. Assuming that five items selected from a random-number table are 700, 444, 15, 323, and 120, identify the first 15 sample items to be selected.

2-17. If a population N contains 100 checks and a sample n of 10 is desired, how many random numbers will be needed from a random-number table for a random systematic sampling application? What is the range within which random numbers will be selected?

2-18. Systematic sampling is always applied in a sampling without replacement mode. Do you agree?

2-19. Describe the selection approach an auditor should follow if probability-proportional-to-size sampling is used.

2-20. When using the probability-proportional-to-size selection method, the auditor must first stratify the population. Do you agree?

2-21. Contrast "unrestricted random sampling" with "stratified selection."

2-22. Use a spreadsheet program to produce random numbers for the following situations.

   a. Generate ten random numbers for a population numbered 10484 to 21896.

   b. Generate 20 random numbers for an inventory stored in four separate warehouses. Each inventory listing for each warehouse contains a different number of pages. Each page, however, contains ten product lines.

Warehouse Number	Number of Pages—Inventory Listing
1	280
2	82
3	240
4	124

MULTIPLE-CHOICE QUESTIONS FROM PROFESSIONAL EXAMINATIONS

2-23. In examining cash disbursements, an auditor plans to select a sample using systematic selection with a random start. The primary advantage of such a systematic selection is that population items:

   a. That include irregularities will *not* be overlooked when the auditor exercises compatible reciprocal options.

   b. May occur in a systematic pattern, thus making the sample more representative.

   c. May occur more than once in a sample.

   d. Do *not* have to be prenumbered in order for the auditor to use the technique.

2-24. An auditor plans to examine a sample of 20 purchase orders for proper approvals as prescribed by the client's internal control procedures. One of the purchase orders in the chosen sample of 20 cannot be found, and the auditor is unable to use alternative procedures to test whether that purchase order was properly approved. The auditor should:

   a. Choose another purchase order to replace the missing purchase order in the sample.

   b. Consider this test of control invalid and proceed with substantive tests since internal control *cannot* be relied upon.

   c. Treat the missing purchase order as a deviation for the purpose of evaluating the sample.

   d. Select a completely new set of 20 purchase orders.

2-25. An underlying feature of random-based selection of items is that each:

   a. Stratum of the accounting population be given equal representation in the sample.

   b. Item in the accounting population be randomly ordered.

   c. Item in the accounting population have an opportunity to be selected.

   d. Item be systematically selected using replacement.

2-26. An auditor initially planned to use unrestricted random sampling with replacement in the examination of accounts receivable. Later, the auditor decided to use unrestricted random sampling without replacement. As a result only of this decision, the sample size should:

a. Increase.

b. Remain the same.

c. Decrease.

d. Be recalculated using a binomial distribution.

2-27. An auditor desires to use a table of random digits to select a sample from a population of documents that have the following broken number sequences: 0001–1000, 2000–5000, and 8000–11000. Which of the following is the most efficient approach to overcome the problem of the broken number sequences?

a. Deduct four-digit constant values from the second and third sequences, choose the appropriate random numbers, and add the constants back to the individual numbers.

b. Skip through the entire random-number tables until large blocks of digits appear that will fit within the three different number sequences.

c. Choose appropriate random numbers from the tables without any modification of the approach and recognize that a large selection of unusable numbers will occur.

d. Select three different starting points in the random tables and vary the selection pattern to obtain needed numbers in the three different sequences.

2-28. Which of the following statistical selection techniques is *least* desirable for use by an auditor?

a. Systematic selection.

b. Stratified selection.

c. Block selection.

d. Sequential selection.

2-29. In a sampling application, the group of items about which the auditor wants to estimate some characteristic is called the:

a. Population.

b. Attribute of interest.

c. Sample.

d. Sampling unit.

2-30. To test the operating effectiveness of a policy regarding sales returns recorded during the most recent year, an auditor systematically selected 5 percent of the actual returns recorded in March and April. Returns during these two busiest months of the year represented about 25 percent of total annual returns. Error projections from this sample have limited usefulness because:

    a. The small size of the sample relative to the population makes sampling risk unacceptable.

    b. The failure to stratify the population according to sales volume results in bias.

    c. The systematic selection of returns during the two months is not sufficiently random.

    d. The error rates during the two busiest months may not be representative of the whole year.

2-31. Using random numbers to select a sample:

    a. Is required for a variables sampling plan.

    b. Is likely to result in an unbiased sample.

    c. Results in a representative sample.

    d. Allows auditors to use smaller samples.

2-32. In obtaining a sample for the purpose of reaching a conclusion about the population from which it is drawn, the auditor:

    a. Can statistically quantify the sample results only if the sample was selected in such a way that each population item has an equal or known probability of selection.

    b. Should use judgmental sampling and concentrate on high-risk items.

    c. Cannot use random sampling procedures unless the items to be sampled are available in machine-readable form.

    d. Will usually use random sampling with replacement.

CASES

Case 2-1   Selecting a Sample

(Estimated time to complete: 20 minutes)

 The following table (Table C2.1) is a partial listing of the sales transactions for the Watson Distributing Company for the year ended December 31, 200X. Select the first three sample items from the population using the following techniques.

    a. The systematic selection technique with a random starting point of 13 and a sampling interval of 30.

    b. The probability-proportional-to-size sampling selection technique with a random starting dollar of $17,240 and a sampling interval of $220,000.

    c. The random-number table selection technique using Figure 2.1 on pp. 24–25. Using the last four digits of the invoice number, begin at row (0004) and column (01), continuing across the row and then down to the beginning of the next row.

TABLE C2.1

Invoice Number	Amount	Cumulative Amount	Invoice Number	Amount	Cumulative Amount
23246	$ 5,687.90	$ 5,687.90	23291	$ 79.98	$261,276.88
23247	$ 123.45	$ 5,811.35	23292	$ 4,328.88	$265,605.76
23248	$ 2,323.89	$ 8,135.24	23293	$23,444.65	$289,050.41
23249	$ 289.00	$ 8,424.24	23294	$ 344.77	$289,395.18
23250	$ 1,211.76	$ 9,636.00	23295	$ 1,298.76	$290,693.94
23251	$ 2,256.77	$ 11,892.77	23296	$ 9,653.40	$300,347.34
23252	$23,543.30	$ 35,436.07	23297	$ 110.11	$300,457.45
23253	$ 333.45	$ 35,769.52	23298	$26,544.45	$327,001.90
23254	$ 9,000.00	$ 44,769.52	23299	$22,455.00	$349,456.90
23255	$ 899.90	$ 45,669.42	23300	$ 12.71	$349,469.61
23256	$ 4,566.75	$ 50,236.17	23301	$ 222.93	$349,692.54
23257	$ 454.68	$ 50,690.85	23302	$ 2,256.00	$351,948.54
23258	$12,745.66	$ 63,436.51	23303	$ 6,482.25	$358,430.79
23259	$ 4,444.50	$ 67,881.01	23304	$ 1,199.90	$359,630.69
23260	$11,009.00	$ 78,890.01	23305	$ 3.75	$359,634.44
23261	$ 2,223.45	$ 81,113.46	23306	$12,309.55	$371,943.99
23262	$ 8,956.66	$ 90,070.12	23307	$ 999.54	$372,943.53
23263	$ 444.87	$ 90,514.99	23308	$ 3,330.88	$376,274.41
23264	$ 33.60	$ 90,548.59	23309	$ 22.34	$376,296.75
23265	$33,545.86	$124,094.45	23310	$65,900.00	$442,196.75
23266	$ 96.66	$124,191.11	23311	$ 999.90	$443,196.65
23267	$ 343.76	$124,534.87	23312	$ 2,323.44	$445,520.09
23268	$ 1,232.67	$125,767.54	23313	$ 1,000.00	$446,520.09
23269	$ 763.81	$126,531.35	23314	$ 9,900.11	$456,420.20
23270	$ 12.50	$126,543.85	23315	$ 3,399.99	$459,820.19
23271	$ 23.44	$126,567.29	23316	$13,700.00	$473,520.19
23272	$ 1,111.45	$127,678.74	23317	$12,500.90	$486,021.09
23273	$20,700.50	$148,379.24	23318	$ 222.99	$486,244.08
23274	$ 333.11	$148,712.35	23319	$ 121.40	$486,365.48
23275	$ 5,550.29	$154,262.64	23320	$ 19.20	$486,384.68
23276	$12,122.76	$166,385.40	23321	$ 700.32	$487,085.00
23277	$ 789.90	$167,175.30	23322	$ 810.89	$487,895.89
23278	$ 4,334.98	$171,510.28	23323	$ 9,476.50	$497,372.39
23279	$ 3,333.75	$174,844.03	23324	$ 8,999.00	$506,371.39
23280	$ 878.87	$175,722.90	23325	$ 35.50	$506,406.89
23281	$43,588.00	$219,310.90	23326	$ 4,506.21	$510,913.10
23282	$ 32.45	$219,343.35	23327	$ 555.50	$511,468.60
23283	$ 110.00	$219,453.35	23328	$15,900.71	$527,369.31
23284	$ 6,127.00	$225,580.35	23329	$ 1,111.84	$528,481.15
23285	$ 200.00	$225,780.35	23330	$ 777.89	$529,259.04
23286	$ 1,198.99	$226,979.34	23331	$ 3,344.67	$532,603.71
23287	$ 2,323.00	$229,302.34	23332	$ 980.00	$533,583.71
23288	$ 7,772.34	$237,074.68	23333	$ 1,423.00	$535,006.71
23289	$ 988.03	$238,062.71	23334	$ 981.25	$535,987.96
23290	$23,134.19	$261,196.90	23335	$21,322.32	$557,310.28

Case 2-2   Adams Supply Company

(Estimated time to complete: 20 minutes)

Assume that the table on this page (Table C2.2) is a partial listing of inventory items for Adams Supply Company for the year ended December 31, 200X. Select the first three sample items from the population using the following techniques.

a. The random-number table selection technique using Figure 2.1 on pp. 24–25. The part numbers run from A-01 to D-76. In selecting the sample, assign a number to the letter in the part number with A=1, B=2, C=3, etc. Use the last three digits and begin at column (02) and row (0001), continuing down to the end of the column and then beginning at the top of the next column.

b. The systematic selection technique with a random starting point of 4 and a sampling interval of 12.

c. The probability-proportional-to-size sampling selection technique with a random starting dollar of $25,621 and a sampling interval of $95,000.

TABLE C2.2

Part Number	Number of Items	Cost	Extended Cost	Cumulative Amount
A-01	45	$ 345.00	$15,525.00	$ 15,525.00
A-02	456	$ 54.30	$24,760.80	$ 40,285.80
A-03	628	$ 21.20	$13,313.60	$ 53,599.40
A-04	29	$ 567.00	$16,443.00	$ 70,042.40
A-05	22	$ 775.00	$17,050.00	$ 87,092.40
A-06	333	$ 99.85	$33,250.05	$ 120,342.45
A-07	342	$ 112.50	$38,475.00	$ 158,817.45
A-08	984	$ 23.40	$23,025.60	$ 181,843.05
A-09	44	$ 356.50	$15,686.00	$ 197,529.05
A-10	234	$ 98.40	$23,025.60	$ 220,554.65
A-11	67	$ 635.80	$42,598.60	$ 263,153.25
A-12	29	$ 898.00	$26,042.00	$ 289,195.25
A-13	167	$ 10.50	$ 1,753.50	$ 290,948.75
A-14	9	$ 232.50	$ 2,092.50	$ 293,041.25
A-15	223	$ 9.50	$ 2,118.50	$ 295,159.75
A-16	123	$ 65.22	$ 8,022.06	$ 303,181.81
A-17	872	$ 78.50	$68,452.00	$ 371,633.81
A-18	34	$ 900.00	$30,600.00	$ 402,233.81
A-19	65	$ 654.30	$42,529.50	$ 444,763.31
A-20	847	$ 78.00	$66,066.00	$ 510,829.31
A-21	23	$ 455.30	$10,471.90	$ 521,301.21
A-22	18	$ 772.90	$13,912.20	$ 535,213.41
A-23	93	$ 878.20	$81,672.60	$ 616,886.01
A-24	22	$ 778.20	$17,120.40	$ 634,006.41

TABLE C2.2 (Continued)

Part Number	Number of Items	Cost	Extended Cost	Cumulative Amount
A-25	3	$ 745.20	$ 2,235.60	$ 636,242.01
A-26	877	$ 85.50	$74,983.50	$ 711,225.51
A-27	889	$ 94.30	$83,832.70	$ 795,058.21
A-28	2231	$ 35.50	$79,200.50	$ 874,258.71
A-29	11	$ 220.00	$ 2,420.00	$ 876,678.71
A-30	1123	$ 23.30	$26,165.90	$ 902,844.61
A-31	879	$ 99.20	$87,196.80	$ 990,041.41
A-32	976	$ 76.30	$74,468.80	$1,064,510.21
A-33	2453	$ 34.00	$83,402.00	$1,147,912.21
A-34	2	$1,090.00	$ 2,180.00	$1,150,092.21
A-35	79	$ 234.00	$18,486.00	$1,168,578.21

3 ATTRIBUTE SAMPLING

LEARNING OBJECTIVES

After a careful study and discussion of this chapter, you will be able to:

1. Relate attribute sampling plans to audit objectives.
2. Describe the relationship of attribute sampling to the auditor's assessment of control risk.
3. Define and select appropriate attributes for tests of controls.
4. Identify areas of professional judgment inherent in an attribute sampling application.
5. Define and apply the concepts of risk of assessing control risk too low, tolerable rate, and expected rate.
6. Use fixed-sample-size attribute sampling, sequential sampling, and discovery sampling plans to test controls.
7. Perform deviation analysis and discuss its importance.
8. Provide suitable documentation in audit work papers of attribute sampling applications.
9. Describe how fixed-sample-size attribute sampling and sequential sampling results are evaluated and correlated with substantive tests.
10. Recognize the limitations of attribute sampling plans.

This chapter defines, explains, and illustrates the three statistical sampling plans categorized as attribute sampling plans. Also, a review of the audit process with particular emphasis on attribute sampling and understanding and assessing internal control is presented. The judgmental aspects of an attribute sampling application (e.g., setting tolerable rates) are discussed at appropriate points throughout the chapter.

ATTRIBUTE SAMPLING PLANS

As we discussed in Chapter 1, the term **attribute sampling** refers to one of three related sampling plans.

1. Fixed-sample-size attribute sampling also is called attribute estimation and is used when the auditor wishes to perform a test of controls to estimate the deviation rate of a population.

2. Sequential attribute sampling is also referred to as stop-or-go sampling. It is an alternative to fixed-sample-size attribute sampling and may be used when the auditor does not have a reasonable estimate of the expected rate of deviations. It is especially efficient when the population deviation rate is relatively low.

3. Discovery sampling is used when the audit objective is to observe at least one deviation whenever the true deviation rate equals or exceeds some stated rate. It is used when the population or occurrence rate is very low.

All three attribute sampling plans deal with qualitative characteristics of the population. Variable sampling answers the question, "How much?" whereas attribute sampling answers the question, "How many?" Fixed-sample-size attribute sampling and sequential sampling are used primarily by internal and external auditors in tests of controls when the auditor wants to assess the extent to which prescribed internal control procedures are being followed.

Fixed-sample-size attribute sampling and sequential sampling might be used in the following areas:

- **Cash Disbursement Tests.** Discounts not taken, invoice quantities not in agreement with receiving information, and payments in excess of specified limits.
- **Sales Tests.** Invoice quantities not in agreement with shipping data, missing purchase order information, invalid part number, and no credit approval.
- **Payroll Tests.** Misstatements in hours, rates, extensions, deductions, lack of appropriate approvals, or excessive vacation time.
- **Inventory Tests.** Inventory items not properly priced and misstatements in perpetual inventory records.

- **Cash Receipts Tests.** Erroneous discounts allowed and unusual amounts of cash receipts.

In executing a test of controls, the auditor is generally concerned with the frequency of deviations from prescribed controls. When using attribute sampling, items being tested or evaluated must be either indicative of a deviation in performance or not a deviation in performance. There are no degrees of deviation; it is a yes or no situation. The objective of attribute sampling as it is used for tests of controls or special-purpose studies is to obtain a reasonable level of confidence that the population deviation rate is not beyond a certain level.

ATTRIBUTE SAMPLING AND THE INDEPENDENT AUDITOR'S ASSESSMENT OF CONTROL RISK

The auditor's responsibility to consider an entity's internal control is explained in SAS No. 55, as amended by SAS No. 78 and SAS No. 94, *Consideration of Internal Control in a Financial Statement Audit* (AU 319). This standard requires the auditor to obtain an understanding of internal control sufficient to plan the audit and to assess control risk. Although an entity's internal control includes the controls established to provide reasonable assurance that all the objectives of the organization concerning (a) reliability of financial reporting, (b) effectiveness and efficiency of operations, and (c) compliance with applicable laws and regulations are achieved, only certain of these controls are relevant to an audit. Generally, the pertinent controls are primarily those that affect the entity's ability to record, process, summarize, and report financial data that is consistent with management's assertions embodied in the financial statements. For purposes of a financial statement audit, an entity's internal control may be viewed as consisting of the following five interrelated components:

- **Control Environment.** The foundation for all other components of internal control, providing discipline and structure. It sets the tone of an organization and influences the control consciousness of personnel. It includes integrity and ethical values, commitment to competence, board of directors or audit committee participation, management's philosophy and operating style, organizational structure, assignment of authority and responsibility, and human resource policies and practices.
- **Risk Assessment.** An entity's identification and analysis of risks relevant to achievement of its objectives that forms a basis for determining how the risks should be managed. For financial reporting purposes, the relevant risks are those related to the preparation of financial statements, such as the possibility of unrecorded transactions.
- **Control Activities.** The policies and procedures that help ensure that management directives are carried out. The control activities that generally have

audit relevance include performance reviews, information processing controls, physical controls, and segregation of duties.

- **Information and Communication.** The identification, capture, and exchange of information in a form and time frame that enables people to carry out their responsibilities. For financial reporting purposes, the relevant information system consists of the methods and records used to record, process, summarize, and report entity transactions, conditions, and events and to maintain accountability for the related assets, liabilities, and equity. The information system includes the accounting system and related means of preparing reliable financial reports.

- **Monitoring.** A process that assesses the quality of internal control performance over time. It involves assessing the design and operation of controls on a timely basis and taking necessary corrective action. It may be accomplished by ongoing activities, separate evaluations, or a combination of those two. In many entities, internal auditors contribute to monitoring activities.

Figure 3.1 is designed to illustrate a conceptually logical approach to the auditor's consideration of an entity's internal control, especially as it relates to performing tests of controls and assessing control risk.

As indicated, the auditor begins consideration of internal control by obtaining an understanding of the five interrelated components sufficient to plan the audit. The auditor's understanding of the procedures prescribed by the client ordinarily is obtained by inquiry or reference to written instructions, and an understanding of their function and limitations is based on the auditor's training, experience, and judgment. The auditor's understanding of internal control is documented using a flowchart, internal control questionnaire, or written narrative. Based on this information, the auditor makes a preliminary assessment of the effectiveness of the prescribed controls, assuming that controls are operating effectively (see Judgment No. 1 in Figure 3.1). At this point, the auditor may decide that it is not efficient to perform additional internal control work. Then, he or she will assess control risk based solely on the evidence obtained while obtaining an understanding of internal control. *Audit sampling (e.g., attribute sampling) is not applicable to this phase of the process.*

If the auditor decides that it is efficient to obtain additional evidence about internal control, he or she will make a judgment about the planned assessed level of control risk (Judgment No. 2 in Figure 3.1), and the planned tests of controls needed to support that level of control risk. Implicit in this judgment is a consideration of the cost and benefits of the tests of controls. A particular control will be tested only if the cost of testing the control is less than the benefit obtained from reduced substantive testing.

Judgment No. 3 in Figure 3.1 involves the determination by the auditor of which tests of controls may be performed using audit sampling. If a control does not leave evidence of performance, audit sampling usually cannot be employed to test its operating effectiveness. According to SAS No. 39 (AU 350.32):

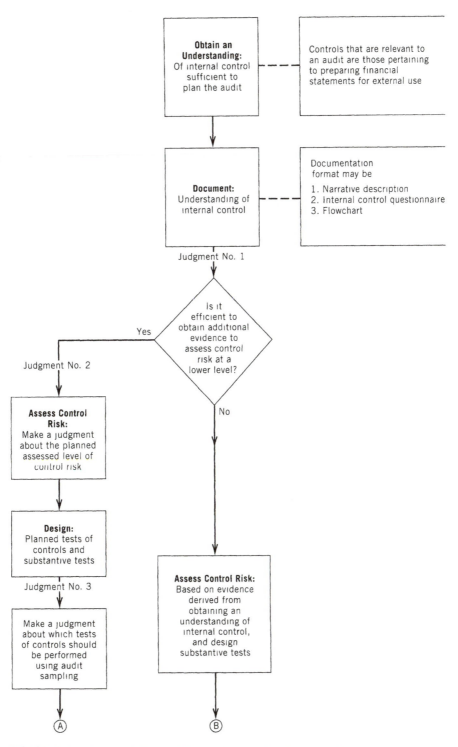

FIGURE 3.1   Internal Control Consideration in the Audit Process

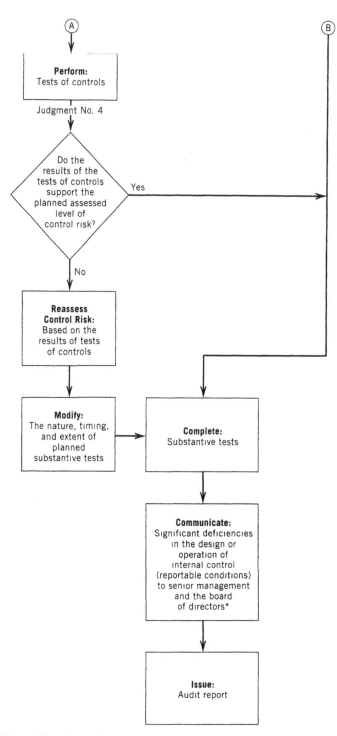

FIGURE 3.1   (Continued)

Sampling generally is not applicable to tests of controls that depend primarily on appropriate segregation of duties or that otherwise provide no documentary evidence of performance. In addition, sampling may not apply to tests of certain documented controls. Sampling may not apply to tests directed toward obtaining evidence about the design or operation of the control environment or the accounting system. For example, inquiry or observation of explanation of variances from budgets when the auditor does not desire to estimate the rate of deviation from the prescribed control.

After the tests of controls are completed (perhaps using fixed-sample-size attribute or sequential attribute sampling), the auditor will consider whether the test results support the planned assessed level of control risk (Judgment No. 4 in Figure 3.1). If the tests of controls disclose that internal controls are not operating sufficiently to support the planned assessed level of control risk, the auditor will revise the assessed level of control risk and the nature, extent, or timing of the related substantive tests.

PLANNING CONSIDERATIONS FOR TESTS OF CONTROLS

Several matters need to be considered when a test of controls using audit sampling is planned. SAS No. 39 (AU 350.31) describes these matters:

- The relationship of the sample to the objective of the test of controls.
- The maximum rate of deviations from prescribed controls that would support his or her planned assessed level of control risk.
- The auditor's allowable risk of assessing control risk too low.
- Characteristics of the population, that is, the items comprising the account balance or class of transactions of interest.

These considerations are identified by the following shorthand terms commonly used in SAS No. 39 (AU 350) and practice.

- Sample–objective relationship
- Tolerable rate
- Risk of assessing control risk too low
- Expected deviation rate in the population

The relationship between these terms and common statistical terms is explained in Figure 3.2.

ATTRIBUTE AND DEVIATION CONDITIONS

An *attribute* is the evidence of performance of the control that is being tested, and a *deviation* is a departure from adequate performance of the prescribed control. The attribute and deviation conditions must be carefully defined before an auditor begins

Professional Terms **[SAS No. 39 (AU 350)]**	**Statistical Terms**
Sample–Objective Relationship	Attribute Definition and Population Definition
Tolerable Rate	Upper Precision Limit (UPL)
Risk of Assessing Control Risk Too Low	One Minus Reliability (Confidence Level)
Expected Deviation Rate	Expected Rate of Occurrence

FIGURE 3.2   The Relation of Professional and Statistical Terms for Attribute Sampling

to execute attribute sampling. Defining them can be difficult and is a matter of professional judgment. Considerable care must be exercised. For example, if the sampling unit is a check and the audit test is concerned with whether the check is properly supported, one of the attributes reviewed for proper support may be a receiving report. A deviation may be defined as a check unsupported by a properly signed receiving report. However, some disbursements for services received (such as rent payments) are not typically supported by receiving reports. The auditor may handle this problem in two ways. First, the attribute definition may be structured so that checks selected relating to certain service acquisitions are excluded from the population. A second way to address this problem is to define the attribute broadly as a properly supported check with identification of what constitutes proper support. Thus, a check not requiring a receiving report but properly supported by a lease agreement would not be a control deviation. Of course, when performing audit tests, the auditor must be alert to the possibility of undefined deviations. Audit awareness is essential in all sampling applications—statistical or nonstatistical.

POPULATION DEFINITION

In an attribute sampling application, the auditor should consider whether the population being sampled is homogeneous. Homogeneity means that all the items in the population should have similar characteristics. If, for example, export and domestic sales transactions for a given company are processed in a different manner, the auditor is faced with the evaluation of two different control situations and therefore two separate populations. Although all the branch operations of a company may be similar, the branches are run by different people. If the auditor is interested in the internal control and staff of individual branches, he or she will be dealing with separate populations for each branch. On the other hand, if the auditor is not concerned about the individual branches but with the operations of the entity as a whole, and there are sufficient similarities among controls of branches, the company may be viewed as a single population.

JUDGMENT IN A STATISTICAL TEST OF CONTROLS

The importance of judgment in statistical sampling was emphasized in Chapter 1. As previously stated, statistical sampling does not eliminate professional judgment. However, it does require quantification of some of the auditor's judgmental decisions.

Figure 3.3 delineates the steps in a nonstatistical test of controls compared with those in a statistical test of controls. Note that quantification of judgment occurs at step 4 (setting risk of assessing control risk too low and tolerable rate), step 5 (determining sample size), and step 8 (evaluating sample findings quantitatively). Step 6 (pertaining to sample selection) also might be different in a statistical test of controls. As discussed in Chapter 2, before a sample can be evaluated statistically it should be selected randomly.

Step 6 in Figure 3.3 indicates that the sample should be selected from at least the first nine months of the fiscal year. The nine months criterion is a guide used by many practitioners. The rationale for its use is that year-end substantive procedures include many transactions generated during the later months of the year and, therefore, will generate both substantive and tests of controls evidence (dual-purpose tests). SAS No. 55, as amended by SAS No. 78 and SAS No. 94 (AU 319.99), states that when the auditor obtains evidential matter about the design or operation of internal control policies and procedures during an interim period, he or she should make a judgment about the additional evidential matter that should be obtained for the remaining period. In making this judgment, the auditor should consider factors such as the significance of the assertion involved, the specific control being tested, the results of the tests of controls performed at the interim period, the length of the remaining period, and any evidence about operating effectiveness that will be obtained from the auditor's substantive tests.

Step 4 of Figure 3.3 indicates that for statistical testing the risk of assessing control risk too low (reliability level) and a tolerable deviation rate should be predefined. The risk of assessing control risk too low is determined in accordance with the maximum sampling risk that is acceptable. The tolerable deviation rate is based on guidelines adopted from practice. Both the risk of assessing control risk too low and the tolerable deviation rate (acceptable upper precision limit) are discussed and defined later in this chapter.

Step 8 of Figure 3.3 states that the sample findings must be evaluated quantitatively (statistically) and qualitatively. In fact, performing a qualitative deviation analysis on each observed deviation may be more strategically important to the auditor than a statistical projection based on the selected sample. For example, an auditor in a statistical test of controls may define a deviation as a sales invoice that is footed (totaled) incorrectly. Consequently, if in a sample of 100 sales invoices, two footing errors are observed—one for $10 and one for $5988—statistically, both deviations are treated equally. However, audit judgment may indicate that even with a 2-percent deviation rate, an accounting system that permits a large error to go undetected cannot be considered reliable.

Steps in a Nonstatistical Test of Controls	*Steps in a Statistical Test of Controls*	*Illustrative Statistical Test of Controls*
1. Define the objective(s) of the audit test.	Same.	Ascertain if invalid sales transactions are recorded in the sales journal that would affect the existence and valuation assertions for accounts receivable.
2. Define the relevant population(s) from which to sample, the attributes to be tested, and deviation conditions.	Same.	All transactions recorded in the sales journal from 1/1/0X through the interim test date. Testable attributes are accuracy of invoiced quantities and prices for sale transactions. Deviations are conditions in which the invoiced quantities do not agree with shipping documents or invoiced prices do not agree with approved price lists.
3. Determine that the physical representation of the population is complete.	Same.	Reconcile the total transactions recorded in the sales journal from 1/1/0X to the interim date to total sales for that period.
4. Make judgments about the risk of assessing control risk too low, the tolerable deviation rate, and the expected deviation rate.	Quantify the risk of assessing control risk too low, the tolerable deviation rate (acceptable upper precision limit), and expected deviation rate.	Set the risk of assessing control risk too low at 10% (reliability of 90%) and tolerable rate at 5%. Zero deviations are expected.
5. Determine the sample size judgmentally.	Determine the sample size using a mathematically derived sampling table.	Minimum sample size, if zero occurrences are observed, is 45 sales transactions.
6. Select a representative sample using a random-based method or haphazard selection.	Select the sample at random from at least the first nine months of the fiscal year.	Use a random-number table to select a sample of sales transactions from the sales journal.
7. Apply audit procedures to selected items—be alert for conditions not defined as deviations.	Same.	For each sample item examine the sales invoice and trace quantities to shipping documents and prices to approved price lists.

FIGURE 3.3   Comparison of Nonstatistical and Statistical Tests of Controls

Steps in a Nonstatistical Test of Controls	Steps in a Statistical Test of Controls	Illustrative Statistical Test of Controls
8. Evaluate evidence from the sample.	Evaluate sample evidence quantitatively and qualitatively.	Zero deviations noted; therefore, conclude that there is only a 10% risk that the actual rate of invalid sales and accounts receivable is more than 5%.
9. Combine the evidence from this test with the results of other relevant tests of controls to assess control risk for the existence and valuation assertions for accounts receivable. Ascertain the effect on the nature, timing, and extent of substantive auditing procedures.	Same.	Control risk is assessed at a low level: therefore, the sample size for the confirmation of accounts receivable is set relatively low. Accounts receivable can be confirmed at an interim date.

FIGURE 3.3   (Continued)

SETTING RISK OF ASSESSING CONTROL RISK TOO LOW (RELIABILITY LEVEL)

Generally, risk is the complement of reliability. In other words, one minus reliability is risk. The authoritative auditing literature [SAS No. 39 (AU 350)] is usually phrased in terms of risk, but in statistics the term *reliability* is more commonly used. Also, in statistics, the terms **reliability level** and **confidence level** are used interchangeably. *Reliability* refers to the probability of being right in making a conclusion about the operating effectiveness of a control. For example, if an auditor selects a 95 percent reliability level, he or she has a 5 percent chance (risk) of assessing control risk too low.[1] If the auditor decides that a 90 percent reliability level is acceptable, he or she has a 10 percent statistical chance of concluding that the control is operating effectively when it is not. In brief, the reliability level is the probability that the auditor's statistical conclusion will be correct. As Figure 3.4 depicts, the complement of reliability (1.0 − reliability) is the risk that the auditor will inappropriately conclude that the operating effectiveness of the control is sufficient to support the auditor's

---

[1]This assumes that the statistical evaluation and qualitative (judgmental) evaluation are the same.

Sample Results Indicate: Control Procedure Tested Is:

	Operating Effectively	Not Operating Effectively
Accept	Correct Decision	Risk of Assessing Control Risk Too Low
Reject	Risk of Assessing Control Risk Too High	Correct Decision

FIGURE 3.4   Tests of Control Sampling—Risk Matrix

planned assessed level of control risk. This risk is referred to as the **risk of assessing control risk too low.**

Figure 3.4 shows another risk—the **risk of assessing control risk too high.** The consequence of assessing control risk too high is that substantive tests are unnecessarily extensive. Audit efficiency is affected, but not audit effectiveness. The more serious error is assessing control risk too low. Therefore, attention will be focused on controlling that risk.

When tests of controls using audit sampling provide the primary evidence to support the auditor's assessed level of control risk, a low level of risk of assessing control risk too low is appropriate, usually 5 or 10 percent. Some CPA firms establish policy guidelines about the appropriate level of risk to be used for tests of controls that employ audit sampling.

TOLERABLE RATE (UPPER PRECISION LIMIT)

The **tolerable rate** [upper precision limit (UPL)] represents the maximum deviation rate established that the auditor would be willing to accept. Deviations in excess of that rate would cause the auditor to increase his or her assessed level of control risk. In determining the tolerable rate, the auditor should consider (*a*) the planned assessed level of control risk for the assertion being tested, and (*b*) the extent of assurance desired by the evidential matter in the sample. If, for example, the auditor plans to assess control risk at a low level, and he or she desires a large degree of evidence from the sample (i.e., no other tests of controls for the assertion are planned), a tolerable rate of 5 percent or lower might be considered appropriate. If the auditor either plans to assess control risk at a higher level or desires less evidence from the sample (i.e., other tests of controls are performed on the same assertion), a tolerable rate of 10 percent or more might be appropriate. The following table provides overlapping tolerable deviation rates based on the planned assessed level of control risk:

Planned Assessed Level of Control Risk	*Tolerable Rate*
Low	2%–7%
Moderate	6%–12%
Slightly below the maximum	11%–20%
Maximum	Omit test

In setting the tolerable deviation rate, the auditor also should consider that while deviations from the performance of control procedures increase the risk of misstatements in the accounting records, such deviations do not necessarily result in misstatements. For example, a cash disbursement that is not specifically approved may still be a properly authorized and recorded transaction.

Actually, in a fixed-sample-size or sequential attribute application, two upper precision limits are considered. The one described thus far is **acceptable (or desired) UPL.** Acceptable UPL is predefined and is referred to as the tolerable rate in SAS No. 39 (AU 350). The second UPL, referred to herein as **achieved (or calculated) UPL,** is calculated after the selected sample has been tested by using an appropriate mathematical calculation or attribute sampling evaluation table. Generally, if the test results are to support the auditor's planned assessed level of control risk, the tolerable rate (acceptable UPL) must be greater than or equal to the achieved UPL. However, the auditor's qualitative evaluation based on the statistical evaluation and error analysis may result in acceptance of the results, even though the specified tolerable rate (acceptable UPL) is less than achieved UPL, or vice versa. The auditor's conclusion, especially when he or she accepts the test results when the quantitative (statistical) evaluation indicates a rejection decision, should be adequately documented in the audit work papers.

Other actions that can be considered when the tolerable rate (acceptable UPL) is less than the achieved UPL are:

1. Review the definition of a deviation (error) to make sure it is consistent with the original purpose of the audit test.
2. Review each sampling unit considered to be a deviation in order to be certain it is a deviation as defined. (This action reduces nonsampling errors as discussed in Chapter 1.)

3. Perform expanded substantive tests. (Increase the planned assessed level of control risk.)

4. Increase the sample size until achieved UPL is less than or equal to the tolerable rate. (Normally, this will not be successful and is not cost effective except when the initial sample is small.)

FIXED-SAMPLE-SIZE ATTRIBUTE SAMPLING

As previously discussed for controls that leave an audit trail, the extent of testing might be objectively determined by using fixed-sample-size attribute sampling. Recall from Figure 3.3 that before the extent of testing decision is reached, the auditor must have already defined the objective(s) of the audit test, defined the population and testable attributes, and determined the direction of the audit test. To facilitate determination of the sample size for fixed-sample-size attribute sampling, tables will be used. In addition, tables also will be used to evaluate sample findings.

Tables 3.1 to 3.4 are based on the binomial distribution. The tables are exact only when sampling is *with* replacement. When sampling *without* replacement is used, the hypergeometric distribution is appropriate. Tables are not, however, easily constructed for the latter. Although auditors usually sample without replacement, Tables 3.1 to 3.4 still may be used. When sampling without replacement, the binomial tables produce valid, but conservative results.

Fixed-sample-size attribute sampling is employed when the auditor desires to estimate the population deviation rate (sample deviations divided by the sample size) and the achieved upper precision limit.

The first two tables (Tables 3.1 and 3.2) are used to determine sample size; Tables 3.3 and 3.4 are used to evaluate sample findings. *To determine sample size* (Tables 3.1 and 3.2), three requirements must be estimated or known. The auditor must:

1. Establish the reliability level. This decision is based on the risk of assessing control risk too low that the auditor is willing to accept.

2. Estimate the population deviation rate in percent. To establish this, the auditor may use prior knowledge or experience.

3. Define the tolerable rate (acceptable upper precision limit). This is a percent (rate) that is equated to the maximum permissible deviation rate. It is not one minus reliability, and it must be determined judgmentally by the auditor rather than computed.

To illustrate fixed-sample-size attribute sampling, assume that an auditor wants to test credit approvals on 20,000 sales invoices processed during the year. He or she needs a statistical sample that will give 95 percent confidence that not more than 5 percent of the sales invoices were not approved. The auditor estimates from

TABLE 3.1   Determination of Sample Size: Reliability, 90%
(Risk of Assessing Control Risk Too Low 10%)
(Allowable number of deviations in parentheses)

Expected Population Deviation Rate	Tolerable Rate										
	2%	3%	4%	5%	6%	7%	8%	9%	10%	15%	20%
0.00%	114(0)	76(0)	57(0)	45(0)	38(0)	32(0)	28(0)	25(0)	22(0)	15(0)	11(0)
0.25	194(1)	129(1)	96(1)	77(1)	64(1)	55(1)	48(1)	42(1)	38(1)	25(1)	18(1)
0.50	194(1)	129(1)	96(1)	77(1)	64(1)	55(1)	48(1)	42(1)	38(1)	25(1)	18(1)
0.75	265(2)	129(1)	96(1)	77(1)	64(1)	55(1)	48(1)	42(1)	38(1)	25(1)	18(1)
1.00	*	176(2)	96(1)	77(1)	64(1)	55(1)	48(1)	42(1)	38(1)	25(1)	18(1)
1.25	*	221(3)	132(2)	77(1)	64(1)	55(1)	48(1)	42(1)	38(1)	25(1)	18(1)
1.50	*	*	132(2)	105(2)	64(1)	55(1)	48(1)	42(1)	38(1)	25(1)	18(1)
1.75	*	*	166(3)	105(2)	88(2)	55(1)	48(1)	42(1)	38(1)	25(1)	18(1)
2.00	*	*	198(4)	132(3)	88(2)	75(2)	48(1)	42(1)	38(1)	25(1)	18(1)
2.25	*	*	*	132(3)	88(2)	75(2)	65(2)	42(1)	38(1)	25(1)	18(1)
2.50	*	*	*	158(4)	110(3)	75(2)	65(2)	58(2)	38(1)	25(1)	18(1)
2.75	*	*	*	209(6)	132(4)	94(3)	65(2)	58(2)	52(2)	25(1)	18(1)
3.00	*	*	*	*	132(4)	94(3)	65(2)	58(2)	52(2)	25(1)	18(1)
3.25	*	*	*	*	153(5)	113(4)	82(3)	58(2)	52(2)	25(1)	18(1)
3.50	*	*	*	*	194(7)	113(4)	82(3)	73(3)	52(2)	25(1)	18(1)
3.75	*	*	*	*	*	131(5)	98(4)	73(3)	52(2)	25(1)	18(1)
4.00	*	*	*	*	*	149(6)	98(4)	73(3)	65(3)	25(1)	18(1)
5.00	*	*	*	*	*	*	160(8)	115(6)	78(4)	34(2)	18(1)
6.00	*	*	*	*	*	*	*	182(11)	116(7)	43(3)	25(2)
7.00	*	*	*	*	*	*	*	*	199(14)	52(4)	25(2)

Note: This table assumes a large population.

*Sample size is too large to be cost effective for most audit applications.

Source: AICPA, Auditing Guide, *Audit Sampling* (New York, 2001).

TABLE 3.2   Determination of Sample Size: Reliability, 95%
(Risk of Assessing Control Risk Too Low 5%)
(Allowable number of deviations in parentheses)

Expected Population Deviation Rate	Tolerable Rate										
	2%	3%	4%	5%	6%	7%	8%	9%	10%	15%	20%
0.00%	149(0)	99(0)	74(0)	59(0)	49(0)	42(0)	36(0)	32(0)	29(0)	19(0)	14(0)
0.25	236(1)	157(1)	117(1)	93(1)	78(1)	66(1)	58(1)	51(1)	46(1)	30(1)	22(1)
0.50	*	157(1)	117(1)	93(1)	78(1)	66(1)	58(1)	51(1)	46(1)	30(1)	22(1)
0.75	*	208(2)	117(1)	93(1)	78(1)	66(1)	58(1)	51(1)	46(1)	30(1)	22(1)
1.00	*	*	156(2)	93(1)	78(1)	66(1)	58(1)	51(1)	46(1)	30(1)	22(1)
1.25	*	*	156(2)	124(2)	78(1)	66(1)	58(1)	51(1)	46(1)	30(1)	22(1)
1.50	*	*	192(3)	124(2)	103(2)	66(1)	58(1)	51(1)	46(1)	30(1)	22(1)
1.75	*	*	227(4)	153(3)	103(2)	88(2)	77(2)	51(1)	46(1)	30(1)	22(1)
2.00	*	*	*	181(4)	127(3)	88(2)	77(2)	68(2)	46(1)	30(1)	22(1)
2.25	*	*	*	208(5)	127(3)	88(2)	77(2)	68(2)	61(2)	30(1)	22(1)
2.50	*	*	*	*	150(4)	109(3)	77(2)	68(2)	61(2)	30(1)	22(1)
2.75	*	*	*	*	173(5)	109(3)	95(3)	68(2)	61(2)	30(1)	22(1)
3.00	*	*	*	*	195(6)	129(4)	95(3)	84(3)	61(2)	30(1)	22(1)
3.25	*	*	*	*	*	148(5)	112(4)	84(3)	61(2)	30(1)	22(1)
3.50	*	*	*	*	*	167(6)	112(4)	84(3)	76(3)	40(2)	22(1)
3.75	*	*	*	*	*	185(7)	129(5)	100(4)	76(3)	40(2)	22(1)
4.00	*	*	*	*	*	*	146(6)	100(4)	89(4)	40(2)	22(1)
5.00	*	*	*	*	*	*	*	158(8)	116(6)	40(2)	30(2)
6.00	*	*	*	*	*	*	*	*	179(11)	50(3)	30(2)
7.00	*	*	*	*	*	*	*	*	*	68(5)	37(3)

Note: This table assumes a large population.

*Sample size is too large to be cost effective for most audit applications.

Source: AICPA, Auditing Guide, *Audit Sampling* (New York, 2001).

TABLE 3.3   Evaluation of Results: Reliability, 90%
(Risk of Assessing Control Risk Too Low 10%)
Table Presents Achieved Upper Precision Limit: Percent Rate of Deviation

Sample Size	*Actual Number of Deviations Found*										
	0	*1*	*2*	*3*	*4*	*5*	*6*	*7*	*8*	*9*	*10*
20	10.9	18.1	*	*	*	*	*	*	*	*	*
25	8.8	14.7	19.9	*	*	*	*	*	*	*	*
30	7.4	12.4	16.8	*	*	*	*	*	*	*	*
35	6.4	10.7	14.5	18.1	*	*	*	*	*	*	*
40	5.6	9.4	12.8	16.0	19.0	*	*	*	*	*	*
45	5.0	8.4	11.4	14.3	17.0	19.7	*	*	*	*	*
50	4.6	7.6	10.3	12.9	15.4	17.8	*	*	*	*	*
55	4.1	6.9	9.4	11.8	14.1	16.3	18.4	*	*	*	*
60	3.8	6.4	8.7	10.8	12.9	15.0	16.9	18.9	*	*	*
70	3.3	5.5	7.5	9.3	11.1	12.9	14.6	16.3	17.9	19.6	*
80	2.9	4.8	6.6	8.2	9.8	11.3	12.8	14.3	15.8	17.2	18.6
90	2.6	4.3	5.9	7.3	8.7	10.1	11.5	12.8	14.1	15.4	16.6
100	2.3	3.9	5.3	6.6	7.9	9.1	10.3	11.5	12.7	13.9	15.0
120	2.0	3.3	4.4	5.5	6.6	7.6	8.7	9.7	10.7	11.6	12.6
160	1.5	2.5	3.3	4.2	5.0	5.8	6.5	7.3	8.0	8.8	9.5
200	1.2	2.0	2.7	3.4	4.0	4.6	5.3	5.9	6.5	7.1	7.6

Note: This table presents upper limits as percentages. This table assumes a large population.

*Over 20 percent.

Source: AICPA, Auditing Guide, *Audit Sampling* (New York, 2001).

previous experience that about 1 percent of the sales have deviations (are not approved).

$$\text{Expected deviation} = 1\%$$
$$\text{Tolerable rate} = 5\%$$
$$\text{Reliability level (one minus risk of assessing control risk too low)} = 95\%$$

The appropriate table to use (see Tables 3.1 and 3.2) is determined by the predefined reliability (one minus risk of assessing control risk too low). Table 3.2 corresponds with 95 percent reliability. According to Table 3.2, the required sample size (*n*) is 93. As shown in the table on page 60, "To Determine Sample Size for 95% Reliability," this is determined by the intersection of the 1 percent "expected percent rate of deviation" row with the 5 percent "tolerable rate" column. The number of deviations that may be contained in the sample without requiring the auditor to increase his or her assessed level of control risk is shown in parentheses as 1.

TABLE 3.4   Evaluation of Results: Reliability, 95%
(Risk of Assessing Control Risk Too Low 5%)
Table Presents Achieved Upper Precision Limit: Percent Rate of Deviation

Sample Size	*Actual Number of Deviations Found*										
	0	*1*	*2*	*3*	*4*	*5*	*6*	*7*	*8*	*9*	*10*
25	11.3	17.6	*	*	*	*	*	*	*	*	*
30	9.5	14.9	19.6	*	*	*	*	*	*	*	*
35	8.3	12.9	17.0	*	*	*	*	*	*	*	*
40	7.3	11.4	15.0	18.3	*	*	*	*	*	*	*
45	6.5	10.5	13.4	16.4	19.2	*	*	*	*	*	*
50	5.9	9.2	12.1	14.8	17.4	19.9	*	*	*	*	*
55	5.4	8.4	11.1	13.5	15.9	18.2	*	*	*	*	*
60	4.9	7.7	10.2	12.5	14.7	16.8	18.8	*	*	*	*
65	4.6	7.1	9.4	11.5	13.6	15.5	17.4	19.3	*	*	*
70	4.2	6.6	8.8	10.8	12.6	14.5	16.3	18.0	19.7	*	*
75	4.0	6.2	8.2	10.1	11.8	13.6	15.2	16.9	18.5	20.0	*
80	3.7	5.8	7.7	9.5	11.1	12.7	14.3	15.9	17.4	18.9	*
90	3.3	5.2	6.9	8.4	9.9	11.4	12.8	14.2	15.5	16.8	18.2
100	3.0	4.7	6.2	7.6	9.0	10.3	11.5	12.8	14.0	15.2	16.4
125	2.4	3.8	5.0	6.1	7.2	8.3	9.3	10.3	11.3	12.3	13.2
150	2.0	3.2	4.2	5.1	6.0	6.9	7.8	8.6	9.5	10.3	11.1
200	1.5	2.4	3.2	3.9	4.6	5.2	5.9	6.5	7.2	7.8	8.4

Note: This table presents upper limits as percentages. This table assumes a large population.

*Over 20 percent.

Source: AICPA, Auditing Guide, *Audit Sampling* (New York, 2001).

In situations where the auditor does not know what the **expected deviation rate** is (1 percent above), a pilot sample of 25 may be selected to estimate the population deviation rate. To illustrate, if a sample of 25 is selected and one deviation is discovered for a given attribute, the estimated population deviation rate is 4 percent (1 ÷ 25). Assuming the reliability level desired is 90 percent (10 percent risk of assessing control risk too low) and the tolerable rate is 8 percent, we note that the sample size from Table 3.1 is equal to 98.

To evaluate sample findings, Tables 3.3 and 3.4 are used. To illustrate, consider the first example above where the sample size is calculated to be 93. Table 3.4 for 95 percent reliability (5 percent risk of assessing control risk too low) is the correct table to employ in evaluating the sampling findings. Since the sample size of 93 does not appear in the table, it is appropriate to use the largest sample size that does not exceed 93, or 90. If three deviations are found in the sample, the achieved upper precision limit is 8.4 percent. This is determined by the intersection of the 90 sample size row with the "3" deviations column.

To Determine Sample Size for 95% Reliability
(Risk of Assessing Control Risk Too Low 5%)

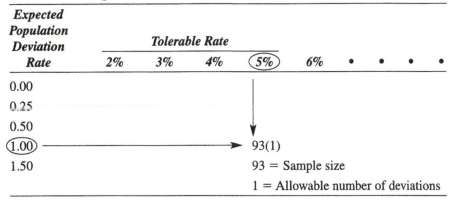

Expected Population Deviation Rate	Tolerable Rate								
	2%	3%	4%	(5%)	6%	•	•	•	•
0.00									
0.25									
0.50									
(1.00)				→ 93(1)					
1.50				93 = Sample size					
				1 = Allowable number of deviations					

Sample Evaluation Table for 95% Reliability
(5% Risk of Assessing Control Risk Too Low)

Sample Size	Actual Number of Deviations Found										
	0	1	2	(3)	4	5	6	7	8	•	•
10											
20											
•											
•											
(90)				→ 8.4 = Achieved upper precision limit							

Other findings from Table 3.4 for the sample size of 90 are evaluated as follows:

Deviations Discovered	Achieved UPL on Deviation Rate
0	3.3%
1	5.2% (5% based on 93 items)
2	6.9%
6	12.8%

Of course, since the tolerable rate (acceptable UPL) was 5 percent, two or more deviations usually would cause the auditor to conclude that this control was not operating sufficiently to justify the planned assessed level of control risk. As indicated in the table, the achieved UPL for 1 deviation is 5.2 percent. However, this results from the fact that a sample size of 90 was evaluated, which is less than the actual sample size of 93. If a sample size of 93 could be evaluated by Table 3.4, we would find that the achieved UPL with 1 deviation is 5 percent.

Notice that the achieved UPL incorporates an allowance for sampling risk. One deviation in a sample of 93 is a rate of 1.1 percent, but the upper limit on the deviation rate at a 5 percent risk of assessing control risk too low is 5 percent. The difference between the achieved UPL of 5 percent and the actual sample deviation rate of 1.1 percent (at a sample size of 93) is 3.9 percent. This is the allowance for sampling risk.

SEQUENTIAL (STOP-OR-GO) ATTRIBUTE SAMPLING

Under fixed-sample-size attribute sampling, the auditor examines a single sample of a specified size; under sequential attribute sampling, the sample may be selected in several steps; each step relies on the results of the previous step. The auditor may gain efficiency by applying sequential sampling. Sequential sampling is used when the auditor expects a zero or very low rate of deviations. By selecting sequential sampling, the auditor may halt sampling if zero or a defined number of **occurrences** are observed. The sample items are examined in groups until the cumulative evidence is sufficient to achieve a predefined reliability and an acceptable upper precision limit. In contrast, a fixed-sample-size attribute application requires larger sample sizes, especially if the expected deviation rate is overstated. In a sequential application, the auditor must specify:

1. Risk of assessing control risk too low (one minus desired reliability)
2. Tolerable rate (acceptable upper precision limit)

Tables 3.5 and 3.6 are presented to illustrate sequential sampling. Although the tables are based on sampling with replacement, auditors typically employ sampling without replacement when using them.

TABLE 3.5   Minimum Sample Size Table for Tests of Controls
(Zero Expected Deviations)

	Sample Size Based on Risk of Assessing Control Risk Too Low		
Tolerable Rate	*10%*	*5%*	*2.5%*
10%	24	30	37
9	27	34	42
8	30	38	47
7	35	43	53
6	40	50	62
5	48	60	74
4	60	75	93
3	80	100	124
2	120	150	285
1	240	300	370

TABLE 3.6   Attribute Sampling Table for Determining Sequential Sample Sizes and Upper Precision Limit of Population Deviation Rate Based on Sample Results

Number of Deviations	Risk Factors for Risk of Assessing Control Risk Too Low		
	10%	*5%*	*2.5%*
0	2.4	3.0	3.7
1	3.9	4.8	5.6
2	5.4	6.3	7.3
3	6.7	7.8	8.8
4	8.0	9.2	10.3
5	9.3	10.6	11.7
6	10.6	11.9	13.1
7	11.8	13.2	14.5
8	13.0	14.5	15.8
9	14.3	16.0	17.1
10	15.5	17.0	18.4
11	16.7	18.3	19.7
12	18.0	19.5	21.0
13	19.0	21.0	22.3
14	20.2	22.0	23.5
15	21.4	23.4	24.7
16	22.6	24.3	26.0
17	23.8	26.0	27.3
18	25.0	27.0	28.5
19	26.0	28.0	29.6
20	27.1	29.0	31.0
21	28.3	30.3	32.0
22	29.3	31.5	33.3
23	30.5	32.6	34.6
24	31.4	33.8	35.7
25	32.7	35.0	37.0
26	34.0	36.1	38.1
27	35.0	37.3	39.4
28	36.1	38.5	40.5
29	37.2	39.6	41.7
30	38.4	40.7	42.9
31	39.1	42.0	44.0
32	40.3	43.0	45.1
33	41.5	44.2	46.3
34	42.7	45.3	47.5
35	43.8	46.4	48.8
36	45.0	47.6	49.9

TABLE 3.6   (Continued)

Number of Deviations	Risk Factors for Risk of Assessing Control Risk Too Low		
	10%	5%	2.5%
37	46.1	48.7	51.0
38	47.2	49.8	52.1
39	48.3	51.0	53.4
40	49.4	52.0	54.5
41	50.5	53.2	55.6
42	51.6	54.5	56.8
43	52.6	55.5	58.0
44	54.0	56.6	59.0
45	55.0	57.7	60.3
46	56.0	59.0	62.6
47	57.0	60.0	63.7
48	58.0	61.1	63.7
49	59.7	62.2	64.8
50	60.4	63.3	65.0
51	61.5	64.5	67.0

Source: Adapted from a table developed by Marvin Tummins and Robert H. Strawser, "A Confidence Limits Table for Attribute Sampling," *Accounting Review* (October 1976), pp. 907–912.

Table 3.5 presents the minimum sample sizes that should be used for risks of assessing control risk too low of 10, 5, and 2.5 percent and the tolerable rates of 10 percent through 1 percent. The final sample may be larger than the initial sample specified in Table 3.5—if the auditor expects or finds deviations.

Table 3.6 permits estimation of the achieved UPL. An estimate of the achieved UPL is derived by dividing the proper *risk factor* taken from Table 3.6 by the sample size used to evaluate the population. The risk factor is determined by the intersection of the "risk" column with the "number of deviations" row. For example, using 5 percent risk of assessing control risk too low and a sample size of 200 with 14 deviations yields 22.0. This represents an achieved upper precision limit of 11 percent (22.0 ÷ 200).

Table 3.6 is particularly applicable when:

$$N > 1000$$

$$n > 20$$

$$n/N < 10\%, \text{ and}$$

the estimated population deviation rate < 20 percent, where:

$$N = \text{population size}$$

$$n = \text{sample size}$$

If Table 3.6 is used in other sampling situations, however, the only error made is a conservative estimate of the achieved UPL and an overestimate of the risk of assessing control risk too low. This, of course, means that the auditor may reject the results and apply unnecessary substantive procedures. In this situation, audit cost may increase, but audit risk does not. As previously discussed, this concept is referred to as the risk of assessing control risk too high.

To apply sequential sampling, the auditor typically initiates the application via a three-step process.

Step 1. Specify the tolerable rate (acceptable upper precision limit) and the risk of assessing control risk too low (reliability level) desired.

> *For example, a 5 percent tolerable rate and a 5 percent risk of assessing control risk too low.*

Step 2. Use Table 3.5 to determine your initial sample.

> *Minimum sample from Table 3.5 = 60*

Step 3. Construct a stop-or-go decision table using Table 3.6 as explained below.

If the auditor finds one deviation in a sample of 60, the achieved upper precision limit at a 5 percent risk of assessing control risk too low is 8 percent ($4.8 \div 60$). This is greater than the 5 percent tolerable rate specified in step 1. The auditor can determine the sample size for the next step by dividing the risk factor from Table 3.6 by the tolerable rate and subtracting the initial sample size. Therefore, the auditor may decide to extend the sample by an additional 36 items to a total sample of 96 ($4.8 \div 0.05$ tolerable rate). If zero occurrences are observed in the 36 additional sample items, the auditor can conclude that he or she is 95 percent confident that the population deviation rate is not greater than 5 percent ($4.8 \div 96$). There is a 5 percent risk that the population deviation rate exceeds 5 percent.

If, on the other hand, the auditor finds two deviations in the initial sample of 60, the achieved upper precision limit is 10.5 percent ($6.3 \div 60$). This is again greater than the 5 percent tolerable rate specified in step 1. Therefore, the auditor may decide to extend the sample by an additional 66 ($6.3 \div 0.05$ tolerable rate minus 60). If zero deviations are observed in the 66 additional sample items, the auditor can conclude that he or she is 95 percent confident that the population deviation rate does not exceed 5 percent. If, instead, the auditor observed one more deviation (total deviations now equal three), the achieved upper precision limit is 6.2 percent ($7.8 \div 126$). The auditor must then decide whether to extend the sample by an additional 30 items ($7.8 \div 0.05 = 156$ total sample). Another possibility the auditor has is to use the approximate sample deviation rate of 3 percent ($3 \div 126$) as an estimate of the expected deviation rate in order to use fixed-sample-size attribute sampling.

In designing a sequential application, the auditor will not typically extend the sample to more than three times the initial sample size. On reaching that point, the auditor might consider increasing the planned assessed level of control risk or shifting to fixed-sample-size attribute sampling. Also, after each iteration the auditor should perform a **qualitative deviation analysis;** that is, do the nature and cause of deviations lead to the conclusion that a material misstatement could exist in the financial statements and not be detected by the system? Qualitative analysis may indicate that the particular attribute cannot be relied on to limit substantive testing. On the other hand, rather than extend the initial sample, the auditor might decide that it is more efficient to assess control risk at the maximum and expand substantive tests. In no circumstance should sequential sampling be mechanically applied.

To apply sequential sampling, the auditor may construct a decision table similar to the following:

Step	Cumulative Sample Size to Use:	Stop If Cumulative Deviations Are Equal to:	Sample More If Deviations Are:	Go to Step 5 If Deviations Are at Least:
1	30	0	1–3	4
2	48	1	2–3	4
3	63	2	3	4
4	78	3		4
5	Consider increasing assessed level of control risk or using fixed-sample-size attribute sampling.			

From the above discussion and illustrations, note that Table 3.6 may be used in two ways. First, in evaluation, to determine achieved UPL, the appropriate risk factor from the table is divided by the sample size.

$$\text{Acheived UPL} = \frac{\text{Risk factor at desired risk of assessing control risk too low for deviations observed}}{\text{Sample size}}$$

Second, in planning, to determine total sample size, the appropriate risk factor is divided by the tolerable rate (acceptable UPL).

$$\text{Sample size} = \frac{\text{Risk factor at desired risk of assessing control risk too low for number of deviations expected}}{\text{Tolerable rate}}$$

1. Define deviation as critical or noncritical to audit scope.
2. Determine the nature and cause of each critical deviation.
   a. Intentional or unintentional
   b. Carelessness or misunderstood instructions
   c. Frequent or infrequent
   d. Systematic or random
   e. Likely or actual dollar effect, if any
3. Evaluate the worst possible effect of each critical deviation.
4. Decide whether the critical deviations were consistent or inconsistent with the planned assessed level of control risk and modify it, accordingly.
5. Determine the effect of the deviations on other tests of controls and substantive tests. (Keep in mind that auditors are concerned with the population deviations, not the sample deviations).
6. Suggest improved procedures to the client, preferably in writing.
7. *Remember:* Even when the statistical evaluation conclusions are within acceptable limits, deviation analysis should be performed.

FIGURE 3.5   Qualitative Analysis Model

Table 3.6 is especially useful in practice, because any sample size (e.g., 53, 49, 86) can be evaluated. The practicing auditor's planned sample size is sometimes reduced because of discards or voids.

QUALITATIVE ANALYSIS IN ATTRIBUTE SAMPLING APPLICATIONS

All **deviations** detected while doing tests of controls, whether control deviations or monetary misstatements, should be analyzed regardless of *their statistical impact.* To determine what impact a deviation might have on audit scope, if any, can be a difficult problem. Given a certain type of deviation, the auditor has to determine the potential financial statement impact, the range and related probabilities of misstatement, and the type(s) of substantive test(s) that could be used to determine if the financial statements were misstated.

The basic decision model employed by auditors in **deviation analysis** is presented in Figure 3.5. To distinguish a **critical deviation** from a **noncritical deviation,** the auditor should clearly understand the distinction between a control deviation and a monetary deviation. Control deviations do not necessarily produce monetary misstatements in the financial statements. For example, an unapproved disbursement voucher may nevertheless be a valid transaction that was properly paid and recorded. Control deviations increase the risk of monetary misstatements, but certainly not in a one-to-one ratio.

Some attributes are critical to audit scope, but others are not. For example, the failure of a client to take cash discounts may be evaluated in a disbursements test.

Whether the client takes cash discounts has virtually no impact on audit scope. Of course, the failure to take cash discounts may be an item that should be included in a letter to management on possible improvements in operations or controls.

Some attributes are more critical than others. Generally, the more likely a control deviation is to produce a monetary deviation, the more critical it is. For example, the auditor may be more tolerant of a high deviation rate in credit limit reviews than for accuracy on sales invoices.

ILLUSTRATIVE ATTRIBUTE SAMPLING APPLICATION

To demonstrate work paper documentation and the relationship of control testing to substantive testing, an illustrative detail sales test is presented. *The audit objective is to determine if internal controls are operating effectively and are adequate to provide proper control over shipments and billings to customers and the distribution thereof in the accounts. The population consists of sales invoices for the period 1/1/0X to 10/12/0X. The sampling frame is the sales invoice number recorded in the sales journal. Sequential sampling will be used with 95 percent reliability or 5 percent risk of assessing control risk too low and 10 percent tolerable rate.* The following attributes were predefined.

1. Were supporting documents (customer purchase order, shipping document, and freight bill) agreed to sales invoice details?
2. Were prices in agreement with the approved current price list in effect at the date of sale or other price authorization—for example, sales contract, bid proposal, and the like?
3. Were the charges recorded properly in the accounts receivable subsidiary ledger?
4. Were all documents tested for clerical accuracy?
5. Was credit memo for returns or allowances (if any) properly approved?
6. Was credit approved by the credit manager?

Actual test results were as follows:

Attribute Number	Actual Sample Size	Number of Deviations	Achieved UPL (in percent)
1	30	0	10
2	63	2	10
3	50	3	16
4	78	3	10
5	30	0	10
6	48	1	10

Before a decision to accept the results can be made concerning any of the six attributes tested, qualitative deviation analysis must be performed on *all* deviations noted. Qualitative analysis data can be analyzed and documented as follows:

Attribute Number	Number of Deviations	Nature of Deviations	Effect on Audit Scope
1	—	—	—
2	2	In both instances, the sales price was mistakenly obtained from the approved price list instead of the sales contract. The total overbilling was $150.	No expansion of tests of controls or substantive tests is needed.
3	3	In each instance, the amount was erroneously added to the receivable detail of different company.	Because of the potential significance of this type of deviation, the confirmation of accounts receivable will be expanded. Control risk will be assessed at a moderate level rather than a low level for determining the sample size for confirmation purposes.
4	3	All three of the deviations noted were extension errors apparently due to haste and multiplication mistakes. The extension errors were less than $100 each, except one that resulted in overbilling of $325.	Extension errors appear to be excessive, even though the achieved UPL is 10%. Because of the potential significance of this deviation, the 50 largest sales transactions will be reviewed for computational errors.
5	0	—	—
6	1	Credit was not approved for a new customer.	Credit manager indicated that this rarely happens. Review five new customer invoices to test representation.

Based on quantitative evaluation and qualitative evaluation, attributes 1, 2, and 5 can be relied on to reduce the assessed level of control risk and limit substantive tests (i.e., positive receivable confirmations). Attributes 3 and 4 cannot be relied on to reduce the assessed level of control risk, and, accordingly, audit scope must be modified as indicated. Attribute 6 must be tested further (as indicated) to determine if it is operating effectively. Also, as required by SAS No. 60, *Communication of Internal Control Related Matters Noted in an Audit* (AU 325), the auditor should consider whether reportable conditions exist related to attributes 3 and 4. These significant deficiencies should be communicated to senior management and the audit committee of the board of directors.

DISCOVERY SAMPLING

Just as sequential sampling is a special kind of attribute sampling, so is discovery sampling. In *selected* situations, the auditor may apply a discovery sampling technique. **Discovery sampling** is used when the auditor believes that the population occurrence rate is near zero.[2] But in case the occurrence rate is not zero, discovery sampling applications are designed to yield a large enough sample size so that at least one occurrence will be produced. Actually, two conditions should generally exist before discovery sampling is used. They are:

- When the auditor's best judgment of the population occurrence rate is zero or near zero percent.
- When the auditor is looking for a *very* critical characteristic (e.g., payroll padding) that, if discovered, might be indicative of more widespread fraud or serious errors in the financial statements.

Discovery sampling also is useful in substantive testing. If the auditor's objective is to discover at least one example of a type of misstatement having a potentially material effect on an account balance, then discovery sampling should be considered. In this instance, discovery sampling may be more effective than trying to design a variable sampling application concerned with both misstatement identification and estimation. In practice, discovery sampling often is used in confirming account balances in large banks and savings and loan institutions that have very effective internal control (i.e., few misstatements are expected).

In a discovery sampling application, the following prerequisites must be defined:

1. Characteristic to be evaluated
2. Reliability desired
3. Maximum acceptable occurrence rate (upper precision limit)
4. Definition and size of population

---

[2]Typically, in discovery sampling applications, an occurrence is defined as a monetary misstatement or a control deviation.

TABLE 3.7   Discovery Sampling Tables: Probability in Percent of Including at Least One Occurrence in a Sample
(for populations between 2000 and 5000)

Sample Size	*Upper Precision Limit: Critical Rate of Occurrence*							
	0.3%	*0.4%*	*0.5%*	*0.6%*	*0.8%*	*1%*	*1.5%*	*2%*
50	14%	18%	22%	26%	33%	40%	53%	64%
60	17	21	26	30	38	45	60	70
70	19	25	30	35	43	51	66	76
80	22	28	33	38	48	56	70	80
90	24	31	37	42	52	60	75	84
100	26	33	40	46	56	64	78	87
120	31	39	46	52	62	70	84	91
140	35	43	51	57	68	76	88	94
160	39	48	56	62	73	80	91	96
200	46	56	64	71	81	87	95	98
240	52	63	71	77	86	92	98	99
300	61	71	79	84	92	96	99	99+
340	65	76	83	88	94	97	99+	99+
400	71	81	88	92	96	98	99+	99+
460	77	86	91	95	98	99	99+	99+
500	79	88	93	96	99	99	99+	99+
600	85	92	96	98	99	99+	99+	99+
700	90	95	98	99	99+	99+	99+	99+
800	93	97	99	99	99+	99+	99+	99+
900	95	98	99	99+	99+	99+	99+	99+
1000	97	99	99	99+	99+	99+	99+	99+

Source: Used with permission of the AICPA.

Tables 3.7 to 3.9 are discovery sampling tables.[3] To determine which of the three tables to use in a discovery sampling application, first define the population to be sampled and its size. Assume that for a given application, the auditor has a population size N equal to 6500 payroll checks; therefore, Table 3.8 is the correct table to use *to determine sample size.*

Next, the auditor defines reliability and maximum acceptable occurrence rate. Assume that reliability is set at 95 percent and that the maximum acceptable occurrence rate is set at 1 percent. To determine sample size, the auditor goes down the 1 percent column until the desired reliability factor is located (or the next highest reliability level if the one he or she is searching for is not in the table). The sample size n is 300.

[3]Tables 3.7 to 3.9 are taken from "Sampling for Attributes: Estimation and Discovery." Supplementary Section. *An Auditor's Approach to Statistical Sampling,* Volume 2 (New York: AICPA. 1974).

TABLE 3.8 Discovery Sampling Tables: Probability in Percent of Including at Least One Occurrence in a Sample
(for populations between 5000 and 10,000)

Sample Size	Upper Precision Limit: Critical Rate of Occurrence							
	0.1%	0.2%	0.3%	0.4%	0.5%	0.75%	1%	2%
50	5%	10%	14%	18%	22%	31%	40%	64%
60	6	11	17	21	26	36	45	70
70	7	13	19	25	30	41	51	76
80	8	15	21	28	33	45	55	80
90	9	17	24	30	36	49	60	84
100	10	18	26	33	40	53	64	87
120	11	21	30	38	45	60	70	91
140	13	25	35	43	51	65	76	94
160	15	28	38	48	55	70	80	96
200	18	33	45	56	64	78	87	98
240	22	39	52	62	70	84	91	99
300	26	46	60	70	78	90	95	99+
340	29	50	65	75	82	93	97	99+
400	34	56	71	81	87	95	98	99+
460	38	61	76	85	91	97	99	99+
500	40	64	79	87	92	98	99	99+
600	46	71	84	92	96	99	99+	99+
700	52	77	89	95	97	99+	99+	99+
800	57	81	92	96	98	99+	99+	99+
900	61	85	94	98	99	99+	99+	99+
1000	65	88	96	99	99	99+	99+	99+
1500	80	96	99	99+	99+	99+	99+	99+
2000	89	99	99+	99+	99+	99+	99+	99+

Source: Used with permission of the AICPA.

The third step is to select 300 payroll checks at random from the population of 6500 payroll checks and to substantively test each sample item. Finally, the evaluation stage is reached. If no misstatements are discovered in the sample examined, the auditor can immediately state that the sampling plan criterion has been achieved; that is, the auditor can state that he or she is 95 percent certain that the worst likely misstatement rate in the population does not exceed 1 percent.

On the other hand, if one or more misstatements are located, the auditor cannot make the above statistical statement. Perhaps no statistical conclusion will be expressed. Expanded audit procedures may be applied. Client employees under audit supervision might examine every one of the remaining population items. If the sole objective is discovery, the auditor may stop auditing the sample items as soon as he or she finds an occurrence. For example, if the auditor merely wishes to find

TABLE 3.9   Discovery Sampling Tables: Probability in Percent of Including at Least One Occurrence in a Sample
(for populations over 10,000)

Sample Size	Upper Precision Limit: Critical Rate of Occurrence							
	0.01%	0.05%	0.1%	0.2%	0.3%	0.5%	1%	2%
50		2%	5%	9%	14%	22%	39%	64%
60	1%	3	6	11	16	26	45	70
70	1	3	7	13	19	30	51	76
80	1	4	8	15	21	33	55	80
90	1	4	9	16	24	36	60	84
100	1	5	10	18	26	39	63	87
120	1	6	11	21	30	45	70	91
140	1	7	13	24	34	50	76	94
160	2	8	15	27	38	55	80	96
200	2	10	18	33	45	63	87	98
240	2	11	21	38	51	70	91	99
300	3	14	26	45	59	78	95	99+
340	3	16	29	49	64	82	97	99+
400	4	18	33	55	70	87	98	99+
460	5	21	37	60	75	90	99	99+
500	5	22	39	63	78	92	99	99+
600	6	26	45	70	84	95	99+	99+
700	7	30	50	75	88	97	99+	99+
800	8	33	55	80	91	98	99+	99+
900	9	36	59	83	93	99	99+	99+
1000	10	39	63	86	95	99	99+	99+
1500	14	53	78	95	99	99+	99+	99+
2000	18	63	86	98	99+	99+	99+	99+
2500	22	71	92	99	99+	99+	99+	99+
3000	26	78	95	99+	99+	99+	99+	99+

Source: Used with permission of the AICPA.

one misstatement and to review the nature of the discrepancy, the sampling process might stop if the auditor observed a misstatement in the tenth sample item, even though a sample size of 300 was indicated. Conversely, a misstatement might not be discovered until the 299th item was randomly selected. The point is, if the auditor simply wants to find one misstatement and evaluate it, the sampling process might stop, and, as a result, the audit tests may be substantially modified.

In other discovery sampling situations, the auditor may continue with the sample selection, even though a misstatement or deviation was found. The auditor then could use attribute tables (Tables 3.3, 3.4, or 3.6) to project a misstatement rate in the population.

RELATING ATTRIBUTE SAMPLING RESULTS TO MONETARY MISSTATEMENT

It can be difficult to make dollar conclusions (as opposed to proportion or percent conclusions) when any of the attribute sampling models (fixed-sample-size, sequential, or discovery) are used. Three techniques of *limited accuracy* to translate attribute information into dollar estimates are discussed below. Before studying these techniques, remember that the primary objective of attribute sampling is not dollar estimation.

1. If the sample deviation rate is 2 percent in a fixed-sample-size application, and the achieved upper precision limit is 5 percent at 95 percent reliability, the auditor can be 95 percent sure that the maximum exposure of book value would be the total dollar amount of the largest 5 percent of the population items. To the extent that any of the largest 5 percent of the population items were found acceptable in the sample, the next items below that point would be included. A listing of population items in descending amount is needed to apply this estimate.

2. Another rough estimate of the probable dollar exposure might be computed by multiplying the sample mean ($\bar{x}$) in dollars by the sample deviation rate (deviations $\div n$) by the number of items in the population; that is, $\bar{x}$ times (deviations $\div n$) times N equals probable dollar exposure.

3. Conservative dollar conclusions also can be produced from a discovery sampling application *if no occurrences are found in the sample*. For example, if 300 payroll checks from a population of 6500 exhibited no calculation errors, at 95 percent reliability the auditor can conclude that no more than 1 percent of the checks are in error (65 checks). If the largest check is $1065, then payroll dollars exposed to errors probably do not exceed $69,225 (65 × $1065), with a risk of being incorrect of 5 percent.

Another important consideration in making audit decisions based on the results of attribute sampling is that the achieved upper precision limit is not the same as assessed control risk. In a variable sampling application, one of the predefined items introduced into the sampling model will be a risk percentage for internal control assessment. This control risk percentage is based in part on the statistical evaluation of a test of controls, *and* input from judgment and other nonsampling tests of controls. Establishing the link between attribute sampling results and control risk as a percentage is largely judgmental. This concept is discussed and explained in Chapter 5.

SUMMARY

Three kinds of attribute sampling models were introduced in this chapter. These models are useful in performing tests of controls or performing special studies.

Attribute sampling on a fixed or sequential basis is used if the auditor wishes to project the sample deviation rate as the population deviation rate. Discovery sampling, on the other hand, is a special type of attribute sampling that is used when the occurrence is extremely critical to audit scope.

The key role played by audit judgment in an attribute sampling application is emphasized throughout this chapter. We also stress methods that the auditor can use to reduce judgmental failures that could weaken the effectiveness of attribute sampling. In fact, qualitative analysis is presented as being more important than its underlying statistical evaluation.

Fixed-sample size, sequential, and discovery sampling may be summarized by typical application characteristics as follows:

| | *Attribute Model* | | |
Application Characteristic	*Fixed Sample Size*	*Sequential*	*Discovery*
1. Typical sample size	Medium	Small	Large
2. Types of testing	Tests of controls	Tests of controls	Special studies and substantive tests
3. Expected control deviations	Low	Zero or very low	Zero or near zero

The primary factors that influence a test of controls sample size are:

| | *Conditions Leading to* | | *Relationship to Sample Size* |
Factor	*Smaller Sample Size*	*Larger Sample Size*	
1. Planned assessed level of control risk*	Higher planned assessed level of control risk	Lower planned assessed level of control risk	Inverse
2. Allowable rate of deviation (tolerable rate)	Higher acceptable rate of deviation for planned assessed level of control risk	Lower acceptable rate of deviation for planned assessed level of control risk	Inverse
3. Risk of assessing control risk too low	Higher risk of assessing control risk too low	Lower risk of assessing control risk too low	Inverse

	Conditions Leading to		
	---	---	---
Factor	Smaller Sample Size	Larger Sample Size	Relationship to Sample Size
4. Expected rate of population deviation[†]	Lower expected rate of deviation in population	Higher expected rate of deviation in population	Direct
5. Degree of assurance desired from sample evidence	Lower degree of assurance desired from sample (non-sampling tests of controls provide substantial evidence)	Higher degree of assurance desired from the sample (nonsampling tests of controls are minimal)	Direct
6. Number of items in population	Virtually no effect on sample size unless population is small		

*Tests of controls are not performed when control risk is assessed at the maximum.

†Larger samples are necessary when deviations occur. However, high deviation rates normally result in assessing control risk at, or near, the maximum (e.g., 100%).

GLOSSARY

Acceptable upper precision limit The statistical term for the predefined critical rate established so that the possibility of deviations in excess of that rate would cause the auditor to increase his or her assessed level of control risk. Also referred to as *ex ante* or *desired UPL*. In audit sampling, generally, the equivalent term is tolerable rate.

Achieved upper precision limit A calculated upper precision limit determined from attribute sample results. Also referred to as *ex post* or *computed UPL*. It is compared to the tolerable rate (acceptable or desired UPL) to determine whether the assessed level of control risk must be increased.

Attribute sampling See Chapter 1 glossary.

Confidence level As used in attribute sampling, the probability of being correct in assessing the level of control risk. The term is used interchangeably with "reliability."

Critical deviation A deviation that would permit material misstatements to occur in the financial statements.

Deviation A failure to comply with or follow a control. Also referred to as *procedural deviation* or *control deviation*.

Deviation analysis A judgmental study or determination of the cause (nature) of observed control deviations. Also referred to as *qualitative analysis*.

Discovery sampling See Chapter 1 glossary.

Expected deviation rate An estimate of a population deviation rate based on prior knowledge or a pilot sample. The expected deviation rate is used to determine sample size in a fixed-sample-size attribute application.

Fixed-sample-size attribute sampling See Chapter 1 glossary.

Initial sample size The start or minimum sample size used in a sequential sampling application. For 5 percent risk of assessing control risk too low (95 percent reliability) and 5 percent tolerable rate (upper precision limit), the minimum sample size is 60.

Occurrence A control deviation. Also sometimes referred to as an *error*.

Precision (Allowance for sampling risk) The range within which the sample result is expected to be accurate. For example, in a fixed-sample-size attribute sampling model, precision is the difference between the sample deviation rate and the achieved upper precision limit.

Qualitative deviation analysis See Deviation analysis.

Reliability level See Confidence level.

Risk of assessing control risk too high The risk that the assessed level of control risk based on the sample is greater than the true operating effectiveness of the control.

Risk of assessing control risk too low The risk that the assessed level of control risk based on the sample is less than the true operating effectiveness of the control.

Sequential attribute sampling See Chapter 1 glossary.

Tolerable rate The maximum rate of deviations from a prescribed control that the auditor would be willing to accept without altering his or her planned assessed level of control risk. See also Acceptable upper precision limit.

REVIEW QUESTIONS

3-1. Indicate whether each one of the following statements is true (T) or false (F).

    a. If the auditor expects zero or near zero deviations in a sample, sequential sampling may be efficient.

    b. Performing a thorough qualitative analysis on each observed deviation may be more informative than a quantitative projection of a sample.

c. It is not necessary to perform qualitative analysis if the achieved UPL is less than or equal to the tolerable rate (acceptable UPL).

d. If the planned assessed level of control risk is low, achieved UPL generally should not exceed 7 percent.

e. The risk of placing reliance on internal control when deviations are excessive is referred to as the risk of assessing control risk too high.

f. If the tolerable rate (acceptable UPL) is less than the achieved UPL in a sequential application, it is generally not in accordance with due professional care to increase the tolerable rate.

g. The minimum sample size for 95 percent reliability and 5 percent tolerable rate for a fixed-sample-size attribute sample is 59.

h. The risk of assessing control risk too low is generally set at 20 percent or higher.

i. To determine the accounts sample size for a discovery sampling application, the approximate population size must be known.

j. The auditor's assessed level of control risk is usually based solely on tests of controls that use audit sampling.

k. The decision to use a fixed or a sequential sampling plan depends on which plan the auditor believes will be most efficient in the circumstances.

3-2. If the auditor's objective is to observe at least one occurrence if the true occurrence rate exceeds a defined level, _____ sampling should be used.

3-3. If the auditor is concerned with whether the population occurrence rate exceeds a predefined tolerable rate _____ sampling should be used.

3-4. If the auditor expects a 2 percent deviation rate, _____ sampling should be used.

3-5. In an attribute sampling application using check numbers as the sampling unit, what should the auditor do when "voided" checks are encountered?

3-6. Attribute sampling does not eliminate professional judgment. Identify the primary areas involving audit judgment in a typical attribute sampling application.

3-7. What is "risk of assessing control risk too low," and how is it controlled and calculated?

3-8. When the tolerable rate (acceptable UPL) is less than achieved UPL, a number of alternate actions are available to the auditor. Identify what actions could be considered acceptable by the auditor when acceptable UPL < achieved UPL.

3-9. For 90 percent reliability and acceptable UPL of 5 percent, what is the minimum sample size for a fixed-sample-size attribute plan?

3-10. Construct a sequential decision table for 5 percent risk of assessing control risk too low and 10 percent tolerable rate. Use the following format:

Step	Cumulative Sample Size to Use	Stop If Cumulative Deviations Are Equal to	Sample More If Deviations Are	Go to Step— If Deviations Are at Least

3-11. Construct a sequential decision table for 2.5 percent risk of assessing control risk too low and 5 percent tolerable rate. Use the format presented in question 3-10.

3-12. If a sample of 128 produced 5 deviations, what is the achieved UPL at 90 percent, 95 percent, and 97.5 percent reliability? Why is Table 3.6 easier to use for this evaluation?

3-13. If a sample of 10 produced 0 deviations, what is the achieved UPL at 10 percent, 5 percent, and 2.5 percent risk of assessing control risk too low? Why is a sample size of 10 insufficient?

3-14. A sample of 80 produces two deviations; what is the estimated population deviation rate?

3-15. What is the "tolerable rate," and what does the auditor consider in setting the rate for test of controls using attribute sampling?

3-16. What pilot size sample should be used to obtain an estimated occurrence rate if the auditor is attempting to project a sample occurrence rate to a population of vouchers and the expected occurrence rate is not known?

3-17. What is the fixed-sample size for each of the following?

	Risk of Assessing Control Risk Too Low	Tolerable Rate	Expected Deviation Rate
a.	10%	7%	0.0%
b.	5%	5%	1.0%
c.	10%	10%	2.0%
d.	10%	15%	1.5%

3-18. Assume that the following control deviations were identified from the sample sizes determined in question 3-17. What is the achieved UPL for each situation?

	Deviations Noted
a.	1
b.	1
c.	0
d.	2

3-19. What conditions should exist before discovery sampling is used?

3-20. Determine discovery sample sizes for each of the following situations.

	Population Size	*UPL*	*Reliability*
a.	6,200	1%	90%
b.	5,000	0.5%	95%
c.	3,200	2%	98%
d.	10,649	0.3%	85%

3-21. If occurrences are observed in a discovery sampling application, what course of action should the auditor pursue?

3-22. Is it possible to convert an attribute sampling conclusion into a dollar or quantity estimate?

3-23. In performing a test of controls for sales order approvals, the auditor stipulates a maximum tolerable rate of 8 percent with a risk of assessing control risk too low of 5 percent. The auditor anticipates a deviation rate of 2 percent.

    a. What type of sampling plan should the auditor use for this test?

    b. Using the appropriate table from this chapter, compute the required sample size for the test.

    c. Assume that the sample indicates four deviations. May the auditor conclude with a 5 percent risk of assessing control risk too low that the population deviation rate does not exceed the maximum tolerable rate of 8 percent?

3-24. An auditor has reason to suspect that fraud has occurred through forgery of the treasurer's signature on company checks. The population under consideration consists of 3000 checks. Can discovery sampling rule out the possibility that any forged checks exist among the 3000 checks? Explain.

MULTIPLE-CHOICE QUESTIONS FROM PROFESSIONAL EXAMINATIONS

3-25. Which of the following statements is correct concerning statistical sampling in tests of controls?

    a. The population size has little or *no* effect on determining sample size except for very small populations.

    b. The expected population deviation rate has little or *no* effect on determining sample size except for very small populations.

    c. As the population size doubles, the sample size also should double.

    d. For a given tolerable rate, a larger sample size should be selected as the expected population deviation rate decreases.

3-26. When assessing the tolerable rate, the auditor should consider that, while deviations from controls increase the risk of material misstatements, such deviations do not necessarily result in misstatements. This explains why:

    a. A recorded disbursement that does *not* show evidence of required approval may nevertheless be a transaction that is properly authorized and recorded.

    b. Deviations would result in misstatements in the accounting records only if the deviations and the misstatements occurred on different transactions.

    c. Deviations from pertinent control procedures at a given rate ordinarily would be expected to result in misstatements at a higher rate.

    d. A recorded disbursement that is properly authorized may nevertheless be a transaction that contains a material misstatement.

3-27. In the audit of the financial statements of Delta Company, the auditor determines that in performing a test of control, the deviation rate in the sample does not support the planned assessed level of control risk when, in fact, the deviation rate in the population does justify such level of risk. This situation illustrates the risk of:

    a. Assessing control risk too high.

    b. Assessing control risk too low.

    c. Incorrect rejection.

    d. Incorrect acceptance.

Items 3-28 and 3-29 are based on the following information:

The diagram below depicts the auditor's estimated deviation rate compared with the tolerable rate, and also depicts the true population deviation rate compared with the tolerable rate.

Auditor's Estimate Based On Sample Results	True State of Population	
	Deviation Rate Exceeds Tolerable Rate	Deviation Rate Is Less Than Tolerable Rate
Deviation Rate Exceeds Tolerable Rate	I.	II.
Deviation Rate Is Less Than Tolerable Rate	III.	IV.

3-28. In which of the two situations would the auditor have properly assessed control risk?

    a. I and II.

    b. II and III.

    c. III and IV.

    d. I and IV.

3-29. As a result of tests of controls, the auditor assessed control risk too high and thereby increases substantive testing. This is illustrated by situation:

    a. I.

    b. II.

    c. III.

    d. IV.

3-30. The tolerable rate of deviations for a test of a control is generally:

    a. Lower than the expected rate of deviations in the related accounting records.

    b. Higher than the expected rate of deviations in the related accounting records.

    c. Identical to the expected rate of deviations in related accounting records.

    d. Unrelated to the expected rate of deviations in the related accounting records.

3-31. An auditor might use discovery sampling to:

    a. Compute the upper precision limit of an infrequently occurring error.

    b. Compute the upper precision limit of a frequently occurring error.

    c. Estimate the dollar value of a fraud.

    d. Determine how many invoices were paid twice.

3-32. When planning an attribute sampling application, the difference between the expected deviation rate and the maximum tolerable deviation rate is the planned:

    a. Precision.

    b. Reliability.

    c. Dispersion.

    d. Skewness.

3-33. An auditor is designing a sampling plan to test the accuracy of daily production reports over the past three years. All of the reports contain the same information except that Friday reports also contain weekly totals and are prepared by managers rather than by supervisors. Production normally peaks near the end of a month. If the auditor wants to select two reports per month using an interval sampling plan, which of the following techniques reduces the likelihood of bias in the sample?

a. Estimating the deviation rate in the population.

b. Using multiple random starts.

c. Increasing the confidence level.

d. Increasing the precision.

3-34. Which of the following factors is (are) considered in determining the sample size for a test of controls?

	Expected Deviation Rate	*Tolerable Deviation Rate*
a.	Yes	Yes
b.	No	No
c.	No	Yes
d.	Yes	No

CASES

Case 3-1   Millar Company, Inc.

(Estimated time to complete: 15 minutes)

Assume that you are working on the audit of Millar Company, Inc., and are examining checks for the presence of an approved supporting voucher. An unsupported check is thus a "deviation." The population is composed of the approximately 4000 checks that were processed by the client during the current year.

You decide that a deviation rate in the population as high as 5 percent would not require any extended audit procedures. However, if the population deviation rate is greater than 5 percent at 5 percent risk of assessing control risk too low, you would want to extend the audit scope.

In each of the following case situations, identify the letter of the sample (i.e., A or B) which, in your judgment, provides better evidence that the deviation rate in the population is 5 percent or less. Do not refer to the tables in the chapter. Use your best estimate. (Assume that each sample observation is selected randomly.)

Situation	Sample	Number of Invoices Examined	Number of Deviations Found in Sample	Percent of Sample Invoices with Deviations
1	A	75	1	1.3
	B	200	4	2.0
2	A	100	1	1.0
	B	125	3	2.4
3	A	150	2	1.3
	B	25	0	0.0
4	A	200	7	3.1
	B	150	4	2.0
5	A	200	6	2.4
	B	75	2	2.0

Source: Adapted from William R. Kinney, "Judgment Error in Evaluation Sample Results," *The CPA Journal* (March 1977), pp. 61–62.

Case 3-2   Eft, Inc.

(Estimated time to complete: 20 minutes)

Calculate the achieved upper precision limits for the five situations presented in Case 3-1, using the appropriate attribute sampling table.

Record your solution and identify the letter of the sample that provides better evidence that the deviation rate in the population is 5 percent or less. Use 5 percent risk of assessing control risk too low.

Situation	Sample
1	A
	B
2	A
	B
3	A
	B
4	A
	B
5	A
	B

Case 3-3   Tech Producers, Inc.

(Estimated time to complete: 20 minutes)

 Tech Producers, a fast-growing electronics manufacturer, has approximately 2000 hourly employees who are paid weekly by check from a payroll imprest fund. In addition to the testing of payroll transactions throughout the year, the auditor, Terri Sinclair, has decided to test the current payroll period. Because of the many additions to the workforce since last year, she is concerned with the possibility of payroll padding as well as less critical deviations, such as minor mistakes in overtime computations, incorrect payroll deductions, and the like. Names will be drawn from the payroll journal at random.

In this particular engagement, the auditor believes that she should be reasonably satisfied that payroll padding to the extent of 10 or more fictitious or unauthorized employees at any one time would be detected by the system itself or by her examination.

Taking into consideration her other payroll procedures and her review of internal control procedures related to the payroll function, the auditor has decided to seek 90 percent assurance that the actual occurrence rate in the current payroll does not exceed 0.5 percent (10 ÷ 2000).

a. $N =$ _____

   Reliability $=$ _____

      UPL $=$ _____

       $n =$ _____

b. Assuming that you find 0 occurrences in your sample, what probabilistic statement can you make?

c. Assuming that you find 1 occurrence, what action(s) should be taken?

d. Could you use an attribute table to evaluate discovery sampling findings?

Case 3-4   Client, Inc.

(Estimated time to complete: 10 minutes)

Client, Inc., operates out of four branches located in Denver, Dallas, New York, and Midland. You are designing a sequential sampling plan to ascertain the effectiveness of internal control over credit sales. One of the problems that you are having is trying to determine how to allocate your total sample to the different branches. All branches have similar accounting systems, but process varying numbers of credit sales invoices during the year.

Branch	Number of Sales Invoices Processed
Denver	24,000
Dallas	4,000
New York	14,000
Midland	2,000
	40,000

Assuming your sample size n is 100:

a. How would you allocate the sample to the four branches?

b. If it is necessary to determine the effectiveness of the system at each branch, how would you allocate the sample?

c. How would your answer change if it is known that the control systems in Denver and Dallas are especially reliable and the control systems in New York and Midland are somewhat less reliable?

Case 3-5   Lewis & Foot, CPAs

(Estimated time to complete: 30 minutes)

Fred Hancock, a senior accountant with Lewis & Foot, CPAs, has just completed a professional development program in statistical sampling. He decided to use statistics in an audit engagement to which he is currently assigned.

He believed it would be appropriate to apply statistical sampling in a purchase transaction test. He decided that an 8 percent tolerable rate at a 5 percent risk of assessing control risk too low would be appropriate. The expected deviation rate was 4 percent, so he took a sample of 100.

Since Fred felt that the larger items deserved more attention than the smaller ones, he decided to include 60 items in the sample with a value of $5000 or more each; the remainder of the 100 items were valued at less than $5000 each. He was very careful to take a random sample of his test month for each of these two types of items.

When testing the sample, he found only five deviations. One deviation was a missing vendor's invoice, so he sent a confirmation to the vendor to make certain that it was a valid invoice. The confirmation indicated no exceptions. Two deviations were simply missing approvals by the authorized official. Fred went to the official who agreed he had failed to sign the invoice because he had been on vacation in May. He reviewed the invoices and stated they were both valid and correct.

The other two deviations both involved dollar errors. One was an error in the extension of the invoice in the amount of $50 and the other a misclassification error of $850. Fred was not particularly concerned about the $50 error because it was not material, but the $850 was fairly large. Fortunately, it was a misclassification between expenses and did not affect net income. He decided to call the last two actual deviations, and concluded that the achieved UPL was 6.3 percent at a 5 percent risk of assessing control risk too low.

Fred concluded that purchases for the year were almost certain to contain fewer errors than the allowable amount. As a result, he accepted the population and decided to reduce the tests in year-end accounts payable.

Fred was pleased with the use of statistical sampling because he had objective results. The reviewing partner, who could not attend the course because he was talking to a prospective client that day, also liked it because it reduced his exposure to legal liability and greatly reduced the time budget to complete the job.

Identify each weakness in this attribute sampling application and state why it is a weakness.

Case 3-6   CPE Associates

(Estimated time to complete: 20 minutes)

CPE Associates is a partnership that provides discussion leaders and technical course materials on accounting, auditing, and taxation. The primary market served by CPE Associates is CPA firms that have requirements for professional personnel to obtain at least 40 hours of continuing professional education a year. CPE Associates has five partners and a staff of ten people for all disbursements except for petty cash disbursements. For this year's annual audit, you wish to use statistical sampling to ascertain if the cash disbursement system is functioning properly. Sequential sampling with 5 percent risk of assessing control risk too low and 5 percent tolerable rate will be used. Identify the attributes that you will test in evaluating the effectiveness of the cash disbursement system. Your attribute definitions should be comprehensive. Assume that the sampling frame will be canceled checks.

Case 3-7   Taylor & Sons, Inc.

(Estimated time to complete: 20 minutes)

You are getting ready to begin the audit of Taylor & Sons, Inc., for the year ended December 31, 20X1. You will function as senior on the engagement. In prior years, nonstatistical sampling was employed for all control testing on the Taylor engagement. In June of this year, however, your firm adopted a policy that all sample sizes for tests of controls should be determined statistically, using a 5 percent risk of assessing control risk too low. The policy statement also stipulated that tolerable rate should be preset from 20 to 5 percent depending on the criticalness of the attribute being tested and the planned assessed level of control risk. Your audit program includes tests of controls for payroll and cash disbursements as presented below. Classify each test as "very critical," "moderately critical," or "least critical."

Selected Payroll *Tests of Controls*	*Selected Cash Disbursement* *Tests of Controls*
1. Examine the time card for the approval of a supervisor.	1. Examine voucher for supporting invoices, receiving reports, etc.
2. Account for a sequence of payroll checks in the payroll journal.	2. Examine supporting documents for evidence of cancellation (marked "paid").
3. Recompute hours on the time card.	3. Ascertain whether cash discounts were taken.
4. Compare the employee name in the payroll journal to personnel department records.	4. Review voucher for clerical accuracy.
5. Review overtime charges for approval of a supervisor.	5. Agree purchase order price to invoice.

Case 3-8   Becker & Warren

(Estimated time to complete: 20 minutes)

Tammy Smith, a new senior auditor, is planning tests of controls for Becker & Warren, a law firm. She has come to you to get help in using audit sampling to test controls over the firm's billing process and has developed the following questions.

a. What are the factors that affect the determination of

(1) Acceptable level of risk of assessing control risk too low.

(2) Tolerable deviation rate.

(3) Expected population deviation rate.

b. State the effect on sample size of an increase in each of the following factors, assuming all other factors are held constant:

(1) Acceptable level of risk of assessing control risk too low.

(2) Tolerable deviation rate.

(3) Expected population deviation rate.

c. Judgmentally evaluate the sample results of a test for attributes if authorizations are found to be missing on 7 billing invoices out of a sample of 100 tested. The population consists of 47,392 invoices, the tolerable deviation rate is 8 percent, and the acceptable level of risk of assessing control risk too low is 5 percent.

d. Explain how statistical sampling may assist Tammy in evaluating the results described in part c, above.

Case 3-9   Dalton Stationery, Inc.

(Estimated time to complete: 20 minutes)

The audit staff on the audit of Dalton Stationery, Inc., has completed a number of tests of controls with the following results:

Test	1	2	3	4	5	6	7	8
Sample Size	35	60	60	65	100	150	125	200
Reliability	90%	90%	90%	95%	95%	95%	95%	95%
Number of Exceptions	1	0	2	1	3	2	0	5
Estimated Exception Rate								
Achieved Upper Precision								

a. For each test determine the estimated deviation rate in the population.

b. Use the appropriate tables in the textbook to determine the achieved upper precision limit for each test.

4 USING VARIABLE SAMPLING FOR ACCOUNTING ESTIMATION

LEARNING OBJECTIVES

After a careful study and discussion of this chapter, you will be able to:

1. Define variable sampling.
2. Define and apply selected statistical concepts such as standard deviation, the central limit theorem, and the distribution of sample means to accounting problems.
3. Distinguish the accounting estimation approach from the audit hypothesis approach.
4. Use variable sampling to project a book value (e.g., inventory balance).
5. Select the most efficient variable sampling model from among unstratified mean per unit, stratified mean per unit, difference estimation, and ratio estimation.

Variable sampling or quantitative estimation is a statistical technique used to estimate the dollar amount of an account balance or some other quantity. When it is used to estimate account balances, the computed result is stated in terms of the dollar amount of the point estimate (the sample mean times the population size) plus and minus the dollar amount of the precision interval at the confidence level desired. As an example, assume that an inventory balance is projected (based on a sample). If the point estimate is projected at $1,200,000 with a $150,000 computed precision interval at a confidence (or reliability) of 95 percent, this means the estimated true value of the inventory balance is between $1,050,000 and $1,350,000 at 95 percent reliability. Later in this chapter we learn how precision limits are calculated. Unlike attribute sampling, where the concern is primarily with the upper precision limit, variable estimation employs both an upper and lower precision limit—an account balance can be understated or overstated.

The primary purpose of this chapter is to review statistical concepts. Estimation sampling, as explained in this chapter, is primarily useful for accounting rather than auditing applications.

PRECISION AND RELIABILITY

Before we proceed, let us review the concepts of precision and reliability. **Precision,** expressed either as a dollar amount or a percentage, defines the maximum degree of misstatement in either direction that will be acceptable. In statistical terms, the precision of an estimate describes the range of values, less and more than the point estimate, within which the **true value** is expected to fall. The lower and upper bounds of this range are referred to as *precision limits* (or *precision interval*). *Reliability,* on the other hand, expresses the probability that the precision interval contains the true value. Statistically, the reliability figure expresses the proportion of cases in which precision intervals would contain the true value if the same estimating procedures were employed a large number of times. Consequently, precision and reliability have no meaning for decision makers unless paired with each other.

A REVIEW OF SELECTED STATISTICAL CONCEPTS

Sampling for variables is a more sophisticated statistical process than attribute, stop-or-go, or discovery sampling. To apply variable sampling properly, the accountant needs some familiarity with statistical theory and terminology. Of particular importance are the following concepts:

1. Mean
2. Median
3. Mode

4. Standard deviation
5. Skewness
6. Normal distribution
7. Distribution of sample means
8. Central limit theorem

Mean

The **mean** is a measure of central tendency that is obtained by totaling all the values and dividing by the number of items. The mean of a *population* is expressed symbolically as $\bar{X}$. The mean of a *sample* is expressed symbolically as $\bar{x}$. To illustrate a sample mean calculation, assume that a sample of ten items is selected. The numeric values are as follows:

x
$10
18
15
20
24
26
26
17
25
19
$\Sigma_{xj} = \$200$

Formula:

$$\bar{x} = \frac{\Sigma_{xj}}{n} = \frac{200}{10} = 20$$

To calculate $\bar{X}$ you have to know the total dollars for every item in the population and the population size. The symbol x refers to an individual observation or sample item; n refers to sample size; and Σ is the summation sign.

Median

The **median** is that value for which half the values are above and half are below. In effect, the median divides the population into two equal sizes. Strictly speaking, a population (or sample) has a middle item only when it has an odd number of items.

For an even number of items, the median can be defined as the average of the two middle numbers. The median for the ten sample items is 19.5.

Mode

The value that occurs most frequently in a distribution is referred to as the **mode.** In the illustration of the mean, the mode is 26. The modal value(s) corresponds to the peak(s) on a frequency distribution.

Standard Deviation

The **standard deviation** is a widely used statistic that is employed to measure the extent to which the values of the items are spread about the mean. To illustrate the calculation of the standard deviation, the sample items selected to illustrate a sample mean calculation are used.

x	$\bar{x}$	$x - \bar{x}$	$(x - \bar{x})^2$	
10	20	− 10	100	
18	20	− 2	4	Equation:
15	20	− 5	25	
20	20	0	0	
24	20	4	16	$SD = \sqrt{\dfrac{\Sigma(x-\bar{x})^2}{n-1}}$
26	20	6	36	
26	20	6	36	
17	20	− 3	9	$SD = \sqrt{\dfrac{252}{9}} = 5.29$
25	20	5	25	
19	20	− 1	1	where:

$$\Sigma(x - \bar{x})^2{}_{xj} = 252 \qquad SD = \text{standard deviation}$$

Notice that the equation for the standard deviation of a sample includes the term $n - 1$. Because the sample standard deviation is used as an estimate of the population standard deviation, the use of $n - 1$ in the denominator is imperative as an adjustment for bias.

The equation for the estimated population standard deviation presented in *Worksheet 1* (Appendix A) is referred to as the shortcut computational equation. The result is the same as the previous equation. The shortcut computational equation is illustrated as follows:

x	x^2
10	100
18	324
15	225
20	400
24	576
26	676
26	676
17	289
25	625
19	361
200	4252

$$\bar{x} = \frac{200}{10} = 20$$

$$SD = \sqrt{\frac{\sum_{j=1}^{n} x_j^2 - n\bar{x}^2}{n-1}}$$

$$SD = \sqrt{\frac{4252 - 10(20)^2}{10-1}}$$

$$SD = \sqrt{\frac{252}{9}} = 5.29$$

Skewness

Skewness refers to the degree of asymmetry or lopsidedness of a distribution. Most accounting populations exhibit some degree of skewness. Skewness in accounting populations usually means that the population contains a few very large items and many small items. Some skewness exists if there are extreme values at one end of a distribution with no counterbalancing values at the other end.

Normal Distribution

The following distribution, because of certain inherent characteristics described, is a **normal distribution.** An important feature of this distribution is that the relative frequency of any interval can be determined by knowing only the sample mean $\bar{x}$

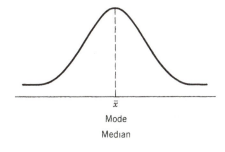

$\bar{x}$
Mode
Median

and the standard deviation *SD*. The interval from $\bar{x} \pm 1$ *SD* contains 68 percent of the items, $\bar{x} \pm 1.96$ *SD* contains 95 percent of the items, and ± 2.58 *SD* contains 99 percent of the items.

Distribution of Sample Means[1]

To illustrate the distribution of sample means, assume that we have a population *N* of nine different merchandise items. The population distribution is

		$20		
	$16	$20	$24	
$12	$16	$20	$24	$28

The standard deviation of this distribution is $4.62.

If a sample size of 2 is selected from this population, there are 36 sample means based on all possible combinations of items, assuming sampling without replacement. These combinations appear as follows:

1. 12 and 16	10. 16 and 20	19. 16 and 24	28. 20 and 24
2. 12 and 16	11. 16 and 20	20. 16 and 24	29. 20 and 24
3. 12 and 20	12. 16 and 20	21. 16 and 28	30. 20 and 28
4. 12 and 20	13. 16 and 24	22. 20 and 20	31. 20 and 24
5. 12 and 20	14. 16 and 24	23. 20 and 20	32. 20 and 24
6. 12 and 24	15. 16 and 28	24. 20 and 24	33. 20 and 28
7. 12 and 24	16. 16 and 20	25. 20 and 24	34. 24 and 24
8. 12 and 28	17. 16 and 20	26. 20 and 28	35. 24 and 28
9. 16 and 16	18. 16 and 20	27. 20 and 20	36. 24 and 28

Given the 36 possible combinations of sample size 2, a mean for each combination may be calculated. The distribution of sample means that results is:

			18	20	22		
			18	20	22		
			18	20	22		
			18	20	22		
		16	18	20	22	24	
		16	18	20	22	24	
	14	16	18	20	22	24	26
	14	16	18	20	22	24	26

[1]The illustrated distributions in this section are from Donald H. Taylor and G. William Glezen, *Auditing: Integrated Concepts and Procedures,* 2nd ed. (New York: John Wiley & Sons, Inc. © 1982), pp. 700–702.

The standard deviation of this distribution, which is called the **standard error of the mean,** is 3.06.

As shown on the previous page, the distribution of sample means will be normally distributed (bell-shaped distribution) if the sample is taken from a normally distributed population. However, as already stated, accounting populations usually are not normally distributed. For example, the population of nine items may be skewed to the right (large dollar items):

$$
\begin{array}{ccccccc}
 & & 20 & & & & \\
 & 14 & 20 & & & & \\
10 & 14 & 20 & 26 & 32 & 42 &
\end{array}
$$

However, even if the population distribution is skewed, the distribution of sample means will approach normality as the sample size increases. For example, a plotted distribution of sample means for all combinations of sample size 3 will be less skewed than one for a sample size of 2, and so on.

In variable sampling applications, the minimum sample size recommended is 30. Statisticians tell us that a sample of at least size 30 will produce a close approximation to normality, even if the population is skewed.

Accountants, of course, do not generate a distribution of sample means. They select one sample and project the same results to the sampled population. Similarly, accountants do not calculate the standard error of the mean based on all possible combinations of samples. An approximation of the standard error of the mean is the estimated population standard deviation (based on a sample) divided by the square root of the sample size. It is calculated by the following equation:

$$
\text{Standard error of the mean (estimated)} = \frac{SD}{\sqrt{n}}
$$

In summary, a distribution of sample means (mean calculated from many samples of the same size) has three properties:

1. The shape of the distribution is approximately normal if the sample is large enough.
2. The distribution is centered at the population mean $\bar{X}$.
3. The estimated standard error of the mean equals the estimated population standard deviation SD, divided by the square root of the sample size.

Central Limit Theorem

According to the **central limit theorem,** for large sample sizes (typically, 30 is a reasonable minimum size), the distribution sample means tends to be normally distributed, almost independently of the shape of the original population. The fact that sample means from a lopsided accounting population converge to a normal distribution is the reason why normal theory is useful in selected accounting or auditing applications. This chapter explains accounting applications, and Chapter 5 explains auditing applications.

An accounting population may be skewed as follows:

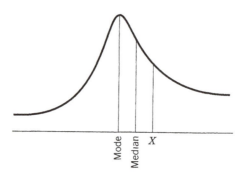

But *if the sample size is large enough,* the distribution of sample means from the skewed accounting population will be normal.

WHAT IS ACCOUNTING ESTIMATION?

In designing a variable sampling application, the accountant or auditor must consider whether the objective is: (1) to make an independent estimate of some amount (e.g., Lifo inventory), or (2) to test the reasonableness of a financial statement representation (e.g., the balance in accounts receivable). When an account balance is to be determined by statistical sampling, the accountant should use an accounting estimation approach. In these instances, the accountant generally intends to propose an adjustment to bring the account balance into agreement with the statistical estimate (point estimate). If an account balance does not exist, the point estimate is simply booked.

When an auditor wants to accept a client's representation without adjustment if it is reasonably correct, or to propose an adjustment only if it is probable that there might be a material misstatement in the amount as stated by the client, an **audit hypothesis approach** should be used. The audit hypothesis approach statistically discriminates between the hypothesis that the amount as represented is correctly stated and the alternative hypothesis that the amount is materially misstated. Chapter 5 explains the audit hypothesis approach.

Remember that the purpose of the accounting estimation is to estimate some amount of interest to the accountant, such as the total cost of inventory on hand. This method is generally used when the resulting estimate is to be entered into the books and records as a substitute for a complete enumeration of the components of an account. Accounting estimation should *not* be used if the client has a book value that an auditor is trying to decide whether to accept or reject. If this type of decision is to be made, the audit hypothesis approach should be used.

When accounting estimation is used, the precision of the estimate must be small enough to result in an **estimated value** (or **point estimate**) of the financial statement amount that is very unlikely to be materially different from the actual (true) amount. A material difference is the largest amount of misstatement of a financial statement item that could exist and still not affect an informed user's decision.

The following statistical accounting estimation models are discussed in this chapter:

- Unstratified mean per unit (unstratified MPU)
- Stratified mean per unit (stratified MPU)
- Difference estimation
- Ratio estimation

Unstratified MPU generally is not efficient because the sample sizes generated are relatively large. It is presented in this chapter for illustrative purposes. The other models are easier to understand and apply when one has studied unstratified mean per unit. Ratio estimation is very similar to difference estimation; consequently, it is presented in a summary fashion without the operational aids (e.g., calculation worksheets) included for difference estimation.

UNSTRATIFIED MEAN PER UNIT

The **unstratified MPU** model is used to project an estimated value from a sample. This method also is called *simple extension*. After a sample is selected and a value is determined for each sample item, the sample mean $\bar{x}$ of sample values is multiplied by the number of items in the population N to produce an estimate of the total dollar value of the sampled population.

Because mean per unit without stratification produces large sample sizes relative to other sampling methods, as previously stated, its use in accounting or auditing is limited. The technique is appropriate when a book value for each population item is not available or when the footed total of the book value is not accurate. Mean per unit is seldom used without stratification, and generally important or material values (e.g., large dollar account balances) are treated separately; that is, large dollar balances or other key items (unusual, obsolete, etc.) are not included within the sampling frame.

In an unstratified MPU application, the objective is to calculate a sample mean to project as the population total. Of course, the $\bar{x} \cdot N$ projection will not correspond exactly to the true (but unknown) population total. But the projection plus and minus a precision limit should contain the true population total with a defined reliability. Consequently, the estimated value must be paired with a reliability percentage and a precision limit.

Before he or she obtains an estimated value, the accountant has to determine the extent of testing. The sample-size equation is derived from the mathematical definition of precision. Mathematically, precision is.

$$A = U_R \cdot SE \cdot N$$

where

A = precision

U_R = confidence level coefficient

SE = estimated standard error of the mean

N = population size

Given the mathematical definition of precision, the sample-size equation can be derived as follows:

$$A = U_R \cdot SE \cdot N$$

$$A = U_R \cdot \frac{SD}{\sqrt{n}} \cdot N$$

$$\sqrt{n} = A = U_R \cdot SD \cdot N$$

$$\sqrt{n} = \frac{U_R \cdot SD \cdot N}{A}$$

$$n' = \left(\frac{U_R \cdot SD \cdot N}{A} \right)^2$$

This is the equation for sample size assuming replacement, with n' denoting the sample size. The n' sample size is larger to compensate for the possibility of including the same sample item in the selection process more than once. If sampling is done without replacement, the sample size can be smaller. A finite population correction factor is applied to n' to yield n, which is sample size without replacement. This adjustment appears as follows:

$$n = \frac{n'}{1 + (n'/N)}$$

To determine the extent of testing (sample size) for an unstratified MPU application, the accountant must predefine U_R, SD, N, and A in the sample-size equation. U_R is based on the amount of sampling risk the accountant is willing to accept. For example, if 95 percent reliability is selected (U_R = 1.96), there is a 5 percent chance that an estimated value ± precision will not contain the true population total. In an accounting estimation application, a high reliability is usually selected. Otherwise, there will be a higher probability that the recorded point estimate (estimated value) will be materially misstated.

The standard deviation is determined by a pilot sample or the accountant's prior knowledge. Statisticians say that a sample of 30 is sufficient in most circumstances to estimate the standard deviation of a population.

N is determined by the sampling objective and is dependent on the part of the population that will be sampled. The total population may be divided into a sampled group and a 100 percent (nonsampled) group. In an accounting application, A (precision) is determined to be the amount material to the account balance in light of the amount that is material to the financial statements taken as a whole.

At this point, the following variables have been predefined: U_R, SD, N, and A. By studying the equation for **acceptable precision,** you can see that we implicitly set an upper limit on SE.

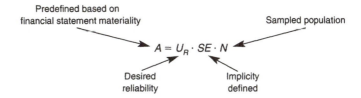

After the sample size is selected, acceptable precision A is compared with **achieved precision** A'. A' is calculated based on the planned U_R, predefined N, and calculated SE (based on the final sample $SD \div \sqrt{n}$). If A' is greater than A, the sample size is insufficient because the precision limit is too wide. In this situation, the sample size would have to be increased to produce an A' equal to or below A. When the sample is deemed sufficient, the mean of the final sample is calculated to determine estimated value.

STEPS IN APPLYING UNSTRATIFIED MEAN PER UNIT

We present a 16-step approach to applying unstratified MPU in this section. Afterward, we discuss stratified MPU, difference estimation, and ratio estimation.

Unstratified Mean per Unit

1. Define reliability level. Generally, a high reliability level should be used (99–90%).

2. Based on the following table, convert step 1 into a U_R coefficient (reliability factor).

Reliability	U_R Coefficient
0.99	2.58
0.95	1.96
0.90	1.65

3. Set acceptable precision equal to the amount of material for the application.

$$\text{Acceptable precision} = A$$

Note: This is the *desired* precision and not a calculated amount.

4. Calculate required sample size *with replacement*.

$$n' = \left(\frac{U_R \cdot SD \cdot N}{A} \right)^2$$

where

n' = sample size with replacement

SD = standard deviation

If the standard deviation SD is known from prior sampling work, use that as an estimate. If SD is unknown, an estimate must be made. To estimate SD:

a. Select a pilot random sample of 30 items from the population on a without replacement basis.

b. Use *Worksheet 1* in Appendix A or the following equation to calculate SD:

$$SD = \sqrt{\frac{\sum_{j=1}^{n} x_j^2 - n\bar{x}^2}{n - 1}}$$

c. Substitute B into the n' equation.

5. Adjust step 4 to sample size *without replacement* (finite population correction factor).

$$n = \frac{n'}{1 + (n'/N)}$$

Note: n is more efficient (i.e., smaller) than n' because of the finite population correction factor. However, n' must be calculated before n can be determined.

6. If n is greater than 30, randomly select the additional sample items using computer generation, random-number table, or systematic selection. (See Chapter 2 for a discussion of sample selection techniques.)

7. Select the additional sample items and calculate the following sample results.

8. Calculate the standard deviation of the total sample, (*Worksheet 1* in Appendix A may be used to calculate the standard deviation.)

9. Calculate the standard error using the following equation:

$$SE = \frac{SD}{\sqrt{n}}$$

10. Calculate achieved precision A' based on the following equation (use SE from step 9):

$$A' = U_R \cdot SE \cdot N \sqrt{1 - (n/N)}$$

11. If $A' \leq A$, go to step 13; otherwise, go to step 12.

12. Increase the sample size according to the following equation (afterward, go back to step 6):

$$\text{Adjusted } n = \left(\frac{U_R \cdot (\text{step 8}) \cdot N}{A} \right)^2$$

13. Calculate the mean $\bar{x}$ of the total sample.

$$\bar{x} = \frac{\text{Sum of each audited sample}}{n}$$

14. Calculate estimated value, EV.

$$EV = \bar{x} \cdot N$$

15. Conclude that you believe that at the reliability level specified in step 1 the true book value is within $EV \pm A'$. Your conclusion should also address the effectiveness of the procedures used to generate the projected amount and whether or not accounting personnel applied the procedures correctly.

16. State book value at EV (step 14).

Caution

1. Do not use this approach if the client has a book value that you are trying to decide whether or not to accept. (It is not appropriate to make a statistical estimate of a population total and, finding the book value somewhere within the precision interval, to accept the book value as materially correct. If this type of decision procedure is to be used, the audit hypothesis approach should be employed.)

2. Do not use this approach if you can stratify the population or use difference or ratio estimation.

DEMONSTRATION OF UNSTRATIFIED MEAN PER UNIT

To illustrate simple extension, let us assume that Red Raider, Inc., is trying to estimate the total dollars in inventory for a particular subsidiary. The subsidiary does not have perpetual records or a book total for inventory. Red Raider, Inc., decides that a material misstatement would be $60,000. They desire 95 percent reliability and plan to use unrestricted random sampling (unstratified) without replacement. To estimate the standard deviation of the inventory population, a pilot sample of 30 items from the total population of 2000 items was selected. The pilot sample produced an arithmetic mean of $4000 and a standard deviation of $150.

1. Reliability is set equal to 95 percent. Red Raider, Inc., is willing to tolerate a 5 percent chance of sampling error. That is, 5 percent of the time, if they repeat this process over and over again, a projection would be produced plus and minus precision A' that would not include the true population total.
2. Based on 95 percent reliability, the reliability coefficient (U_R) is 1.96.
3. Precision (A) is judgmentally set equal to $60,000—the amount considered material for this application.

4. $n' = \left(\dfrac{1.96 \cdot \$150 \cdot 2000}{\$60,000} \right)^2$

   $n' = 96$ (rounded)

5. $n = \dfrac{96}{1 + (96/2000)}$

   $n = 92$ (rounded)

6. Sixty-two additional sample items are added to the pilot sample of 30 to yield the total sample of 92.
7. The 62 additional sample items are selected.
8. A standard deviation based on 92 items is calculated. Assume that the result is a standard deviation of $136.

9. $SE = \dfrac{\$136}{\sqrt{92}} = 14.18$ (rounded).

10. $A' = (1.96) \cdot (14.18) \cdot (2000) \cdot \sqrt{1 - \dfrac{92}{2000}} = \$54,292.$

11. Calculated precision A' is less than or equal to predefined precision A; therefore, go to step 13.
12. It is not necessary to increase the sample size. Skip step 12.
13. The mean of the 92 inventory items is calculated as follows, assuming the sample totals $370.977:

$$\bar{x} = \frac{\$370,977}{92} = \$4032.36$$

14. $EV = \$4032.36 \cdot 2000 = \$8,064,720.$
15. Red Raider, Inc., is 95 percent certain that the true inventory balance of all 2000 inventory items is within $8,064,720 ± $54,292.
16. Red Raider, Inc., should book $8,064,720 as their subsidiary's ending inventory.

STRATIFIED MEAN PER UNIT

When a population is highly variable (large standard deviation), unstratified MPU (unrestricted random sampling) may produce very large sample sizes. Stratification of the population produces an estimate that has a desired level of precision with a reduced sample size. Such a sampling approach is more efficient than unstratified MPU. **Stratified MPU** may be applied to populations where no monetary misstatements are expected, or where a moderate rate and amount of monetary misstatements are expected. Stratified MPU is widely used in practice.

Stratified sampling increases efficiency because the weighted sum of the stratum standard deviations is less than the standard deviation for the whole population. To illustrate, suppose a population consists of seven items—five have a value of $1 each and two have a value of $3 each. The standard deviation of this population is close to $1, but by forming two strata with the five items of value $1 and the remaining two items of value $3 in the other stratum, the standard deviation of each stratum is 0 and the weighted sum is also 0. By grouping sampling units with similar characteristics into the same strata, stratified MPU sampling reduces the variability among the items in a stratum.

To use stratified sampling, the accountant should adhere to three rules:

1. Every element must belong to one and only one stratum.
2. There must be a tangible, specifiable difference that defines and distinguishes the strata.
3. The *exact* number of elements in each stratum must be known.

The accountant can select the stratum boundaries as desired *if* all three of the above criteria are satisfied. If logical divisions exist in the population, they can be used (e.g., product line, type of item, location, and geographic areas). However, there must be some reason to expect the standard deviation of each stratum to be less than the standard deviation of the total population. As is explained below, the usual basis for stratification is the dollar amount of sample units.

In stratifying a population, one useful approach is to select stratum boundaries so that each stratum contains approximately the same total dollars [except the 100 percent (nonsampled) stratum]. To use dollar stratification, the total population amount is reduced by the 100 percent stratum and the remainder is divided by the number of strata desired. This yields a target dollar amount. The stratum boundaries then are selected so that each stratum has nearly the desired dollar amount. Usually three to five strata, including the 100 percent stratum, is reasonable.[2]

In defining strata and their boundaries, consideration must be given to the cost (implementation expense) and benefit (efficiency in resulting sample size). From a cost perspective, recorded book amounts are widely used as a basis for population stratification. Likewise, if possible, manual stratification of a large population should be avoided, because it is time-consuming and expensive. One reason that accounts for the popularity of stratified MPU application in practice is that the method can be easily computerized. Because of the use of computer programs, most stratifying is done on a quantitative field (e.g., book recorded amount).

Most accountants, even in nonstatistical sampling, treat separately all population units that are individually significant. Statistically, there are two reasons for this:

1. It reduces the variability of the population to be sampled, thus reducing the sample size.
2. It improves the stability of the standard error of the mean, thus maintaining the target risk levels of the sampling plan.

A useful rule of thumb is to place all sampling units with amounts greater than four or five times the mean of the total sample into the 100 percent stratum. Some accounting populations, however, may not contain any of these key items.

Two methods are used to allocate a total sample to individual strata. One method is known as **proportional allocation**. In this method, the percentage of the sample allocated to each stratum is the same as the percentage of the total population accounted for by that stratum. That is,

$$n_i = n \cdot N_i / N$$

where n_i represents the sample size for the ith stratum, n the total sample size, N_i the number of population items in the ith stratum, and N the total population size.

A more precise method, however, is **optimal allocation.** Optimal allocation allocates the total sample to the individual stratum on the basis of the relative stratum size N and the stratum standard deviation SD.

---

[2]According to Roberts. "In some limited empirical work. it was found that using up to about five strata can be expected to result in large savings in sample size. With more strata, the incremental saving persists but becomes appreciably smaller because a few differences of larger size than anticipated can adversely affect the sample evaluation," Donald M. Roberts, *Statistical Auditing* (New York: AICPA, 1978). p. 96.

$$n_i = n \cdot \frac{N_i SD_i}{\Sigma N_i SD_i}$$

where

n_i = sample size per stratum i

n = total sample

N_i = population size of stratum i

SD_i = standard deviation of stratum i

Worksheet 2 in Appendix A is based on optimal allocation.

In summary, stratified sampling makes it feasible to sample a nonhomogeneous population without requiring an extremely large sample size. To ascertain whether or not stratified sampling should be used, consider the following:

1. The range of items in the population.
2. The shape of the population (compare with a normal curve).
3. The sample size produced via nonstratified sampling.

STEPS IN APPLYING STRATIFIED MEAN PER UNIT

1. Define the reliability level. Generally, a high reliability level should be used (99–90%).
2. Based on the following table, convert step 1 into a U_R coefficient.

Reliability	U_R *Coefficient*
0.99	2.58
0.95	1.96
0.90	1.65

3. Set acceptable precision equal to an amount material for the application.
4. Define each stratum.
   a. Every population element must belong to one and only one stratum.
   b. There must be a tangible, specifiable difference that defines and distinguishes the strata.
   c. The exact number of elements in each stratum must be known.
   d. One approach to use in stratifying a population is to select the stratum boundaries so that each stratum contains approximately the same total dollars.
   e. The top stratum generally should be sampled 100 percent.

5. Calculate required sample size *without replacement* by using *Worksheet 2* in Appendix A. If you cannot estimate the standard deviation of each stratum, draw a random sample of 30 items from each stratum (use sampling without replacement) and use *Worksheet 1* in Appendix A to estimate the standard deviations. Instead of using *Worksheet 2* and *Worksheet 1*, the following equations may be used to calculate stratum standard deviation and sample size:

$$SD = \sqrt{\frac{\sum\limits_{j=1}^{n} x_j^2 - n\bar{x}^2}{n-1}}$$

$$n_i = \frac{(N_i SD_i)(\Sigma N_i SD_i)}{(A/U_R)^2 + \Sigma N_i SD_i^2}$$

If any n_i is greater than N_i, set that stratum sample size equal to its population size and recalculate the sample sizes for the remaining strata. The saturated stratum may be excluded from *Worksheet 2*.

6. Randomly select the additional sample elements (if pilot samples were used) using computer generation, the random number table, or systematic selection.

7. Select the additional sample items.

8. Calculate achieved precision A' by using *Worksheet 3* in Appendix A or use the following equation:

$$A' = U_R \sqrt{\Sigma \frac{N_i SD_i^2 (N_i - n_i)}{n_i}}$$

Note that a 100 percent audited stratum (a saturated stratum) has no effect on A'. Thus, a saturated stratum should be omitted from the A' calculation.

9. If $A' \leq A$, go to step 11; otherwise, go to step 10.

10. Use *Worksheet 2* in Appendix A to recalculate and reallocate sample size. Use the standard deviations of each stratum based on the total sample from each stratum. *Worksheet 1* in Appendix A may be employed to calculate the standard deviation of each stratum. Go back to step 6 after the recalculated (larger) sample size is determined.

11. Calculate the mean $\bar{x}$ of each stratum based on n_i for each stratum.

12. Calculate the **estimated population value** total according to the following.

$$\bar{x} \cdot N_1 = \bar{x}_1 N_1$$
$$\bar{x} \cdot N_2 = \bar{x}_2 N_2$$
$$\underline{\bar{x}_3 \cdot N_3 = \bar{x}_3 N_3}$$

$$\Sigma \bar{x}_i N_i = EV \text{ for sampled stratum}$$

$EV = EV$ for sampled stratum *plus* total for any 100 percent nonsampled stratum

where

$$\bar{x}_i = \text{the mean of a defined stratum}$$
$$N_i = \text{the total number of items per a defined stratum}$$
$$\sum \bar{x}_i N_i = \text{sum of } (\bar{x}_i N_i)$$

13. Conclude that you believe that at the reliability level specified in step 1 the true book value is within $EV \pm A'$ (step 8). Your conclusion should also address the effectiveness of procedures used to generate the projected amount and whether or not accounting personnel applied the procedures correctly.
14. State book value at EV (step 12).

Caution

Do not use this approach if the client has a book value that you are trying to decide whether to accept. (It is not appropriate to make a statistical estimate of a population total and, finding the book value somewhere within the precision interval, to accept the book value as materially correct. If this type of decision procedure is to be used, the audit hypothesis approach should be employed.)

If you understand the Red Raider, Inc., problem as is illustrated in applying simple extension, stratified simple extension should not be difficult to comprehend. The only additional reminder concerns step 12, where the estimated population total EV is calculated. For a 100 percent stratum, the estimated value is increased by the total of that stratum. Similarly, calculated precision A' is not affected by a 100 percent stratum.

DIFFERENCE ESTIMATION

Difference estimation is a model used to estimate dollar amounts, similar to unstratified and stratified MPU. Difference estimation, however, is sometimes more efficient (i.e., smaller sample size). Instead of computing the mean value and the standard deviation of the sample item values as in MPU, the mean value and standard deviation of the individual *differences* between each sample item's value and book value are computed. A **difference** is defined to be the sample item value minus book value and will be zero if these quantities are equal. Algebraically, a positive difference indicates an understated book value, but a negative difference indicates an overstated book value. As we discuss later, difference estimation can be used with or without stratification.

Difference estimation may be appropriate and advantageous when:

1. There is a book value for each population item.
2. The total book value is known and corresponds to the addition of all the individual book values. (Before using difference estimation, the book values *must* be footed.)

For difference estimation to be efficient and effective, the sample size should be large enough for the distribution of sample mean differences to be approximately normal. Whether or not practical sample sizes that approximate normality are produced depends on: (1) the proportion of sample units with nonzero differences, and (2) the distribution of these differences in terms of their magnitude (dollar amount) and their algebraic sign (understated or overstated).

Unstratified difference estimation works effectively if the population and sample units contain a large proportion of nonzero differences. Also, the differences should be nearly equally divided between overstatement and understatement, and the misstatements should be fairly constant in amount. If differences are highly skewed, stratified difference estimation or ratio estimation should be considered.

Before the standard deviation can be safely estimated, a minimum number of nonzero differences must be observed. What is the minimum number of differences? According to Roberts:

There is no simple answer to this question. A small number would suffice if all the nonzero differences are nearly equal whereas a large number would be necessary when the differences vary widely. Whatever the number, the auditor should be reasonably satisfied that the observed differences appear to be typical for the particular situation. In that case, recognizing that any numerical guideline has exceptions, the auditor might use 15 or 20 as a minimum number.[3]

We recommend a minimum of about 30 differences to ensure a good estimate of the standard deviation of differences. For illustration purposes, a minimum of 30 will be used in this text.

The mean of the differences for unstratified difference estimation is calculated as:

$$\bar{d} = \frac{\Sigma di}{n}$$

where

$$\bar{d} = \text{mean of the differences}$$

$$\Sigma di = \text{sum of observed differences considering signs}$$

---

[3]Donald M. Roberts, *Statistical Auditing,* p. 74. See also J. H. McCray, "Ratio and Difference Estimation in Auditing," *Management Accounting* (December 1973), p. 47.

After calculating the mean of the differences, the estimated population difference is obtained by

$$\hat{D} = N\bar{d}$$

where

$$\hat{D} = \text{estimated population difference}$$

An estimate of the total value is calculated as

$$EV = \text{book value} + \hat{D} \text{ (if net differences are positive) or}$$
$$- \hat{D} \text{ (if net differences are negative)}$$

The standard deviation of the differences then is used to compute the precision of the total observed value at some predetermined reliability level.

The approach to a difference estimation application is essentially the same as the approach used in unstratified MPU. The primary difference as depicted by the following model is that the mean of the differences $\bar{d}$ and the standard deviation of differences SD_d is used instead of $\bar{x}$ and SD. Thus, difference estimation improves the efficiency (smaller sample size) and precision (tighter precision) vis-à-vis other estimation techniques.

Stratified difference estimation may further enhance the efficiency of difference estimation. In fact, unless nonzero differences are reasonably small in dollar amount, unstratified difference estimation probably should not be used.

Three to five strata are commonly employed in stratified difference applications, with stratum boundaries selected so that each stratum contains nearly an equal dollar amount—except the top stratum, which is the 100 percent nonsampled stratum. The only change in the stratified MPU model is that d is substituted for $\bar{x}$ and SD_d for SD for each stratum. Also, if stratified difference estimation is used, several differences should be observed in each stratum. After the sample has been selected and sample item values established, the estimated total difference is calculated according to the following equation, assuming three strata:

$$\hat{D} = N_1\bar{d}_1 + N_2\bar{d}_2 + N_3\bar{d}_3$$

Because of the qualifying misstatement conditions that are necessary before difference estimation can be used, its application is sometimes limited. For example, in large banks, savings and loan institutions, and public utilities characterized by strong internal control, differences between sample item values and book values may be rare. One widely used application is in the area of Lifo inventory. If a company maintains Fifo records that are converted to Lifo at year-end, difference estimation, stratified or unstratified, is very useful in making this conversion.

STEPS IN APPLYING UNSTRATIFIED DIFFERENCE ESTIMATION

1. Define reliability level. Generally a high reliability level should be used (99–90%).
2. Based on the following table convert step 1 into a U_R coefficient.

Reliability	U_R Coefficient
0.99	2.58
0.95	1.96
0.90	1.65

3. Set acceptable precision equal to an amount material for the application.
4. Calculate required sample size *with replacement*.

$$n' = \left(\frac{U_R \cdot SD_d \cdot N}{A}\right)^2$$

where

n' = sample size with replacement

SD_d = standard deviation (based on prior knowledge or random sample).

Worksheet 4 in Appendix A delineates the steps involved in calculating a standard deviation of differences from a sample. The size of the pilot sample must be large enough to contain several nonzero differences. Otherwise, SD_d would be zero and n' could not be computed. The pilot sample (if used) should be selected without replacement.

5. Adjust step 4 to sample size *without replacement*.

$$n = \frac{n'}{1 + (n'/N)}$$

6. Randomly select additional samples (if pilot sample was used) by using computer generation, a random-number table, or systematic selection.
7. Determine the difference between sample item values and book values. Examine the cause of observed misstatements to ascertain that any unobserved misstatements that might exist are likely to be in about the same range of values as observed misstatements.
8. Calculate the standard deviation of the sample differences. *Worksheet 4* in Appendix A may be used to calculate the standard deviation of the differences, or the following equation may be used.

$$SD_d = \sqrt{\frac{\Sigma d_i^2 - n\bar{d}^2}{n - 1}}$$

9. Calculate the standard error of the differences by using the following equation:

$$SE_d = \frac{SD_d}{\sqrt{n}}$$

10. Calculate achieved precision A' based on the following equation. Use SE_d from step 9,

$$A' = U_R \cdot SE_d \cdot N\sqrt{1 - \frac{n}{N}}$$

11. If $A' \leq A$, go to step 13; otherwise, go to step 12.
12. Increase the sample size according to the following equation. Afterward, go back to step 6.

$$\text{Adjusted } n = \left(\frac{U_R \cdot SD_d(\text{step 8}) \cdot N}{A} \right)^2$$

13. Calculate the mean of the differences $\bar{d}$ of the total sample.

$$\bar{d} = \frac{\Sigma d_i}{n}$$

14. Calculate the estimated population difference $\hat{D}$

$$\hat{D} = N \cdot \bar{d}$$

15. Calculate estimated value, EV.

$EV = $ book value (footed) $+ \hat{D}$ (if net differences are positive) or $- \hat{D}$ (if net differences are negative).

16. Conclude that you believe that at the reliability level specified in step 1 the true book value is within $EV \pm A'$. Your conclusion should also address the effectiveness of procedures used to generate the projected amount and whether or not accounting personnel applied the procedures correctly.
17. State book value at EV (step 15).

Caution

1. Do not use this approach if the client has a book value that you are trying to decide whether to accept.
2. The *observed* misstatement rate (sample item value minus book value) in the final sample must include at least a minimum of 30 differences. *Otherwise,* consider using stratified MPU or probability-proportional-to-size sampling.

RATIO ESTIMATION

Ratio estimation is applied in much the same fashion as difference estimation. Because of its close similarity to difference estimation and the complexity involved in manual calculations, only a brief introduction is presented here.

Like difference estimation, ratio estimation may be appropriate and efficient when a book value exists for each population item, and differences between sample item values and book values are not rare. Ratio estimation assumes that the book values are all positive.

To apply ratio estimation, a sample is selected from a population and the observed sample item value *OV* of each item is determined along with the corresponding book value *BV*. From the selected random sample, the estimated population ratio $\hat{R}$ is calculated as follows:

$$\hat{R} = \frac{\Sigma OV_i}{\Sigma BV_i}$$

The estimated value (point estimate) for the population total is

$$EV = \hat{R} \cdot \text{book value}$$

If $\hat{R}$ is less than one, the sample evidence indicates that book value is overstated; but if $\hat{R}$ is greater than one, the book value appears to be understated.

Ratio estimation will be more efficient relative to unstratified MPU if the standard deviation of ratios SD_r is smaller than the *SD* of the sample item values. Similarly, ratio estimation may, in certain situations, be more efficient than difference estimation if SD_r is less than SD_d. Ratio estimation is favored relative to difference estimation when the absolute differences (sample item values—book values) are nearly a constant percentage of book values. That is, if each sample item value is nearly proportional to book value, ratio estimation produces a more efficient sample size. Recall that difference estimation tends to be more efficient when the absolute differences are nearly the same amount (without regard to book value). To illustrate, the following situation would favor ratio estimation:

Sample Item Value	Book Value	Difference
$ 2,000	$ 1,800	$ 200
4,000	4,480	(480)
10,000	10,000	0
3,000	3,390	(390)
12,000	10,800	1,200
$31,000	$30,470	$ 530

Conversely, the next situation would favor difference estimation, relative to ratio estimation.

Sample Item Value	Book Value	Difference
$ 2,000	$ 1,730	$ 270
4,000	4,300	(300)
10,000	10,000	0
3,000	2,680	320
12,000	11,760	240
$31,000	$30,470	$ 530

The tedious manual calculations inherent in ratio estimation applications perhaps can best be appreciated by the equation for SD_r.

$$SD_r = \left[\frac{\Sigma OV^2 + R^2 \Sigma BV^2 - 2R\Sigma(OV)(BV)}{n-1} \right]^{1/2}$$

SUMMARY

When the accountant is faced with a situation requiring the projection of a total quantity or total dollars based on a mean of a sample, accounting estimation is the appropriate tool to use. By using estimation sampling, a projection can be made of the estimated population value that becomes the booked amount. The estimated population value plus and minus calculated precision is expected to contain the true but unknown value at a defined reliability level.

Four estimation models are discussed in this chapter. They are: (1) unstratified mean per unit, (2) stratified mean per unit, (3) difference estimation, and (4) ratio estimation. Ranked in order of efficiency (smallest sample size), stratified difference estimation or ratio estimation would most likely produce the most efficient sample size. Unstratified difference estimation would be next, followed by stratified mean per unit. Unstratified mean per unit is the most inefficient accounting estimation model; consequently, it is infrequently used.

Stratified mean per unit is probably more widely used in practice than the other accounting estimation models discussed in this chapter. Extensive use of stratified mean per unit occurs primarily because qualifying misstatement conditions that are necessary for using difference and ratio estimation are somewhat limiting.

GLOSSARY

Accounting estimation A statistical model used to estimate a dollar balance or quantity total when the point estimate is to be entered into the accounting records.

Achieved precision A calculated precision A' determined by multiplying reliability (U_R) times the standard error SE times the population size N.

Audit hypothesis approach A statistical model used to determine if an already existing book value or quantity is misstated by a material amount.

Central limit theorem A theorem that states that if a large number of samples are drawn from a given population, the distribution of sample means tends to be normally distributed, almost independently of the shape of the original population distribution.

Difference The sample item value minus its book value.

Difference estimation See Chapter 1 glossary.

Estimated population value A positive or negative total determined by multiplying the difference mean $\bar{d}$ times the population size N yielding an estimated population difference $\hat{D}$.

Estimated value A point estimate determined by multiplying the sample mean $\bar{x}$ times the population size N or adding/subtracting the estimated population difference $\hat{D}$ to a footed book value total.

Mean The arithmetic average—the total of all items divided by the number of items.

Median The midpoint of a population or sample.

Mode The value that occurs most frequently in a distribution.

Normal distribution A frequency distribution in which item values tend to congregate around the mean with no tendency for deviation toward one side rather than the other. A normal distribution is represented graphically by a bell-shaped curve.

Optimal allocation A method to determine strata sample sizes based on the relative size of each stratum and its standard deviation.

Point estimate The same as estimated value (EV).

Precision A measure of closeness of a sample estimate to the corresponding population characteristic. A range of values around a point estimate within which the true value is expected to fall. It is a probabilistic measure in that the precision of an estimate A' can only be made for a specified reliability.

Precision interval If the precision of an estimate EV is A', the interval from $EV + A'$ to $EV - A'$ is the precision interval.

Proportional allocation A method to determine strata sample sizes based only on the relative size of each stratum.

Ratio estimation   A variable sampling model whereby a ratio $\hat{R}$ of the sum of observed sample item values divided by the sum of book values is calculated from a sample. The ratio is multiplied by the total book value to yield a point estimate of the population total.

Skewness   The degree of asymmetry or lopsidedness of a distribution. Typical accounting populations are skewed because there are many small to medium amounts and a few very large amounts.

Standard deviation   A unit of measure of the variability of a frequency distribution. In a normal distribution, 68 percent of all item values fall within $\pm$ 1 standard deviation, 95 percent within $\pm$ 1.96 standard deviations, and 99 percent within $\pm$ 2.58 standard deviations.

Standard error of the mean   The standard deviation of the distribution of sample means. The estimated standard error of a sample mean is equal to the standard deviation of the sample divided by the square root of the sample size.

Stratified mean per unit   See Chapter 1 glossary.

True value   An account balance determined by a complete examination of the account details (without the use of sampling).

Unstratified mean per unit   See Chapter 1 glossary.

REVIEW QUESTIONS

4-1. Each of the following assumes the uses of unrestricted random sampling without replacement. State whether each one is true (T) or false (F).

a. If an accountant wishes to use a table of random digits to select a random sample, he or she must first find a table that conforms to the numbering employed by the items in the population the accountant wishes to sample.

b. If a usable number appears more than once in the table of random digits during the selection of the sample, the item should be included in the sample only once and another number should be selected from the table.

c. A random sample of at least 50 items would have to be discarded if it produced one item disproportionately large in relation to the other items selected.

d. The effect of the inclusion by chance of a very large or a very small item in a random sample can be lessened by increasing the size of the sample.

e. The reliability specified by the accountant for a sample estimate expresses the degree of confidence that the true value will be within the computed precision interval.

f. The standard deviation is a measure of variability of items in the population.

g. Variability of items in the population is a factor that usually causes the point estimate of the population and its true value to be different.

h. It is necessary to determine the true standard deviation for a population to determine the size of the sample to be drawn from that population.

i. The standard error of the mean generally will be less than the estimated standard deviation computed on the basis of a sample.

j. Precision and reliability have no meaning unless paired with each other.

k. Variable sampling is used primarily for tests of controls.

4-2. What is variable sampling?

4-3. What is the primary difference in accounting estimation versus audit hypothesis testing?

4-4. Calculate the standard deviation of the following sample items.

$\overline{x}$
8
15
2
34
16

4-5. Why is the unstratified mean per unit sometimes referred to as simple extension?

4-6. Is the standard error of the mean smaller or larger than the standard deviation? Explain.

4-7. If calculated precision A' is larger than predefined precision A, the sample size has to be increased. Why?

4-8. Prove that the mathematical defintion of precision is equal to the sample size formula. That is,

$$A = U_R \cdot SE \cdot N \text{ equals } n' = \left(\frac{U_R \cdot SD \cdot N}{A} \right)^2$$

4-9. List the three rules that must be followed if stratified mean per unit is to be used correctly.

4-10. What are two methods used to allocate a total sample to individual strata? Which one is recommended in the text?

4-11. The Clay Corporation is applying simple statistical sampling to estimate their receivable balance. They have four strata. The stratum containing the largest accounts was not sampled. It totals $88,900. The other three strata produced the following results:

Stratum	$\bar{x}$	N
1	238	250
2	154	600
3	53	1500

Calculated precision (A') is $20,000. What is the estimated value?

4-12. Determine the sample size for each stratum using (a) proportional allocation and (b) optimal allocation.

Stratum	Stratum Boundaries	Size	Standard Deviation
1	0–300	5500	80
2	301–800	2000	150
3	801–1600	500	200
4	1601–3000	300	400

4-13. Difference estimation often is more efficient than unstratified MPU. However, before difference estimation can be used, two conditions must be met. What are these conditions? What is the minimum number of observed differences that are recommended in the text before difference estimation can be safely used?

4-14. If a population of size N is footed and yields $10,000 and the mean of differences $\bar{d}$ is +$50, what is the estimated population difference if $N = 100$?

4-15. If the estimated population difference $\hat{D}$ is −$500, what is the estimated value if the footed book value is $10,000?

4-16. What causes difference estimation to be more efficient than unstratified MPU? What could cause ratio estimation to be more efficient than difference estimation?

4-17. Calculate the mean of the following differences.

Sample Item Value	Book Value
$20	18
40	40
36	38
21	36
15	15

MULTIPLE-CHOICE QUESTIONS FROM PROFESSIONAL EXAMINATIONS

4-18. In applying variables sampling, an auditor attempts to:

   a. Estimate a qualitative characteristic of interest.

   b. Determine various rates of occurrence for specified attributes.

   c. Discover at least one instance of a critical deviation.

   d. Predict a monetary population value within a range of precision.

4-19. In estimation sampling for variables, which of the following must be known in order to estimate the appropriate sample size required to meet the auditor's needs in a given situation?

   a. The qualitative aspects of misstatements.

   b. The total dollar amount of the population.

   c. The number of misstatments in the population.

   d. The estimated deviation rate in the population.

4-20. An internal auditor is using variables estimation as the statistical sampling technique to estimate the monetary value of a large inventory of parts. Given a sample standard deviation of $400, a sample size of 400, and a 95 percent two-tail confidence level, what precision can the auditor assign to the estimate of the mean dollar value of a part?

   a. $\pm$ $39.

   b. $\pm$ $2.

   c. $\pm$ $52.

   d. $\pm$ $20.

4-21. A statistical sample from an inventory containing a total of 10,000 items produced a sample mean equal to $25 and a standard error of the mean equal to $1. What is the interval estimate of the total value of the inventory at the 95 percent confidence level (assume that $U_R = 2.0$)?

   a. $230,000 to $270,000.

   b. $240,000 to $260,000.

   c. $240,450 to $259,550.

   d. $250,000 to $270,000.

4-22. In estimating the total value of supplies on repair trucks. Baker Company draws random samples from two equal-sized strata of trucks. The mean value of the inventory stored on the larger trucks (stratum 1) was computed at $1500, with a standard deviation of $250. On the smaller trucks (stratum 2), the mean value of inventory was computed as $500, with a standard deviation of $45. If Baker had drawn an unstratified sample from the entire population of trucks, the expected mean value of inventory per truck would be $1000, and the expected standard deviation would be:

    a. Exactly $147.50.

    b. Greater than $250.

    c. Less than $45.

    d. Between $45 and $250, but not $147.50.

4-23. An auditor's finding was stated as follows: "Twenty of 100 randomly selected items tested revealed that $200 of cash discounts on purchases were lost." This variables sampling finding is deficient because the:

    a. Recommendation specifies no action.

    b. Sampling methodology is not defined.

    c. Amount is not material.

    d. Probable effect on the entire population is not provided.

4-24. In a sampling application, the standard deviation represents a measure of the:

    a. Expected error rate.

    b. Level of confidence desired.

    c. Degree of data variability.

    d. Extent of precision achieved.

4-25. In determining the sample size for variables sampling, the internal auditor requires some knowledge of the variability of the population. In obtaining this preliminary information, the internal auditor:

    a. Can seldom rely on the results of prior years' sample results since they pertain only to the prior years' populations.

    b. Frequently takes a convenience pilot sample of 30 to 50 items and uses this to estimate the variability of the population.

    c. Frequently takes a random pilot sample of 30 to 50 items, applies audit tests to these items, and uses the variability in these items to estimate the variability in the population of audit values. The pilot sample is then discarded and the real sample is taken from the remaining population.

    d. Will frequently take a random pilot sample of 30 to 50 items, compute the range in this sample, and use this range as an estimate of the population variability for purposes of computing sample size.

Use the following information to answer questions 4-26 and 4-27.

A construction company has an inventory of 1000 homes under construction with a recorded book value of $22,222,222. The population standard deviation was initially estimated to be $3000; desired precision and confidence level were $247,500 and 90 percent, respectively. A sample of 400 homes was taken for use in mean-per-unit estimation. Audit results revealed an estimated inventory value of $22 million with a precision of $291,176.

4-26. The sample standard deviation, which is different from that originally estimated, affected which of the following?

   a. Estimated inventory value of $22 million.

   b. Calculated precision of $291,176.

   c. Calculated sample size of 400.

   d. Desired precision of $247,500.

4-27. The finite population correction factor was not used to calculate the required sample size. The application of the finite correction factor to the precision interval will cause:

   a. The precision interval to become smaller.

   b. The precision interval to become larger.

   c. The reliability to decrease.

   d. The reliability to increase.

CASES

Case 4-1   Empress Cosmetique Case*

(Estimated time to complete: 4 hours)

 Empress Cosmetique markets inexpensive, quality cosmetics for the mature woman. Well established in the state, Empress maintains five regional warehouses with approximately equal stock levels.

   Until recently, Naomi Van Diver, the company's founder and director, followed traditional management practices by insisting on the pricing of all inventory items in each warehouse. Now under new management, Empress Cosmetique is considering the use of statistical sampling techniques for estimating its inventory for financial reporting purposes.

   The company's inventory consists of 100 different beauty products in each of the five warehouses. For inventory control purposes, perpetual inventory counts for each product are maintained for each warehouse location.

   The new plan will consist of randomly selecting inventory lots for count and comparison with the perpetual record. Using statistical sampling, an estimate of the inventory value will be made that provides 95 percent assurance that the estimated value is within ± $58,000 of the actual amount.

   A list of perpetual inventory units by lot as of June 30 (pages 123–135 and a product price schedule (page 136) are provided. Assume that there are no differences in physical and perpetual inventory counts.

---

*This case was prepared by Doyle Z. Williams, Dean, College of Business Administration. University of Arkansas, and Dale A. Stewart, BBA Accounting, Texas Tech University, and is copyrighted by Doyle Z. Williams. It is reproduced here with permission.

REQUIREMENTS

For each of the following, prepare complete, well-organized, and documented work papers.

  a. As the chief accountant for Empress Cosmetique, describe the sampling plan appropriate for estimating the June 30 inventory.

  b. Using appropriate statistical sampling techniques, estimate the value of the June 30 inventory that will meet the $58,000 precision and 95 percent confidence level indicated. If you use a random-number table, the illustration on page 24 may be employed. The price list for the inventory appears on page 136.

  c. By using the data obtained from your preliminary sample of 30 items, calculate the required sample size (n'), assuming the desired levels of precision and reliability in each case are as follows:

Case	Reliability	Precision
1	95%	$60,000
2	90%	$30,000
3	90%	$14,000
4	85%	$60,000

  d. If you were the auditor of Empress Cosmetique, could you accept the use of a statistical sampling model instead of a 100 percent inventory count? Consult your Statements on Auditing Standards for authoritative support.

Inventory

	Empress Cosmetique		
Line Number	Item Number	Quantity	Description
	A001R	1103	Lipstick Red
	B001R	1250	
	C001R	1301	
	D001R	1012	
5	E001R	1212	
	A001P	1062	Lipstick Pink
	B001P	1013	
	C001P	1081	
	D001P	1039	
10	E001P	1072	
	A001M	1017	Lipstick Mocha
	B001M	1041	
	C001M	1101	
	D001M	1013	

Inventory (Continued)

	Empress Cosmetique		
Line Number	*Item Number*	*Quantity*	*Description*
15	E001M	1076	
	A001W	1001	Lipstick Wine
	B001W	1031	
	C001W	1114	
	D001W	1061	
20	E001W	1103	
	A101R	1143	Nail Polish Red
	B101R	1116	
	C101R	1189	
	D101R	1135	
25	E101R	1147	
	A101P	1481	Nail Polish Pink
	B101P	1414	
	C101P	1539	
	D101P	1564	
30	E101P	1491	
	A101M	1521	Nail Polish Mocha
	B101M	1416	
	C101M	1429	
	D101M	1497	
35	E101M	1465	
	A101W	1270	Nail Polish Wine
	B101W	1128	
	C101W	1252	
	D101W	1148	
40	E101W	1165	
	A002BK	1465	Eye Liner Black
	B002BK	1471	
	C002BK	1461	
	D002BK	1488	
45	E002BK	1450	
	A002BR	1273	Eye Liner Brown
	B002BR	1285	
	C002BR	1314	
	D002BR	1269	
50	E002BR	1298	
	A202BR	1199	Eye Brow Pencil Brown
	B202BR	1265	
	C202BR	1233	
	D202BR	1301	

Inventory (Continued)

Empress Cosmetique			
Line Number	Item Number	Quantity	Description
55	E202BR	1277	
	A202BK	1414	Eye Brow Pencil Black
	B202BK	1459	
	C202BK	1504	
	D202BK	1499	
60	E202BK	1517	
	A202G	1777	Eye Brow Pencil Gray
	B202G	1711	
	C202G	1734	
	D202G	1741	
65	E202G	1768	
	A003B	1503	Eye Shadow Blue
	B003B	1507	
	C003B	1487	
	D003B	1475	
70	E003B	1496	
	A003G	1749	Eye Shadow Green
	B003G	1696	
	C003G	1765	
	D003G	1731	
75	E003G	1677	
	A003W	1916	Eye Shadow White
	B003W	1959	
	C003W	2001	
	D003W	1966	
80	E003W	1940	
	A003CG	1633	Eye Shadow Charcoal Gray
	B003CG	1617	
	C003CG	1576	
	D003CG	1621	
85	E003CG	1588	
	A003T	1501	Eye Shadow Topaz
	B003T	1520	
	C003T	1511	
	D003T	1469	
90	E003T	1471	
	A003Y	1851	Eye Shadow Oyster
	B003Y	1913	
	C003Y	1857	
	D003Y	1901	

Inventory (Continued)

	Empress Cosmetique		
Line Number	*Item Number*	*Quantity*	*Description*
95	E003Y	1862	
	A003M	1702	Eye Shadow Mauve
	B003M	1727	
	C003M	1727	
	D003M	1714	
100	E003M	1682	
	A003L	1611	Eye Shadow Lavender
	B003L	1661	
	C003L	1587	
	D003L	1634	
105	E003L	1550	
	A303C	1299	Blusher Copper
	B303C	1324	
	C303C	1349	
	D303C	1377	
110	E303C	1409	
	A303LO	1439	Blusher Light Orange
	B303LO	1522	
	C303LO	1491	
	D303LO	1486	
115	E303LO	1500	
	A303R	1616	Blusher Rose
	B303R	1644	
	C303R	1677	
	D303R	1579	
120	E303R	1663	
	A303P	1625	Blusher Pearlie Pink
	B303P	1721	
	C303P	1755	
	D303P	1760	
125	E303P	1641	
	A303DR	1193	Blusher Dawn Red
	B303DR	1212	
	C303DR	1206	
	D303DR	1187	
130	E303DR	1197	
	A303B	1076	Blusher Beige
	B303B	1111	
	C303B	1057	
	D303B	1082	

Inventory (Continued)

Empress Cosmetique			
Line Number	**Item Number**	**Quantity**	**Description**
135	E303B	1124	
	A316P	1024	Hair Rinse Platinum
	B316P	1036	
	C316P	1048	
	D316P	1031	
140	E316P	1054	
	A316SM	1114	Hair Rinse Silver Mist
	B316SM	1196	
	C316SM	1174	
	D316SM	1165	
145	E316SM	1159	
	A316A	1117	Hair Rinse Auburn
	B316A	1124	
	C316A	1106	
	D316A	1131	
150	E316A	1119	
	A316BN	1227	Hair Rinse Brownette
	B316BN	1234	
	C316BN	1221	
	D316BN	1241	
155	E316BN	1236	
	A316BL	1179	Hair Rinse Blonde
	B316BL	1184	
	C316BL	1214	
	D316BL	1166	
160	E316BL	1193	
	A316BR	1634	Hair Rinse Brunette
	B316BR	1586	
	C316BR	1599	
	D316BR	1649	
165	E316BR	1651	
	A316SF	1786	Hair Rinse Silver Flake
	B316SF	1759	
	C316SF	1741	
	D316SF	1697	
170	E316SF	1681	
	A366	1083	Nail File
	B366	1076	
	C366	1074	
	D366	1085	

Inventory (Continued)

	Empress Cosmetique		
Line Number	Item Number	Quantity	Description
175	E366	1036	
	A367	1029	Nail File
	B367	1001	
	C367	1093	
	D367	1033	
180	E367	1097	
	A368	1032	Nail File
	B368	1003	
	C368	1005	
	D368	1059	
185	E368	1033	
	A369	1976	Nail File
	B369	2043	
	C369	1903	
	D369	2072	
190	E369	1968	
	A370	1321	Nail File
	B370	1383	
	C370	1391	
	D370	1395	
195	E370	1366	
	A410	1136	Emery Board Fine
	B410	1159	
	C410	1127	
	D410	1147	
200	E410	1161	
	A411	1132	Emery Board Fine
	B411	1103	
	C411	1115	
	D411	1159	
205	E411	1330	
	A420	1377	Emery Board Medium
	B420	1405	
	C420	1411	
	D420	1389	
210	E420	1394	
	A421	1316	Emery Board Medium
	B421	1324	
	C421	1339	
	D421	1331	

Inventory (Continued)

Empress Cosmetique			
Line Number	Item Number	Quantity	Description
215	E421	1306	
	A430	1387	Emery Board Coarse
	B430	1374	
	C430	1391	
	D430	1398	
220	E430	1377	
	A431	1283	Emery Board Coarse
	B431	1290	
	C431	1349	
	D431	1301	
225	E431	1297	
	A440	1314	Tweezers
	B440	1324	
	C440	1311	
	D440	1301	
230	E440	1332	
	A450	1214	Tweezers
	B450	1187	
	C450	1212	
	D450	1196	
235	E450	1210	
	A460	1354	Tweezers
	B460	1339	
	C460	1362	
	D460	1341	
240	E460	1350	
	A500	1080	Depilatory Unscented
	B500	1068	
	C500	1030	
	D500	1067	
245	E500	1070	
	A501	1021	Depilatory Scented
	B501	1062	
	C501	1001	
	D501	1079	
250	E501	1075	
	A520S	1018	Deodorant Spray
	B520S	1053	
	C520S	1029	
	D520S	1065	

Inventory (Continued)

	Empress Cosmetique		
Line Number	*Item Number*	*Quantity*	*Description*
255	E520S	1019	
	A520P	1085	Deodorant Powder
	B520P	1068	
	C520P	1011	
	D520P	1062	
260	E520P	1056	
	A520R	1063	Deodorant Roll-on
	B520R	1064	
	C520R	1039	
	D520R	1034	
265	E520R	1088	
	A530S	1025	Antiperspirant Spray
	B530S	1076	
	C530S	1042	
	D530S	1066	
270	E530S	1021	
	A530P	1082	Antiperspirant Powder
	B530P	1025	
	C530P	1011	
	D530P	1076	
275	E530P	1063	
	A530R	1467	Antiperspirant Roll-on
	B530R	1455	
	C530R	1301	
	D530R	1357	
280	E530R	1477	
	A601	1427	Hair Spray Mist
	B601	1314	
	C601	1260	
	D601	1276	
285	E601	1372	
	A602F	1925	Hair Spray Fine Hold
	B602F	1864	
	C602F	1862	
	D602F	1912	
290	E602F	1964	
	A602R	1311	Hair Spray Regular Hold
	B602R	1473	
	C602R	1360	
	D602R	1493	

Inventory (Continued)

	Empress Cosmetique		
Line Number	*Item Number*	*Quantity*	*Description*
295	E602R	1375	
	A602H	1407	Hair Spray Hard-to-Hold
	B602H	1305	
	C602H	1577	
	D602H	1442	
300	E602H	1457	
	A603	1878	Hair Spray Unscented
	B603	1961	
	C603	1896	
	D603	1929	
305	E603	1836	
	A650	1865	Shampoo Dandruff
	B650	1882	
	C650	1892	
	D650	1816	
310	E650	1828	
	A652D	1145	Shampoo Dry
	B652D	1192	
	C652D	1163	
	D652D	1101	
315	E652D	1162	
	A652N	1295	Shampoo Normal
	B652N	1291	
	C652N	1292	
	D652N	1213	
320	E652N	1218	
	A652Y	1311	Shampoo Oily
	B652Y	1284	
	C652Y	1395	
	D652Y	1348	
325	E652Y	1273	
	A654	1795	Shampoo Color Treated
	B654	1549	
	C654	1784	
	D654	1634	
330	E654	1665	
	A660	1123	Creme Rinse Lemon
	B660	1076	
	C660	1077	
	D660	1114	

Inventory (Continued)

| | Empress Cosmetique | | |
Line Number	Item Number	Quantity	Description
335	E660	1115	
	A662	1710	Creme Rinse Unscented
	B662	1712	
	C662	1758	
	D662	1679	
340	E662	1793	
	A670R	1936	Setting Gel Regular
	B670R	1895	
	C670R	1827	
	D670R	1843	
345	E670R	1937	
	A670H	1708	Setting Gel Hard-to-Hold
	B670H	1620	
	C670H	1763	
	D670H	1661	
350	E670H	1742	
	A672R	1631	Setting Lotion Regular
	B672R	1635	
	C672R	1636	
	D672R	1729	
355	E672R	1748	
	A672H	1021	Setting Lotion Hard-to-Hold
	B672H	1004	
	C672H	1062	
	D672H	1069	
360	E672H	1087	
	A701	1228	Hand Lotion
	B701	1121	
	C701	1197	
	D701	1137	
365	E701	1234	
	A702	1039	Hand Creme
	B702	1086	
	C702	1064	
	D702	1069	
370	E702	1017	
	A712	1017	Skin Moisturizer
	B712	1097	
	C712	1076	
	D712	1088	
375	E712	1087	

Inventory (Continued)

	Empress Cosmetique		
Line Number	**Item Number**	**Quantity**	**Description**
	A714	1358	Body Lotion
	B714	1399	
	C714	1345	
	D714	1224	
380	E714	1205	
	A750	1262	Bath Oil
	B750	1120	
	C750	1275	
	D750	1190	
385	E750	1180	
	A751	1474	Bath Oil
	B751	1439	
	C751	1362	
	D751	1426	
390	E751	1492	
	A752	1311	Bath Oil
	B752	1493	
	C752	1365	
	D752	1480	
395	E752	1456	
	A761	1651	Bubble Bath Beads
	B761	1694	
	C761	1572	
	D761	1681	
400	E761	1688	
	A762	1576	Bubble Bath Powder
	B762	1627	
	C762	1437	
	D762	1489	
405	E762	1578	
	A763	1859	Bubble Bath Liquid
	B763	1968	
	C763	1804	
	D763	1886	
410	E763	1998	
	A800	1946	Makeup Remover
	B800	1903	
	C800	1900	
	D800	1908	
415	E800	1951	
	A810	1623	Cold Creme

Inventory (Continued)

	Empress Cosmetique		
Line Number	*Item Number*	*Quantity*	*Description*
	B810	1732	
	C810	1632	
	D810	1722	
420	E810	1605	
	A814	1541	Medicated Lotion
	B814	1670	
	C814	1793	
	D814	1804	
425	E814	1908	
	A815	1534	Medicated Creme
	B815	1527	
	C815	1518	
	D815	1571	
430	E815	1563	
	A824	1770	Hair Texturizer
	B824	1765	
	C824	1773	
	D824	1745	
435	E824	1791	
	A830	1592	Nail Polish Remover
	B830	1526	
	C830	1588	
	D830	1565	
440	E830	1591	
	A831	1347	Nail Polish Remover
	B831	1395	
	C831	1393	
	D831	1356	
445	E831	1421	
	A860B	1456	Mascara Black
	B860B	1472	
	C860B	1476	
	D860B	1453	
450	E860B	1360	
	A860LB	1097	Mascara Light Brown
	B860LB	1026	
	C860LB	1074	
	D860LB	1037	
455	E860LB	1033	
	A860DB	1052	Mascara Dark Brown
	B860DB	1068	
	C860DB	1073	

Inventory (Continued)

Line Number	Item Number	Quantity	Description
		Empress Cosmetique	
	D860DB	1016	
460	E860DB	1098	
	A901	1372	Skin Be Gone
	B901	1370	
	C901	1361	
	D901	1331	
465	E901	1333	
	A911	1378	Nails Hard
	B911	1401	
	C911	1373	
	D911	1407	
470	E911	1466	
	A990B	1006	Eyelashes Black
	B990B	1024	
	C990B	1088	
	D990B	1017	
475	E990B	1083	
	A990LB	1024	Eyelashes Light Brown
	B990LB	1044	
	C990LB	1004	
	D990LB	1010	
480	E990LB	1067	
	A990MB	1038	Eyelashes Medium Brown
	B990MB	1176	
	C990MB	1119	
	D990MB	1050	
485	E990MB	1045	
	A990DB	1131	Eyelashes Dark Brown
	B990DB	1183	
	C990DB	1142	
	D990DB	1192	
490	E990DB	1132	
	A990A	1146	Eyelashes Auburn
	B990A	1198	
	C990A	1109	
	D990A	1076	
495	E990A	1182	
	A990S	1098	Eyelashes Strawberry
	B990S	1016	
	C990S	1022	
	D990S	1003	
500	E990S	1033	

Price List

		Empress Cosmetique			
Item Number	Price	Item Number	Price	Item Number	Price
001M	$1.35	316SM	$1.39	662	$1.32
001P	$1.39	366	$1.19	670H	$1.34
001R	$1.39	367	$1.29	670R	$1.31
001W	$1.35	368	$1.39	672H	$1.42
101M	$1.25	369	$1.41	672R	$1.41
101P	$1.29	370	$1.45	701	$1.39
101R	$1.29	410	$1.19	702	$1.38
101W	$1.25	411	$1.29	712	$1.50
002BK	$1.40	420	$1.19	714	$1.41
002BR	$1.40	421	$1.29	750	$1.36
202BK	$1.19	430	$1.19	751	$1.40
202BR	$1.19	431	$1.29	752	$1.38
202G	$1.19	440	$1.19	761	$1.41
003B	$1.31	450	$1.29	762	$1.38
003CG	$1.29	460	$1.39	763	$1.39
003G	$1.31	500	$1.40	800	$1.29
003L	$1.35	501	$1.44	810	$1.36
003M	$1.33	520P	$1.29	814	$1.44
003T	$1.33	520R	$1.35	815	$1.41
003W	$1.29	520S	$1.39	824	$1.51
003Y	$1.35	530P	$1.29	830	$1.39
303B	$1.45	530R	$1.35	831	$1.37
303C	$1.40	530S	$1.39	860B	$1.29
303DR	$1.45	601	$1.40	860DB	$1.29
303LO	$1.40	602F	$1.41	860LB	$1.29
303P	$1.38	602H	$1.42	901	$1.79
303R	$1.38	602R	$1.45	911	$1.61
316A	$1.37	603	$1.39	990A	$1.40
316BL	$1.40	650	$1.37	990B	$1.41
316BN	$1.37	652D	$1.39	990DB	$1.37
316BR	$1.40	652N	$1.38	990LB	$1.40
316P	$1.39	652Y	$1.40	990MB	$1.39
316SF	$1.45	654	$1.41	990S	$1.40
		660	$1.34		

CASE

Case 4-2   Stratified Sampling, Inc.

(Estimated time to complete: 45 minutes)

Population: 1600 job orders in process.

Objective: to estimate dollar value of work in process inventory using stratified mean per unit estimation.

Acceptable precision: $7500.

Reliability: 95 percent.

By analyzing book-value data, the following additional data were obtained:

	N	*Standard Deviation*
Stratum 1	100	$500
Stratum 2	500	40
Stratum 3	1000	10

a. What is the sample size for each stratum using the optimum allocation method?

b. Assuming sample sizes of:

100 for Stratum 1

43 for Stratum 2

22 for Stratum 3

90 percent reliability, and standard deviations of $500, $40, and $10 for Stratum 1, 2, and 3, respectively, what is the achieved precision?

c. Is $A' \leq A$?

d. If $\bar{x}$ is $40 and $65 for Stratum 2 and 3, respectively, and the total of Stratum 1 is $200,000, what is EV?

Case 4-3   Foot, Tick, & Tie, CPAs

(Estimated time to complete: 15 minutes)

An audit partner of Foot, Tick, & Tie, CPAs is developing an office training program to familiarize his professional staff with statistical models that are applicable to dollar-value balances. He wishes to demonstrate the relationship of sample sizes to population size and variability and to specifications as to precision and confidence level. The partner prepared the following table to show the comparative population characteristics and specifications of two populations.

	Characteristics of Population 1 Relative to Population 2		Specifications as to a Sample from Population 1 Relative to a Sample from Population 2	
	Size	*Variability*	*Acceptable Precision Interval*	*Specified Confidence Level*
Case 1	Equal	Equal	Equal	Higher
Case 2	Equal	Larger	Wider	Equal
Case 3	Larger	Equal	Narrower	Lower
Case 4	Smaller	Smaller	Equal	Lower
Case 5	Larger	Equal	Equal	Higher

In items 1 to 5 below, indicate for the specific case from the above table the required sample size to be selected from population 1 relative to the sample from population 2.

Your answer choice should be selected from the following responses:

a. Larger than the required sample size from population 2.

b. Equal to the required sample size from population 2.

c. Smaller than the required sample size from population 2.

d. Indeterminate relative to the required sample size from population 2.

(1) In case 1 the required sample size from population 1 is _____

(2) In case 2 the required sample size from population 1 is _____

(3) In case 3 the required sample size from population 1 is _____

(4) In case 4 the required sample size from population 1 is _____

(5) In case 5 the required sample size from population 1 is _____

(AICPA adapted)

Case 4-4   Ace Corporation

(Estimated time to complete: 20 minutes)

Ace Corporation does not conduct a complete annual physical count of purchased parts and supplies in its principal warehouse but instead uses statistical sampling to estimate the year-end inventory. Ace maintains a perpetual inventory record of parts and supplies and believes that statistical sampling is highly effective in determining inventory values and is sufficiently reliable to make a physical count of each item of inventory unnecessary.

REQUIRED

Identify the audit procedures that change, or are in addition to normally required audit procedures, that should be used by the independent auditor when a client uses statistical sampling to determine inventory value, and does not conduct a 100 percent annual physical count of inventory items.

(AICPA adapted)

Case 4-5   Catalog Sales

(Estimated time to complete: 40 minutes)

You are an internal auditor for a company offering both department store and catalog sales. You are designing a variables sampling plan to determine the amount of revenue resulting from catalog sales. Company records indicate that 85,000 catalog sales were completed during the year. The total sales recorded for the same period were equal to $15,682,000. Catalog sales are not separately recorded.

A pilot sample of 30 catalog sales resulted in the following:

$$\text{Estimated population standard deviation} = \$9.00$$
$$\text{Average billing amoun} = \$27.50$$

The appropriate statistical sampling table indicates that a desired precision of $1.38 (5 percent of average billed amount) and the pilot sample standard deviation of $9.00 will require testing a sample of 121 transactions. It is the policy of your department to conduct such tests at the 90 percent confidence level ($U_r = 1.65$).

REQUIRED

a. Can the 30 items used as a pilot sample also be used as part of the sample of 121? Explain.

b. What factors impact the precision of the estimate of a population value?

c. Given the pilot sample results, what can the internal auditor do to decrease the size of the sample standard deviation?

d. The standard error of the mean can be computed by dividing the population standard deviation by the square root of sample size (ignoring the finite population correction factor). Assuming no change in the estimated population standard deviation after considering all 121 items, calculate:

The standard error of the mean

The achieved precision

  e. Assuming no change in the estimated average billing amount after considering all 121 items, compute estimated total catalog sales.

  f. Compute the 90 percent confidence interval for estimated total catalog sales.

(CIA, adapted)

Case 4-6 Sunnytime Snack Company

(Estimated time to complete: 35 minutes)

 Sunnytime Snack Company operates 1,250 snack machines in the Chicago metropolitan area. Each machine has a transmitter that communicates sales and inventory levels to the home office to enable the company to determine when the machine needs to be refilled. The transmitted information generally is accurate but may vary from actual amounts if the device is not working properly or the service attendant does not fill the machine properly. The company is experimenting with using the transmitted information to determine the amount of inventory for financial reporting purposes. Accordingly, the company has selected a sample of 60 machines to count for comparison with the recorded amounts of inventory based on the transmitted information. Information about the sample is presented below. The book value of the total inventory is $292,467.

  a. Using unstratified mean-per-unit sampling:

   (1) Calculate the estimated value of the inventory (EV).

   (2) Calculate the precision of the mean-per-unit estimated value. Assume that the standard deviation of the mean values in the sample is $29.

  b. Using difference estimation:

   (1) Calculate the estimated value of the inventory (EV).

   (2) Calculate the precision of the difference estimate. Assume that the standard deviation of the sample differences is $7.

  c. State which method is a better method of estimation in this situation. Explain your answer.

Sunnytime Snack Company

			Physical Inventory Sample				
Machine Number	**Amount Per Books**	**Amount Per Count**	**Difference**	**Machine Number**	**Amount Per Books**	**Amount Per Count**	**Difference**
24	$227.49	$227.49	$0.00	684	$276.54	$276.54	$0.00
35	$203.06	$203.06	$0.00	692	$194.69	$203.45	$8.76
56	$241.11	$232.33	−$8.78	700	$248.47	$248.47	$0.00
76	$266.91	$234.59	−$32.32	704	$257.55	$260.56	$3.01
92	$264.96	$264.96	$0.00	732	$282.97	$284.50	$1.53
113	$278.33	$278.33	$0.00	749	$232.89	$232.89	$0.00

Sunnytime Snack Company (Continued)

		Physical Inventory Sample					
Machine Number	**Amount Per Books**	**Amount Per Count**	**Difference**	**Machine Number**	**Amount Per Books**	**Amount Per Count**	**Difference**
125	$180.41	$191.23	$10.82	759	$221.91	$219.91	−$2.00
146	$229.15	$229.15	$0.00	797	$251.88	$255.00	$3.12
178	$262.38	$262.38	$0.00	810	$225.47	$230.00	$4.53
199	$207.83	$207.83	$0.00	824	$253.94	$253.94	$0.00
214	$217.74	$201.45	−$16.29	852	$198.90	$220.01	$21.11
256	$192.74	$192.74	$0.00	867	$213.82	$213.82	$0.00
275	$188.83	$188.83	$0.00	889	$196.96	$196.96	$0.00
301	$210.56	$212.34	$1.78	912	$225.93	$225.93	$0.00
340	$215.66	$215.66	$0.00	915	$234.19	$234.19	$0.00
345	$182.05	$170.00	−$12.05	934	$235.70	$230.20	−$5.50
393	$220.80	$220.80	$0.00	945	$226.93	$226.93	$0.00
395	$224.90	$224.90	$0.00	983	$289.86	$289.86	$0.00
424	$238.37	$238.37	$0.00	999	$191.44	$183.90	−$7.54
436	$225.86	$230.66	$4.80	1008	$216.59	$225.45	$8.86
468	$226.83	$210.34	−$16.49	1034	$170.56	$170.56	$0.00
487	$225.74	$225.74	$0.00	1045	$271.19	$271.19	$0.00
506	$268.57	$268.57	$0.00	1087	$203.01	$203.01	$0.00
513	$232.87	$240.90	$8.03	1112	$218.66	$218.66	$0.00
576	$230.35	$230.35	$0.00	1117	$253.94	$253.94	$0.00
581	$222.17	$227.00	$4.83	1132	$246.67	$246.67	$0.00
621	$284.31	$284.31	$0.00	1151	$256.87	$256.87	$0.00
632	$256.64	$256.64	$0.00	1183	$249.89	$240.00	-$9.89
651	$294.39	$293.00	-$1.39	1201	$200.70	$200.70	$0.00
671	$218.63	$218.63	$0.00	1235	$207.11	$207.11	$0.00
				Total	$13,894.84	$13,863.80	−$31.04

5 USING VARIABLE SAMPLING FOR AUDIT HYPOTHESIS TESTING

LEARNING OBJECTIVES

After a careful study and discussion of this chapter, you will be able to:

1. Use unstratified mean per unit (MPU), stratified MPU, and difference estimation to test a client's book value for material misstatement.

2. Define the various audit risks inherent in sampling, understand the interrelationships among these risks, and be able to control risk in particular fact settings.

3. Explain how the auditor considers overall materiality for an engagement and how this is used to determine tolerable misstatement for substantive tests.

4. Describe what action(s) to take if a variable sampling application does not support a client's book value.

5. Identify areas of judgment involved in using the audit hypothesis model.

Substantive tests are those in which the feature of audit interest is the amount of monetary misstatements that would affect the financial statements being audited, including those due to error and fraud. By definition, therefore, substantive tests are concerned with reaching conclusions about whether financial amounts are materially correct. The variable sampling model is often used for substantive testing. Variable sampling is useful because conclusions are produced that are stated in monetary-unit terms and can be related directly to financial statement impact. Attribute sampling (see Chapter 3), on the other hand, is more readily applicable to tests of controls.

This chapter explains the audit hypothesis approach from a variable sampling perspective. To do so, we explain and demonstrate the concepts of audit risk and its component risks. Following the discussion of these risks, the audit hypothesis testing model is presented and illustrated.

SAMPLING RISK AND AUDIT SAMPLING

SAS No. 39 (AU350.12) is concerned with two aspects of sampling risk in performing a substantive test of details: the **risk of incorrect acceptance** and the **risk of incorrect rejection.** The risk of incorrect acceptance is the risk the auditor is willing to accept that the sample supports the conclusion that the recorded account balance is not materially misstated when it is. It is an aspect of sampling risk for a substantive test of details of an account balance using audit sampling.

In planning the sample, the *risk of incorrect acceptance* is the *detection risk* for that test. The risk of incorrect acceptance is established using a "risk model" presented later in this chapter.

There is another aspect of sampling risk for a substantive test of details of an account balance—the *risk of incorrect rejection*. This is the risk that the sample supports the conclusion that the account balance is materially misstated when it is not. This aspect of sampling risk relates to audit efficiency rather than effectiveness. If the auditor incorrectly concludes that an account balance is materially misstated, the auditor ordinarily expands substantive tests and eventually reaches the appropriate conclusions.

In statistics, the risk of incorrect rejection is called the **alpha risk** and the risk of incorrect acceptance is called the **beta risk.** The relationship between audit terms and statistical terms is summarized as follows:

SAS 39 Term	*Statistical Term*	*Relates to*
Risk of Incorrect Rejection	Alpha Risk	Audit Efficiency
Risk of Incorrect Acceptance	Beta Risk	Audit Effectiveness

Alpha risk is the chance that the statistical evidence might fail to support a materially correct book value. This type of error usually results in testing additional sample items. Alpha risk is the complement of reliability that is specified when calculating sample size.[1] Alpha risk is controlled by decreasing or increasing reliability.

Many practitioners believe that alpha risk should be set at 5 percent or less (U_R = 1.96 reliability coefficient at 95 percent reliability). In audit practice, a 90 to 98 percent range is typical. A higher alpha risk (i.e., lower reliability) may be justified when the cost and effort of selecting additional samples are low and very few differences (audited value minus book value) are expected. Let us consider why this is so. Alpha risk becomes a concern when evaluating audit sample results only if the auditor rejects a client's book value. Consequently, if a rejection decision is made, based on a low reliability level, the auditor's first inclination is to extend the sample. This is especially true if the sample evidence already obtained shows few differences (misstatements). A low reliability level may be tolerated if the cost of selecting additional items at a later date is relatively easy and involves low sampling setup costs.

The second risk inherent in a variable-sampling audit hypothesis model is beta risk. Beta risk is the probability that the statistical evidence might support a lack of material misstatement of a materially misstated book value. Beta risk is controlled by adjusting the ratio of precision A to materiality M. In Chapter 4, beta risk was not considered because we were not trying to decide if a book value was materially misstated. In accounting estimation, the statistical projection is used to determine the book value. In audit hypothesis testing, the auditor's primary concern is controlling beta risk. A simple illustration explains why. Let's first consider the cost of an alpha error. If an auditor rejects the client's recorded inventory value, the client will generally insist on: (1) an increase in sample size, or (2) a search for additional evidence to show that the inventory balance is misstated. The combined evidence available after such additional work may indicate a need for the auditor to reverse his or her initial decision in a small percentage of cases (alpha percent). It is this risk of subsequent reversal or the potential for such a reversal that alpha is usually meant to control. Auditors sometimes refer to alpha as the red face or client's risk. Alpha risk relates to audit *efficiency*.

On the other hand, if the auditor accepts the client's recorded inventory when it is materially misstated (beta risk), the client will not demand an increase in sample size or a search for additional evidence. In fact, the auditor may have done exactly what the client wished. The risk in this situation, of course, emanates from investors and other external financial statement users. The auditor may be sued and possibly could lose his or her right to practice. Beta risk relates to audit *effectiveness*.

The sample mean distribution (Figure 5.1) graphically depicts alpha risk at 95 percent reliability. At 95 percent reliability, alpha equals 5 percent; that is, sampling error will occur 5 times out of 100, causing an auditor to reject a *true* book value.

---

[1]Reliability can be related to beta risk (negative approach) and the level of control risk, or associated with alpha risk (positive approach) and the cost of obtaining evidence. The latter approach is used here. Both approaches generate the same solution. For an excellent discussion of the negative versus the positive approach, see Donald M. Roberts, *Statistical Auditing* (New York: AICPA, 1978), pp. 45–48.

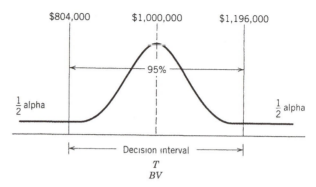

Note: Control alpha errors by varying confidence level (reliability)
Reliability = 95 percent
Alpha risk = 5 percent
True value, T = book value; BV = $1,000,000

FIGURE 5.1   Alpha Risk

The following example will aid an understanding of alpha as is shown in Figure 5.1. The true book value T and the amount recorded by the client BV are equal. The recorded amount is $1,000,000 and the population size N is 1000; thus, $\bar{X}$ times N is $1,000,000. The standard error of the distribution in Figure 5.1 is $100. Figure 5.1 was derived by taking repeat samples of the same size from the population of 1000 items and plotting the sample means times N. Achieved precision is $1.96 \times \$100 \times 1000$ equals $196,000. The **decision interval** is $1,000,000 ± $196,000.

If a sample mean is produced that is between $804 and $1196, the client's book value will be accepted. On the other hand, if a sample mean less than $804 (e.g., $750) or more than $1196 (e.g., $1200) is produced, the true client book value will be rejected. Given that the client's book value is fairly stated at $1,000,000 the distribution in Figure 5.1 shows that there is a 2.5 percent chance in each tail of the distribution where sample results will cause a rejection of a true value. This rejection probability is referred to as an alpha sampling error.

In an actual audit engagement, a distribution of sample means is not produced. Only one set of sample items and, hence, one mean is typically used in projecting the estimated audited value. Figure 5.1 demonstrates the probabilities associated with different possible estimated audited values coming up at different points on the distribution.

Figure 5.2 shows the beta risk of a projected sample mean distribution for an overstatement and an understatement exactly equal to a material amount. Case 1 of Figure 5.2 demonstrates that if precision A is set equal to materiality ($50,000) in planning sample size and the true book value ($950,000) is overstated by exactly a material amount (recorded book value is $1,000,000), beta risk is 50 percent. That is, 50 samples out of 100 samples would lead to an acceptance of a materially overstated book value. Beta risk is depicted by the amount of the distribution that over-

Case 1

Book value overstated by exactly a material amount. Precision *A* equals materiality *M*. *BV* equals book value. *T* equals true value.

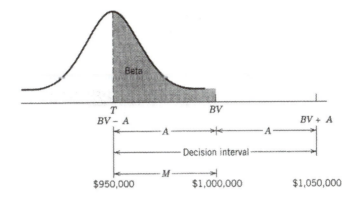

Case 2

Book value understated by exactly a material amount. Precision *A* equals materiality *M*.

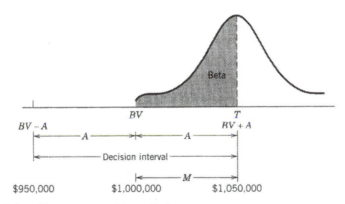

FIGURE 5.2   Illustrations of Beta Risk

laps the decision interval. The decision interval is book value $1,000,000 ± $50,000. Projected sample means ($\bar{x} \cdot N$) falling between $950,000 and $1,050,000 would lead to acceptance, but projected sample means below $950,000 would indicate rejection of the client's book value.

Case 2 of Figure 5.2 indicates that if book value is understated by an amount exactly equal to materiality ($50,000), beta risk again is equal to 50 percent. The auditor will accept a materially understated book value if the projected sample mean falls between $950,000 and $1,050,000. In fact, where precision is set equal to

Case 1

Book value *overstated* by exactly a material amount. Precision A equals one-half materiality M. BV equals book value. T equals true value.

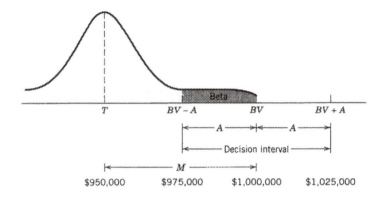

Case 2

Book value overstated by 1 1/2 materiality. Precision A equals one-half materiality M.

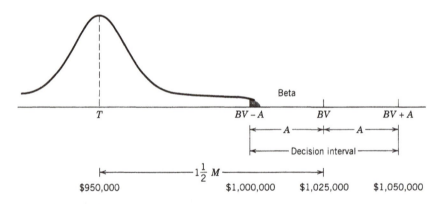

FIGURE 5.3   Other Illustrations of Beta Risk

materiality, the maximum beta risk is 50 percent. That is, there is a fifty-fifty chance of accepting a materially understated book value or a materially overstated book value when the correct decision would be to reject the book value (based on only the sample evidence).

Other beta risk situations are shown in Figure 5.3. Case 1 of Figure 5.3 demonstrates that beta risk is drastically reduced when precision is set equal to one-half of materiality. Precision in Case 1 is $25,000, because materiality is $50,000. The true book value in Case 1 is $950,000, and the recorded book value is $1,000,000. The decision interval is $1,000,000 ± $25,000. A smaller portion of the distribution overlaps the decision interval (above $975,000); thus, a mean projection below $975,000 will cause the book value to be rejected. Beta risk in Case 1 falls to 2 1/2 percent.

Client's Book Value Is:

		Not Materially Misstated	Materially Misstated
Audit Evidence Indicates:	Accept	Correct Decision (1 – Alpha)	Beta Risk
	Reject	Alpha Risk	Correct Decision (1 – Beta)

Remember that in SAS No. 39, *Audit Sampling*, beta risk is the "risk of incorrect acceptance," whereas alpha risk is the "risk of incorrect rejection."

FIGURE 5.4   Alpha and Beta Risk Matrix

Case 2 of Figure 5.3 shows that beta risk is reduced even further if the book value is overstated by 1 1/2 times materiality. In Case 2 the book value is recorded at $1,025,000, but the true value is $950,000. For an acceptance decision to result, a sample mean projection of $1,000,000 or greater must be obtained. The probability of incurring beta in a Case 2 situation is very remote.

Beta risk is always measured and controlled in relation to materiality rather than precision. Consequently, beta risk is expressed as a maximum probability (in a conservative fashion). Figure 5.4 presents an alpha and beta risk matrix. The matrix demonstrates that if alpha occurs, beta cannot occur. Alpha and beta are mutually exclusive. However, in an actual audit the auditor does not know where the true value actually lies; thus, he or she has to control both beta and alpha. As the illustrations show, beta is controlled by varying precision in relation to materiality, but alpha is controlled by varying reliability or confidence. Note that beta risk is controlled with respect to a misstatement of precisely a material amount. In audit sampling, this amount is referred to as tolerable misstatement. It is, conceptually, the maximum monetary misstatement that can exist in a particular account balance without causing the financial statements to be materially misstated.

AUDIT RISK, MATERIALITY, AND SUBSTANTIVE AUDIT TESTS

According to SAS No. 47 (AU 312), *Audit Risk and Materiality in Conducting an Audit,* **audit risk** is the risk that auditors incur if they express an unqualified opinion on materially misstated financial statements. Audit risk at the account balance or class of transactions level is actually a combination of four risks:

1. A material misstatement occurs in the financial statements (i.e., inherent risk).

2. Internal control fails to detect and correct the misstatement (i.e., control risk).

3. The auditor's nonstatistical audit procedures (supplemental procedures) fail to detect the misstatement (i.e., other procedures risk).

4. The auditor's statistical audit procedures fail to detect the misstatement (i.e., test of details (beta) risk).

The underlying rationale of the audit risk model is that the combined risk of a material misstatement remaining undetected is a product of the four independent component risks. This combined risk—the audit risk at the account balance level—should be relatively low; in quantitative terms that would be 5 or 10 percent. Audit risk is given the symbol AR in the risk model equation.

The risk model, including component risks and their corresponding formula symbols, is as follows:

$$AR = IR \times CR \times AP \times TD$$

AR (audit risk)	IR (inherent risk)	CR (control risk)	AP (other procedures risk)	TD (test of details detection risk—beta or risk of incorrect acceptance)

The other procedures risk is the quantification of the detection risk for audit procedures that are relevant to achieving the same audit objective as the substantive test of details being planned. It has the symbol AP because these other procedures frequently are substantive analytical procedures.

To use the model, the auditor has to quantify as a percentage the inherent risk, control risk, and other procedures risk. This is a subjective professional judgment. An approach often used in practice is to associate a percentage with a qualitative level of assessment. Maximum is obviously 100 percent. Specification of the percentage associated with the minimum is a critical professional judgment. It quantifies the lowest degree of risk and, implicitly, the maximum degree of assurance ever attributed to the model component. For example, professional standards indicate that complete reliance should not be placed on internal control. This provides a general guide in establishing the percentage for minimum control risk. In practice the percentages associated with qualitative levels often are established as a matter of CPA firm policy.

Separate assessment of inherent risk (IR) at levels below the maximum is complex. The risk model in SAS No. 39 is presented with inherent risk assumed to be at the maximum (100 percent or 1). SAS No. 47 indicates that if inherent risk is assessed at less than the maximum, the auditor should have an "appropriate basis" for the assessment. Many CPA firms combine the inherent risk and control risk assessments.

At the account balance level, inherent risk (*IR*) is defined as the susceptibility of an account balance to material misstatement given inherent and environmental characteristics, but without regard to internal control. In this book inherent risk is assumed to be at the maximum (100 percent). Control risk (*CR*) is the risk that material misstatement in an account balance may occur and not be prevented or detected on a timely basis by internal control. Detection risk is the risk that an auditor's procedures will lead to the conclusion that material misstatement does not exist in an account balance when the account balance is actually materially misstated. It has two components in the model—*AP* and *TD* (beta risk).

The auditor's approach is to assess the level of control risk (*CR*) and other procedures risk (*AP*), and to adjust beta risk (*TD*) accordingly to restrict the audit risk (*AR*) for the account balance to a relatively low level.

The auditor calculates the desired beta risk by solving the risk model for *TD* as follows:

$$TD \text{ (beta)} = \frac{AR}{CR \times AP}$$

Quantifying Audit Risk (AR)

In practice, the acceptable level of *AR* is predefined. SAS No. 39 (AU 350.19) illustrates an *AR* at 5 percent. Many auditors believe that *AR* should usually be 5 percent and never greater than 10 percent. Variations up to 10 percent might be justified, for example, because the client is a nonpublic entity and the financial statements will not be used by a large number of external users.

Quantifying Control Risk (CR)

Let us now turn to quantifying control risk (*CR*). As we demonstrate later, the smaller the *CR*, the larger allowable beta risk becomes. The control risk (*CR*) is judgmentally determined in practice. *CR* must be determined separately at the assertion level for each transaction cycle (or account balance), because strengths in one assertion do not offset weaknesses in another.

The effectiveness of internal control for a given assertion is judgmentally determined based on the auditor's inquiries, observations, inspections, and reperformance of control procedures. Some CPA firms permit the risk percentage to vary from 10 to 100 percent. The 10 percent limit assumes that even the best internal control system has inherent limitations. The following table depicts feasible *CR* risk ranges.

Auditor's Subjective Assessed Level of Control Risk	Control Risk Percentage (CR)	Control Percentage Effectiveness
Excellent	10	90
Good	30	70
Fair	50	50
Poor	70	30
None (or high potential for management override)	100	0

To illustrate, if an auditor concludes that control risk *(CR)* is 30 percent, the internal controls *for a given assertion over a particular transaction* class are such that there is a 30 percent chance that misstatements could occur to such a degree that the cumulative effect would materially misstate the financial statements. This illustration gives some insight into a very complex judgmental decision process. *CR* should not be equated with the achieved upper precision limit as determined in an attribute sampling plan (see Chapter 3).

Another factor to consider in judgmentally setting *CR* is the potential for management override of the internal control. Although it is impossible to determine with certainty those cases in which management has overridden internal control, it generally should be possible to evaluate this risk through consideration of factors such as the type of organization being audited, the susceptibility of the assertion being examined to misstatement, the requirement for management judgment in determining the amounts in the records, and prior experience in auditing the assertion being examined. If the *potential* for override is deemed significant, the auditor should assess *CR* as high (e.g., 70 or 100 percent).

Quantifying Other Procedures Risk (AP)

Quantifying the risk associated with analytical procedures or other relevant substantive tests is difficult. Any substantive audit procedure that is not part of the variable-sampling statistical test falls into this category. For example, an auditor may decide to use variables sampling to select accounts receivable for confirmation (the existence assertion). He or she may also review collections of accounts receivable subsequent to the balance sheet date and perform certain analytical tests of accounts receivable. All the tests but the confirmation work are by definition other or supplementary procedures.

Analytical procedures usually involve trend analysis, gross margin reviews, comparisons of cost and selling prices of inventory items, review of variance accounts, and so on. Generally, *AP* should be conservatively estimated and probably should rarely be less than 50 percent. If, however, a CPA firm uses a very robust mathematical model for analytical procedures, *AP* should be less than 50 percent. For teaching purposes, we will permit *AP* risk to vary from 50 to 100 percent.

Calculating Beta Risk *(TD)*

As was explained earlier, rearranging the audit risk equation, we have

$$TD\ (\text{beta}) = \frac{AR}{CR \times AP}$$

After the auditor has calculated the desired beta risk, he or she uses the beta risk to determine sample size by figuring out how much precision A has to be reduced in relation to materiality. Beta risk is controlled by reducing precision in the sample-size equation relative to materiality.

To illustrate, let us assume AR = 5 percent, CR = 20 percent, and AP = 90 percent.

$$TD\ (\text{beta}) = \frac{0.05}{0.20 \times 0.90}$$

$$TD\ (\text{beta}) = 28.8\ \text{percent}$$

If beta computes to a value of 1.0 or greater (e.g., CR = 0.10 and AP = 0.50), the auditor may decide to omit the statistical test because AR has already been achieved based on the assessed control risk and other procedures performed. If beta computes to an amount between 1.0 and 0.50, auditors believe that a statistical test should have at least an even chance of detecting a material misstatement. Accordingly, we adopt the policy that is prevalent in practice that beta risk for all statistical tests should be set at 50 percent or less.

Rather than use the beta risk equation, another method of deriving beta used in practice appears in Figure 5.5. The beta outcome resulting from Figure 5.5 should be approximately equal to the previous equation.

The relationship of beta risk calculation to the sample-size equation is as follows:

1. Beta is calculated according to the previous equation.
2. Precision is adjusted in relation to materiality based on the calculated beta risk. (This calculation will be explained in the section that follows.)
3. Precision A is introduced in the sample-size equation to calculate sample size.

$$n' = \left(\frac{U_R \cdot SD \cdot N}{A} \right)^2$$

TOLERABLE MISSTATEMENT

An essential first step in planning a substantive test using audit sampling is to make a preliminary judgment about the amount that will be considered material to the account being tested. This amount is called **tolerable misstatement.** To determine

Assessment of internal control:

- If there is a significant risk that management could override the controls in effect over the areas being examined, enter 0.
- Otherwise, assess the internal controls in effect over the assertion being tested.

_____

If the Controls Are	Enter
Excellent	4
Good	3
Fair	2
Poor	1
Nonexistent	0

Reliance assigned to other procedures:

- Evaluate the other audit procedures that might detect material misstatements of the type being tested for by the statistical tests.
- For each significantly effective additional test allow 2 points, and for each moderately effective additional test allow 1 point. Enter the total (not to exceed 4 points).

Total _____

If the Total Above Is	Use This Beta
0	.05
1	.10
2	.15
3	.30
4	.50
5	.50[b]
6–8	.50[c]

[a]Adapted with permission from Robert K. Elliott and John R. Rogers. "Relating Statistical Sampling to Audit Objectives." _Journal of Accountancy_ (July 1972). p. 50.

[b]In view of these conditions, the auditor may wish to consider increasing the effectiveness of other auditing procedures and omitting the statistical test.

[c]In view of these conditions, the auditor may wish to consider omitting the statistical test.

FIGURE 5.5   Selection of Beta for Hypothesis Test[a]

tolerable misstatement, the auditor generally must first determine what is a material misstatement of the financial statements taken as a whole. In essence, the auditor's goal is to establish an amount that will serve as an approximate dividing line for a material misstatement of financial statements. The auditor wants to be able to conclude, with reasonable assurance, that the financial statements are not misstated by more than this amount.

SAS No. 47, "Audit Risk and Materiality in Conducting an Audit," requires auditors to consider materiality when planning the audit, but they are not required to quantify the amount. However, if the auditor uses a statistical or formal approach to audit sampling, materiality must be quantified, at least at the account balance level.

Quantifying Materiality at the Overall Financial Statement Level

Auditors use various approaches in quantifying a materiality measure for planning audit tests. Some auditors rely upon judgment to estimate the amount that would materially distort the individual financial statements. An auditor may, for example, estimate that a $100,000 misstatement of net income on the income statement is material, while a $200,000 misstatement of total assets on the balance sheet is material. Since most misstatements affect both net income and total assets, the auditor then would design the audit to detect the smallest misstatement that would be material to any one of the financial statements, in this case $100,000. Auditors also may use *rules of thumb* related to a financial statement base, such as net income, total revenues, or total assets, to develop these estimates of overall materiality. Rules of thumb that are commonly used in practice include

- 5 percent to 10 percent of net income before taxes
- 1/2 percent to 2 percent of total assets
- 1/2 percent to 2 percent of total revenues
- 1 percent of total equity

The appropriate financial statement base for computing materiality will vary based on the nature of the client's business. For example, total revenue for a financial institution often is too small to use as the base, in conjunction with the percentages presented above. In addition, if a company is in a near breakeven position, net income for the year will be much too small to be used as the financial statement base. In that situation, the auditors often will choose another financial statement base or use an average of net income over a number of prior years.

Auditors typically use a "sliding scale" for calculating overall materiality. For example, they might use 2 percent of total sales for materiality on the audit of a small business and 1/2 percent of total sales on the audit of a large corporation. This is because the absolute amount of materiality also is important. Consider a small business with $2,000,000 in revenue. If 1/2 percent of total revenue was used as a rule of thumb, $10,000 would be calculated as overall materiality. However, it is unlikely that $10,000 would affect a user's decision about the financial position and

TABLE 5.1   **Materiality Guidelines**

		Larger of Total Revenues or Total Assets Is:				
Over	*But not Over*	*Planning Materiality Is:*	+	*Factor*	×	*Excess Over*
$0	$30 thousand	$0	+	.0593	×	$0
30 thousand	100 thousand	1,780	+	.0312	×	30 thousand
100 thousand	300 thousand	3,960	+	.0215	×	100 thousand
300 thousand	1 million	8,260	+	.0145	×	300 thousand
1 million	3 million	18,400	+	.00995	×	1 million
3 million	10 million	38,300	+	.00674	×	3 million
10 million	30 million	85,500	+	.00461	×	10 million
30 million	100 million	178,000	+	.00312	×	30 million
100 million	300 million	396,000	+	.00215	×	100 million
300 million	1 billion	826,000	+	.00145	×	300 million
1 billion	3 billion	1,840,000	+	.000995	×	1 billion
3 billion	10 billion	3,830,000	+	.000674	×	3 billion
10 billion	30 billion	8,550,000	+	.000461	×	10 billion
30 billion	100 billion	17,800,000	+	.000312	×	30 billion
100 billion	300 billion	39,600,000	+	.000215	×	100 billion
300 billion	....	82,600,000	+	.000148	×	300 billion

Example:

If a company has estimated revenues for the year to be $15 million and estimated assets of $12 million, the planning materiality guideline would be $85,500 + .00461 × $5,000,000 = $108,550. This amount is used by the auditor in planning the audit. Of course, at the end of the audit, the auditor would revaluate the fairness of the financial statements in light of the audit findings. He or she may deem some other amount to be material at that time.

Note: This table is applicable for commercial companies and may need to be adjusted for government and other entities in specialized industries.

Source: AICPA, Auditing Guide, *Auditing Sampling* (New York, 2001).

results of operations of any such company. In addition, it would be impractical to audit the company to that level of precision. Table 5.1 is a materiality table from the AICPA Audit Guide titled *Audit Sampling* that illustrates such a sliding scale.

Qualitative Considerations about Materiality

Qualitative factors also can affect the auditor's consideration of materiality. Materiality depends not only on the amount of the item, but also on its nature. An illegal payment of a relatively small amount, for example, might be considered material to the company's financial statements. Other examples of misstatements that might be qualitatively material include those that

- Reverse trends in profitability.
- Change a net loss into net income.
- Mask violations of loan covenants or government regulations.
- Cause management to make compensation hurdles.
- Cause entities to meet financial analysts' earnings forecasts.

While some qualitative factors related to materiality may be considered when the audit is being planned, most cannot because the auditor does not know what types of misstatements will be found. Of course, the auditor will consider both the quantitative and qualitative aspects of the detected misstatements when subsequently *evaluating the results* of the audit procedures.

Determining Tolerable Misstatement for an Individual Account

Once planning materiality for the overall financial statements has been determined, the auditor must allocate materiality to individual financial statement accounts that are to be tested using audit sampling. When materiality is allocated to a particular account, it is referred to as the amount of **tolerable misstatement** of the account.

When considering the allocation of materiality to individual accounts, it is important to understand that simply allocating materiality to all accounts dollar for dollar, so that the total amount of all the tolerable misstatements is equal to overall planning materiality, is far too conservative. This is because misstatements of various accounts often counterbalance each other. That is, the overstatement of one asset may be offset by the understatement of another. Another reason that materiality should not be allocated dollar for dollar is the double-entry bookkeeping system, which allows detection of misstatements in an account by auditing a related account. For example, if at year-end a purchase of inventory on credit is recorded at an improper amount, the misstatement may be detected by the tests of inventories, accounts payable, or cost of goods sold.

When using audit sampling for a substantive test, the appropriate method of determining tolerable misstatement depends on the sampling technique being used. An informal approach that may used by auditors when applying classical hypothesis testing as described in this chapter involves multiplying the amount of overall planning materiality by some factor, usually from 1.5 to 2.[2] This amount then must be allocated by the auditor to the financial statement accounts.

---

[2]As an alternative, the following mathematical approach, as described in Zuber, G., R.K. Elliott, W. Kinney, and J.J. Leisenring, *Using Materiality in Audit Planning,* Journal of Accountancy, March, 1983, pp. 42–54, may be used:

$$\text{Tolerable Misstatement for a Component} = \text{Planning Materiality less Expected Uncorrected Misstatement} \times \sqrt{\frac{\text{Amount of the Component}}{\text{Total Amount of All Components to Which Materiality is Being Allocated}}}$$

If the auditor uses probability-proportional-to-size sampling, the total amount of planning materiality (adjusted for the expected amount of misstatement) may be used as tolerable misstatement for each sampling application. To illustrate, if the auditor determines that materiality at the financial statement level is $100,000, the auditor may use $100,000 as the amount of tolerable misstatement for both the inventory and accounts receivables that are tested using probability-proportional-to-size sampling. However, the tolerable misstatement amount would have to be adjusted for the amount of expected misstatement in each of the accounts, as illustrated in Chapter 6.

THE AUDIT HYPOTHESIS MODEL

The audit hypothesis model is a series of mathematical-statistical equations. We describe the model with a 22-step approach, beginning with a preliminary assessment of internal control and ending with an accept or reject decision as to the material misstatement of an account balance. The audit hypothesis model can be categorized into four separate phases: phase I, internal control assessment; phase II, substantive test planning; phase III, substantive test execution; and phase IV, substantive test evaluation. Before getting into the details of each distinct step, the objective of each of the four phases is briefly reviewed.

The primary purpose of phase I (internal control assessment) is to assign a risk percentage to *CR* for subsequent use in the beta risk equation. As we discussed previously, to accomplish this the auditor uses his or her preliminary assessment of internal control, the results of sample test of controls, using reperformance and inspection procedures, and test of control evidence produced from inquiries and observations.

Phase II (substantive test planning) of the audit hypothesis model is concerned primarily with the selection of the appropriate sampling plan and calculation of the needed sample size for the statistical test. The appropriate variable sampling plan has to be selected based on audit objectives and population characteristics.

Assuming for illustrative purposes that unstratified MPU will be the sampling plan used, we find that the sample-size equation (with replacement) is

$$n' = \left(\frac{U_R \cdot SD \cdot N}{A} \right)^2$$

In phase II, U_R has to be determined based on acceptable alpha risk; SD may be estimated using a pilot sample of 30; N must be defined; and precision A must be calculated based on desired or calculated beta risk. To calculate A, beta has to be determined by specifying *AR, CR* (from phase I), and *AP*. Also, materiality has to be predefined. The following figure illustrates the decisions that must be made before n' can be determined:

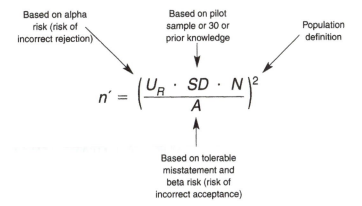

After calculating n', sample size without replacement is determined and phase III commences. Phase III (substantive test execution) has as its major objectives: (1) selecting the sample, (2) auditing the sample, and (3) calculating achieved precision A'. In addition, A″ which is **adjusted precision,** will be calculated using the following equation:

$$A'' = A' + TM (1 - A'/A)$$

where

$$A'' = \text{adjusted precision}$$
$$A' = \text{achieved precision}$$
$$TM = \text{tolerable misstatement}$$
$$A = \text{acceptable precision}$$

The A'' calculation produces an achieved beta risk equal to planned beta. Roberts explains the rationale of A'' as follows:

... the auditor can adjust the precision whenever the achieved precision differs from the planned precision. This occurs when the achieved standard error differs from the standard error used in planning. Without an adjustment, the effective beta risk differs from the planned beta risk whenever the achieved precision is not equal to the planned precision. If the achieved precision is smaller than planned, the effective beta risk is smaller, while an achieved precision larger than planned results in a higher effective beta risk.[3]

In other words, A' will be larger than A whenever SE is larger than planned. The following computations will be smaller than A whenever SE is smaller than planned. The following computations illustrate the A'' concept.

[3]Ibid., p. 43.

Example 1

$$TM - \$100$$

$$A = TM = \$100$$

Beta = 50 percent

$$A' = \$110$$

$$A'' = \$100 + \$100 \left(1 - \frac{\$110}{\$100}\right)$$

$$A'' = \$100$$

Example 2

$$TM = \$100$$

$$A = TM = \$100$$

Beta = 50 percent

$$A' = \$90$$

$$A'' = \$90 + \$100 \left(1 - \frac{\$90}{\$100}\right)$$

$$A'' = \$100$$

Finally, phase IV (substantive test evaluation) is reached. In phase IV, the auditor calculates estimated audit value, constructs a decision interval around the client's book value, and ascertains whether the sample evidence supports or rejects material correctness of that book value. If estimated audit value falls within the constructed decision interval, the auditor concludes that the book value is acceptable.

Before the auditor constructs the decision interval, it may be necessary to adjust the recorded book value for any systematic misstatements discovered. A **systematic misstatement** is a nonrandom misstatement. For example, an error in a computerized inventory program pertaining to the computation of factory overhead may produce an overstatement in inventory. If the audit sample procedure discloses several errors involving erroneous factory overhead computations, the auditor's misstatement analysis investigation may identify the occurrence as systematic. Thus, in looking at additional inventory cost extensions (extended tests of individually significant items), the total adjustment for factory overhead can be established and the recorded inventory corrected accordingly.

Phase I: Internal Control Assessment

1. Complete the internal control questionnaire, flowcharts, or related narrative memoranda for the relevant account balance or transaction class. Make a preliminary assessment of internal control effectiveness.

2. Decide which control policies or procedures you want to test to assess control risk below 100 percent and limit substantive testing for the particular assertion.

3. Set desired risk of assessing control risk too low (10 percent or less) and tolerable rate (e.g., 5 percent or less for substantial assurance desired from sample) for the tests of controls.

4. Perform tests of controls. There is no need for a test of controls when internal controls are assessed as poor or the cost of a test exceeds potential savings from a restriction of the related substantive test.

5. Make a final assessment of control risk *(CR)* based on the evidence provided from the sample tests of controls and the control evidence from inquiries and observations. Concluding that internal controls for a particular assertion permit a *CR* of 0.10 means that there is a 10 percent chance that misstatements could occur on enough transactions or to such a degree that the cumulative effect would be a material misstatement of the account balance.

Phase II: Substantive Test Planning

6. Evaluate (conservatively) the risk of other audit procedures *(AP)* failing to detect a material misstatement $(AP \geq 50$ percent).

7. Select 5 or 10 percent audit risk *(AR)* and calculate maximum planned beta risk.

$$TD \text{ (beta)} = \frac{AR}{CR \times AP}$$

8. Set alpha risk at 5 percent or lower. Alpha risk is the complement of reliability. Reliability should be set between 90 and 99 percent.

9. Based on Table 5.2, convert step 8 into a U_R coefficient.

Reliability	U_R *Factor*
0.99	2.58
0.95	1.96
0.90	1.65

Other U_R coefficients can be calculated from the **normal curve area table** presented on page 163. Table 5.2 can be used to determine additional U_R coefficients by multiplying the numbers in the body of the table by 2, since they are only for one-half of a normal curve starting from the center. For example, 1.96 standard deviations corresponds to an area of 0.4750; 0.4750 × 2 − 95 percent. Also, 90 percent reliability U_R is 1.65 (0.90 ÷ 2 = 0.45); 0.45 in the table is located at 1.65 standard deviations. Likewise, 96 percent reliability U_R is 2.06.

10. Determine tolerable misstatement (materiality for the account balance) as described previously.

11. Determine the amount of acceptable precision to introduce into the sample-size equation. Acceptable precision is based on beta risk specified in step 7, alpha risk specified in step 8, and tolerable misstatement specified in step 10. Use the following equation to calculate acceptable precision.

$$ A = TM \cdot \frac{U_R}{U_R + Z_{\text{beta}}} $$

where

$$
\begin{aligned}
A &= \text{precision} \\
TM &= \text{tolerable misstatement} \\
U_R &= \text{reliability factor} \\
Z_{\text{beta}} &= \text{beta risk coefficient}
\end{aligned}
$$

Table 5.2 (the normal curve area table) can be used in determining the beta risk coefficient (Z_{beta}). Z_{beta} is the normal curve value that includes an area of 0.5 − beta. If, for example, you want to find the Z_{beta} for a 1 percent beta risk, subtract 1 percent (0.01) from 0.5, yielding 0.4900. From the table, 0.4900 corresponds to a Z_{beta} coefficient of 2.33. Next, substitute 2.33 in the equation as Z_{beta} and solve for A. Instead of using the equation for A, which is illustrated here, Table 5.3 may be consulted for the factor to multiply the tolerable misstatement by to determine A.

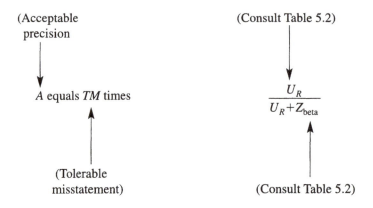

(Acceptable precision

(Consult Table 5.2)

A equals TM times

$$ \frac{U_R}{U_R + Z_{\text{beta}}} $$

(Tolerable misstatement)

(Consult Table 5.2)

TABLE 5.2   Normal Curve Area Table

Standard *Deviation*	*.00*	*.01*	*.02*	*.03*	*.04*	*.05*	*.06*	*.07*	*.08*	*.09*
0.0	.0000	.0040	.0080	.0120	.0159	.0199	.0239	.0279	.0319	.0359
0.1	.0398	.0438	.0478	.0517	.0557	.0596	.0636	.0675	.0714	.0753
0.2	.0793	.0832	.0871	.0910	.0948	.0987	.1026	.1064	.1103	.1141
0.3	.1179	.1217	.1255	.1293	.1331	.1368	.1406	.1443	.1480	.1517
0.4	.1554	.1591	.1628	.1664	.1700	.1736	.1772	.1808	.1844	.1879
0.5	.1915	.1950	.1985	.2019	.2054	.2088	.2123	.2157	.2190	.2224
0.6	.2257	.2291	.2324	.2357	.2389	.2422	.2454	.2486	.2518	.2549
0.7	.2580	.2612	.2642	.2673	.2704	.2734	.2764	.2794	.2823	.2852
0.8	.2881	.2910	.2939	.2967	.2995	.3023	.3051	.3078	.3106	.3133
0.9	.3159	.3186	.3212	.3238	.3264	.3289	.3315	.3340	.3365	.3389
1.0	.3413	.3438	.3461	.3485	.3508	.3531	.3554	.3577	.3599	.3621
1.1	.3643	.3665	.3686	.3708	.3729	.3749	.3770	.3790	.3810	.3830
1.2	.3849	.3869	.3888	.3907	.3925	.3944	.3962	.3980	.3997	.4015
1.3	.4032	.4049	.4066	.4083	.4099	.4115	.4131	.4147	.4162	.4177
1.4	.4192	.4207	.4222	.4236	.4251	.4265	.4279	.4292	.4306	.4319
1.5	.4332	.4345	.4357	.4370	.4382	.4394	.4406	.4418	.4430	.4441
1.6	.4452	.4463	.4474	.4485	.4495	.4505	.4515	.4525	.4535	.4545
1.7	.4554	.4564	.4573	.4582	.4591	.4599	.4608	.4616	.4625	.4633
1.8	.4641	.4649	.4656	.4664	.4671	.4678	.4686	.4693	.4699	.4706
1.9	.4713	.4719	.4726	.4732	.4738	.4744	.4750	.4758	.4762	.4767
2.0	.4773	.4778	.4783	.4788	.4793	.4798	.4803	.4808	.4812	.4817
2.1	.4821	.4826	.4830	.4834	.4838	.4842	.4846	.4850	.4854	.4857
2.2	.4861	.4865	.4868	.4871	.4875	.4878	.4881	.4884	.4887	.4890
2.3	.4893	.4896	.4898	.4901	.4904	.4906	.4909	.4911	.4913	.4916
2.4	.4918	.4920	.4922	.4925	.4927	.4929	.4931	.4932	.4934	.4936
2.5	.4938	.4940	.4941	.4943	.4945	.4946	.4948	.4949	.4951	.4952
2.6	.4953	.4955	.4956	.4957	.4959	.4960	.4961	.4962	.4963	.4964
2.7	.4965	.4966	.4967	.4968	.4969	.4970	.4971	.4972	.4973	.4974
2.8	.4974	.4975	.4976	.4977	.4977	.4978	.4979	.4980	.4980	.4981
2.9	.4981	.4982	.4983	.4984	.4984	.4984	.4985	.4985	.4986	.4986
3.0	.4986	.4987	.4987	.4988	.4988	.4988	.4989	.4989	.4989	.4990
3.1	.4990	.4991	.4991	.4991	.4992	.4992	.4992	.4992	.4993	.4993

12. Calculate the required sample size.

    a. If you are using *unstratified* mean per unit, the following equations are appropriate:

$$n' = \left(\frac{U_R \cdot SD \cdot N}{A}\right)^2$$

$$n = \frac{n'}{1 + n'/N}$$

Worksheet 1 (Appendix A) may be used to estimate the standard deviation based on a pilot sample.

b. If you are using *stratified* mean per unit, define each stratum and use *Worksheet 2* (Appendix A) to calculate the sample size. If the standard deviation of each stratum is not estimable, draw a random sample of 30 items from each stratum (without replacement) and use *Worksheet 1* (Appendix A) to estimate the standard deviation.

c. If you are using *difference* estimation, the following equations are appropriate:

$$n' = \left(\frac{U_R \cdot SD_d \cdot N}{A} \right)^2$$

$$n = \frac{n'}{1 + n'/N}$$

Worksheet 4 (Appendix A) may be used to estimate the standard deviation based on a pilot sample. The pilot sample must contain some differences (misstatements). Otherwise, the pilot sample must be larger.

TABLE 5.3   Tolerable Misstatement Adjustments for Common Alpha and Beta Risk Values

	Tolerable Misstatement Adjustment Factor for:		
Beta Risk Percent	*10 Percent Alpha Risk*	*5 Percent Alpha Risk*	*1 Percent Alpha Risk*
1	.415	.457	.525
2.5	.457	.500	.568
5	.500	.543	.609
7.5	.534	.576	.641
10	.563	.605	.668
15	.613	.653	.712
20	.663	.700	.753
25	.708	.742	.791
30	.757	.787	.829
35	.809	.834	.868
40	.864	.883	.908
50	1.000	1.000	1.000

Phase III: Substantive Test Execution

13. Randomly select the additional sample items by using computer generation, random-number table, or systematic selection.

14. Perform a test of sample representativeness. The sample mean of book values (i.e., sample book values $\div n$) and the population mean of book values (i.e., the client's book value $\div N$) should not be substantially different. For example, if the sample mean of book values is \$100 but the population mean of book values is \$800, barring an arithmetic mistake, the sample may not be representative. Consequently, the first sample should be discarded and a new one selected. The test of sample representativeness helps to control sampling error.

15. Perform audit procedures on sample items selected for substantive tests.

16. Analyze misstatements noted in the sample to determine their cause, nature, and whether a systematic pattern exists. A systematic misstatement is a recurring misstatement that does not occur randomly. For example, an employee pricing inventory may improperly price certain items based on an outdated price list.

17. Calculate achieved precision A'.

   a. *For unstratified simple extension:*

      (1) The standard deviation of the sample *(Worksheet 1)*.

      (2) The standard error using the following equation:

      $$SE = \frac{SD}{\sqrt{n}}$$

      (3) A' (achieved precision) based on the following equation:

      $$A' = U_R \cdot SE \cdot N\sqrt{1 - (n/N)}$$

   b. *For stratified MPU:*

      (1) The standard deviation of each stratum *(Worksheet 1)*.

      (2) A' (achieved precision) by using *Worksheet 3*.

   c. *For difference estimation:*

      (1) The standard deviation of the differences *(Worksheet 4)*.

      (2) The standard error of the differences by using the following equation:

      $$SE_d = \frac{SD_d}{\sqrt{n}}$$

(3) A' based on the following equation:

$$A' = U_R \cdot SE_d \cdot N\sqrt{1 - (n/N)}$$

18. If A' is not equal to A, calculate A'' according to the following equation:

$$A'' = A' + TM\left(1 - \frac{A'}{A}\right)$$

where

TM = tolerable misstatement from step 10.
A' = achieved precision from step 17.
A = acceptable precision from step 11.

This equation gives a new precision yielding a beta risk equal to the planned beta risk in step 7. If $A = A'$, set $A'' = A'$.

19. Calculate estimated audited value, EAV.
For unstratified MPU:
a. Calculate the $\bar{x}$ of the total sample.

$$\bar{x} = \frac{\Sigma \text{ of each audited value}}{n}$$

b. Calculate EAV as:

$$EAV = \bar{x} \cdot N$$

For stratified MPU:
a. Calculate the mean $\bar{x}$ of each stratum based on n_i for each stratum.
b. Calculate EAV as:

$$\bar{x} \cdot N_1 = \bar{x}_1 N_1$$
$$\bar{x} \cdot N_2 = \bar{x}_2 N_2$$
$$\bar{x} \cdot N_3 = \bar{x}_3 N_3$$
$$EAV = \Sigma \bar{x}_i N_i + 100 \text{ percent audited stratum}$$

For difference estimation:

    a. Calculate the mean of the difference $\bar{d}$ of the total sample.

    b. Calculate $\hat{D} = N \cdot \bar{d}$.

    c. Calculate estimated audited value, *EAV*.

$$EAV = \text{book value (footed)} \pm \hat{D}$$

Phase IV: Substantive Test Evaluation

    20. Calculate a **decision interval** as follows:

$$\text{Book value adjusted for any systematic (nonrandom)}$$
$$\text{differences} \pm A''$$

    21. Determine whether sample evidence supports the material correctness of the client's book value. If *EAV* from step 19 falls within the decision interval in step 20, conclude that the statistical evidence supports the book value and stop. If the *EAV* does not fall within the decision interval in step 20, go to step 22.

    22. If statistical evidence does not support the material correctness of the book value and the misstatements (audit values minus book values) do not show a systematic pattern, the client should be requested to perform an investigation of the account balance or class of transaction detail. The client's work, of course, should be tested by the auditor. If the client makes an adjustment after the investigation, the statistical evidence should support the material correctness of the *adjusted* book value. In the event that it does not, the auditor should have enough evidence to reach a judgment conclusion concerning the reasonableness of the adjusted book value.

DEMONSTRATION OF THE AUDIT HYPOTHESIS MODEL

In this section we discuss selected aspects of the audit hypothesis model. For the purpose of illustration, let us assume that John Alderman, CPA, is auditing Axline Corporation's physical inventory. The inventory is recorded on Axline's balance sheet at $1,000,000. It consists of 12,500 kinds of items of approximately equal value. There are no identifiable dollar-value strata. Axline does not use perpetual inventory unit records, but does have a well-planned inventory taking and counting operation. In fact, Axline uses two count teams with the supervision of counting in each department performed by a member of the internal audit department. Moreover, Axline shuts down plant operations for inventory-taking purposes. Based on (1) tests of control of the client's inventory count, (2) observation to ascertain that inventory-taking instructions are followed, and (3) evaluation of the competence and carefulness of client personnel taking inventory, John decides that control risk *(CR)* is no more than 20 percent.

John concludes that the inventory valuation of $1,000,000 will be acceptable if he can be 95 percent confident that the actual inventory is within ± $50,000. The statistical test will consist of recounting, repricing, and extending each sample item selected. Other audit procedures *(AP)* consist of inventory turnover calculations, comparison with prior years, and cutoff tests to ensure that purchases and sales are reflected in inventory in the proper accounting period. John's best guess is that these other procedures have an 80 percent risk. (Remember that *AP* represents the auditor's judgment concerning the risk that such procedures would fail to detect a material misstatement if it existed in the account.)

Having completed the internal control assessment and evaluation of Axline's inventory-taking procedures, John begins his substantive test planning. The primary question to be resolved is what size sample should be selected. To determine sample size according to the sample-size equation,

$$n' = \left(\frac{U_R \cdot SD \cdot N}{A} \right)^2$$

he must determine *SD* and *A*. U_R already has been defined as 1.96 (95 percent reliability), and *N* is given as 12,500 inventory lines. To estimate *SD*, he should take a pilot sample of 30 inventory lines. Let us assume that the standard deviation that results from the pilot sample is $25.

Next, John calculates *A*. To calculate *A*, he needs to know beta risk. Based on audit risk of 5 percent, assessed control risk of 20 percent, and other procedure risk of 80 percent, beta is

$$TD \text{ (beta)} = \frac{0.05}{0.20 \times 0.80} = 0.3125$$

Given that planned beta is 0.3125, the beta risk coefficient is 0.5000 minus 0.3125 equals 0.1875. By using the normal curve area table (see Table 5.2), the appropriate beta risk coefficient of approximately 0.49 can be found in the last column of the fifth row of the table.

Beta is controlled by varying precision *A* in relation to tolerable misstatement *(TM)*. The equation is

$$A = TM \cdot \frac{U_R}{U_R + Z_{\text{beta}}}$$

Thus,

$$A = \$50,000 \cdot \frac{1.96}{1.96 + 0.49}$$

$$A = \$40,000$$

A, of course, is acceptable (planned) precision.

Now, John is ready to calculate sample size. The calculation is

$$n' = \left[\frac{(1.96)(\$25)(12,500)}{40,000} \right]^2 = 235$$

$$n = \frac{235}{1 + (235/12,500)} = 231$$

After the sample size without replacement is calculated, a random sample of 231 items from the 12,500 inventory lines should be selected. Following sample selection, a test of sample representativeness should be applied to control sampling error. This test is applied before any audit work is performed on the sample. If the sample selected appears representative (e.g., the client's book value $\div$ *N* is not substantially different from the sample book value $\div$ *n*), the sample is audited. That is, each sample item is recounted, repriced, and extended. All misstatements identified at this stage should be analyzed to determine their cause.

Following analysis of the misstatements, *A'* is calculated. Before *A'* can be determined, the standard deviation of the 231 sampled items must be calculated along with *SE*. For illustrative purposes, assume that the standard deviation of the 231 sampled items is $28. Therefore, *SE* is $28/$\sqrt{231}$, which equals 1.84 (rounded).

$$A' = (1.96)\,(1.84)\,(122,500)\,\sqrt{1 - \frac{231}{12,500}}$$

$$A' - \$44,662$$

If *A'* is not equal to *A*, *A"* must be determined. *A* is $40,000 and *A'* is $44,662; thus, A" is:

$$A'' = \$44,662 + \$50,000\left(1 - \frac{\$44,662}{\$40,000} \right)$$

$$A'' = \$38,834$$

Estimated audited value is calculated after determination of the value for *A"*. *EAV* is the mean of the 231 sampled items times *N*. Let us say that the mean of the 231 sampled items is $81. Then, *EAV* is $81 $\times$ 12,500 = $1,012,500.

To determine whether the book value of $1,000,000 of Axline's inventory is not materially misstated, a decision interval is constructed. The decision interval is $1,000,000 $\pm$ $38,834. Since *EAV* of $1,012,500 falls within the decision interval, John can conclude that the statistical evidence supports material correctness.

PROPOSING A STATISTICAL ADJUSTMENT

In the event that the substantial evidence does not support material correctness of an *adjusted* client book value, *as a last resort,* a statistical adjustment may be proposed. To propose a statistical adjustment, the sample evidence should meet certain conclusiveness criteria. Conclusiveness is frequently defined as at least 95 percent reliability and no more than 5 percent beta risk. To determine conclusiveness, proceed as follows:

1. Express tolerable misstatement *(TM)* in dollars.
2. Divide A' by U_R.
3. Divide *TM* by the answer in step 2.
4. Ascertain whether the answer in step 3 is equal to or greater than 3.61 (i.e., $1.96 + 1.65$), where 1.96 is U_R and 1.65 is Z_{beta} for 5 percent.

If step 4 is not equal to or greater than 3.61, the sample size should be increased, the client should revalue the account balance, or additional audit procedures should be applied. If step 4 indicates that the sample evidence is conclusive enough to propose an adjustment to the client's book value, the dollar amount of the adjustment should be calculated. To perform this calculation A''' should be calculated if the U_R of A' is different from 1.96. A''' is A' divided by its U_R times 1.96. If A was calculated using 1.96, set A''' equal to A'.

The minimum and maximum adjustments for an *overstated* book value are illustrated as follows:

$$
\overline{\begin{array}{cccc}
\quad\bullet\qquad\quad & \bullet\qquad & \bullet\qquad\quad & \bullet\quad \\
EAV - A''' & EAV & EAV + A''' & BV
\end{array}}
$$

The minimum adjustment is demonstrated by the distance between *BV* (book value) and $EAV + A'''$, and the maximum adjustment is the distance from $EAV - A'''$ to *BV*. If the book value is *decreased* anywhere within $EAV \pm A'''$, the statistical evidence will be in support of the adjusted book value at 95 percent reliability and at a beta risk not exceeding 5 percent. Note that a **precision interval** $(EAV \pm A''')$ approach is used instead of a decision interval $(BV + A''')$ when the statistical evidence indicates the *BV* is materially misstated. By using a precision interval, the range of acceptable book adjustment is easier to determine.

For an *understated* book value, the minimum and maximum adjustments are illustrated as follows:

$$
\overline{\begin{array}{cccc}
\quad\bullet\qquad & \bullet\qquad\quad & \bullet\qquad & \bullet\quad \\
BV & EAV - A''' & EAV & EAV + A'''
\end{array}}
$$

The minimum adjustment is the distance from *BV* to $EAV - A'''$, and the maximum adjustment is the distance from $EAV + A'''$ to *BV*. Note that in this illustration the adjustment is *added* to *BV*, because it is understated.

SUMMARY

In Chapter 5 we present and illustrate three variable sampling models (unstratified MPU, stratified MPU, and difference estimation) that are used to test a client's book value for material correctness—audit hypothesis testing. Two risks are encountered when audit hypothesis testing is used—alpha risk (i.e., the risk of incorrect rejection) and beta risk (i.e., the risk of incorrect acceptance). Alpha risk is the chance that a true book value will be rejected by the auditor's statistical test. Beta risk is the chance that a materially misstated book value will be accepted by the auditor. Alpha risk is controlled by varying reliability, whereas beta risk is controlled by varying precision in relation to tolerable misstatement.

The audit hypothesis model differs from the accounting estimation model introduced in Chapter 4 in the following ways. Risk percentages for audit risk *(AR)*, internal control *(CR)*, and other audit procedures *(AP)* must be predefined to calculate desired beta risk. After beta and alpha risk levels are defined, the amount of precision must be calculated. Precision is determined based on the auditor's judgment about the amount that is material to the account being tested (tolerable misstatement). Once precision is determined, the substantive test sample size is then calculated.

After the sample items selected are audited, the auditor ascertains whether the statistical evidence supports material correctness of the client's book value. A number of alternate procedures are available to the auditor in situations where material correctness is not supported. They are to increase sample size, to request that the client revalue the account balance, to rely on additional audit procedures to determine material correctness or, as a last resort, to propose a statistical adjustment.

An important point to remember is that if the auditor accepts a client's book value, the conditions that correspond with alpha risk are no longer present. Likewise, if the auditor rejects the book value, the conditions that correspond with beta risk are not present. Alpha and beta are mutually exclusive after the final audit decision to accept or to reject the client's book value is made.

SUPPLEMENTARY TOPIC: USING AUDIT SAMPLING FOR COMPLIANCE AUDITING

This section describes some of the unique aspects of using audit sampling for compliance auditing. **Compliance auditing** is a term that is used to describe performing audit procedures to determine whether an entity is complying with specific requirements of laws, regulations, or agreements. A failure to comply with the requirements of a law or regulation is often referred to as a **compliance deviation** or an *illegal act*. Compliance auditing procedures are performed in conjunction with an audit of an entity's financial statements in accordance with generally accepted auditing standards. They also are performed as a part of attestation engagements specifically designed to provide a report on the entity's compliance with specified requirements.

Compliance Procedures in Audits in Accordance with Generally Accepted Auditing Standards

The CPA's responsibility for performing compliance procedures when auditing financial statements in accordance with generally accepted auditing standards is described in SAS No. 54 (AU 317) *Illegal Acts by Clients*. SAS No. 54 divides illegal acts into two types: (1) violations of laws and regulations that have a *direct* effect on amounts in the financial statements, and (2) violations of laws and regulations that have an *indirect* effect on the financial statement amounts. Income tax laws and regulations are examples of those that have a direct effect on financial statement amounts; these laws and regulations directly affect the amounts of the entity's tax provision and the related liability. Examples of laws and regulations that have an indirect effect on the financial statements include those governing securities trading, occupational safety and health, and environmental protection.

The CPA has a responsibility to design the audit to provide reasonable assurance of detecting material misstatements of the financial statements resulting from illegal acts having a direct effect on the financial statements. Therefore, in every audit, the CPA must obtain evidence about compliance with laws and regulations that have a direct and material effect on the entity's financial statements. As shown in Figure 5.6, this evidence may be obtained by performing tests of controls over compliance with laws and regulations or by performing substantive tests of compliance. Audit sampling may be involved in performing either of these types of tests.

When attribute sampling is used to test controls over compliance with laws and regulations, the considerations involved in planning, performing, and evaluating the sample are similar to those involved in performing other tests of controls. The CPA determines the sample size based on the planned assessed level of control risk. More specifically, the sample size is determined by the desired level of risk of assessing control risk too low, the tolerable deviation rate, and the expected deviation rate. As with other applications of attribute sampling, the sample results are evaluated based on the actual deviation rate found in the sample.

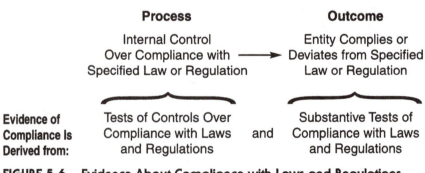

FIGURE 5.6   *Evidence About Compliance with Laws and Regulations*

Since the substantive tests of compliance that are performed in an audit of financial statements are designed to detect misstatements of financial statement amounts, attribute sampling is not generally applicable to the tests. If audit sampling is used for substantive tests of compliance in a financial statement audit, the techniques applied typically are those used to detect dollar misstatements, such as variable sampling or probability-proportional-to-size sampling techniques. These techniques are described in this chapter and Chapters 4 and 6.

Compliance Procedures in Attestation Engagements

Statement on Standards for Attestation Engagements No. 10, Section 600 (SSAE No. 10), *Compliance Attestation,* provides guidance for engagements that are specifically designed to attest to management's assertion about an entity's compliance with laws and regulations. Specifically, SSAE, Section 600 established performance standards for examinations of compliance with specified requirements.[4]

The objective of a CPA's examination of an entity's compliance with laws and regulations is to express an opinion about whether management's assertion about compliance is fairly stated in all material respects based on some established or agreed-upon criteria. A compliance examination engagement is similar to an audit of financial statements. The CPA must obtain sufficient competent evidential matter to support his or her opinion on management's assertion about the entity's compliance with the specified requirements. This evidence may be obtained by performing:

1. Tests of the entity's internal control over compliance with laws and regulations.
2. Substantive tests of compliance with laws and regulations.

The CPA approaches an examination of an entity's compliance with specified requirements in much the same way he or she approaches the audit of an entity's financial statements. In performing these types of engagements, the CPA first assesses the inherent risk that material noncompliance with the specified requirements could occur, assuming there are no internal control policies and procedures. Then, the CPA may perform tests of controls to assess the level of control risk of noncompliance below the maximum. Based on his or her assessments of these risks, the CPA designs sufficient substantive tests of compliance to provide a basis for the opinion. The combined evidence from the CPA's tests of controls over compliance with laws and regulations and substantive tests of compliance must be adequate to reduce attestation risk to a sufficiently low level to justify the CPA's opinion.

The sampling techniques that are appropriate for the substantive tests of compliance with laws and regulations depend on the nature of management's assertion,

---

[4]The term *specified requirements* is used to refer to requirements of specified laws, regulations, rules, contracts, and grants.

that is, whether the assertion about compliance is quantified in monetary terms. If the assertion is quantified in monetary terms, the appropriate sampling techniques are the same as those that are used in the audit of financial statements. The CPA generally uses variable sampling techniques. In those situations, the considerations involved in applying audit sampling to compliance attestation are the same as those involved in applying audit sampling in the audit of financial statement assertions, as described in this chapter and Chapter 6.

If management's assertion about compliance is not quantified in monetary terms, variable sampling techniques are generally not appropriate. Instead, attributes sampling is more appropriate. To illustrate, assume that a CPA has been engaged to attest to management's assertion that a financial institution is in adequate compliance with the federal regulation that requires interest disclosure statements be obtained from borrowers obtaining personal loans. The population consists of 5623 personal loans processed during the year. After considering the nature of the regulation and the controls established by the financial institution over the process of obtaining the disclosure statements, the CPA decides to assess both inherent risk and control risk at the maximum. Based on these assessments and a consideration of the needs and expectations of the users of the compliance report, the CPA decides that the requirements for the substantive test of compliance with this regulation should be 95 percent reliability (i.e., 5 percent risk) with a tolerable compliance deviation rate of 5 percent. In addition, the CPA expects that the rate of noncompliance (i.e., failure to obtain a signed disclosure statement) is 0.5 percent. From Table 3.2 shown on page 58, the CPA finds that the required sample size for the substantive test of compliance is 93. As indicated in the table, the results will provide adequate support for the CPA's opinion provided that the sample is found to contain no more than 1 instance of noncompliance with the regulation (i.e., 1 compliance deviation).

The CPA selects the 93 loan files from the population using a random-number table and examines each file for evidence of compliance with the regulation of having a signed disclosure statement in the file. Only one instance of noncompliance is identified in the sample. Therefore, the results provide adequate support for the CPA's attestation opinion on management's assertion that the institution is in adequate compliance with the regulation of obtaining signed interest disclosure statements from borrowers.

Attribute Sampling in Compliance Auditing Applicable to Recipients of Governmental Financial Assistance

SAS No. 74, *Compliance Auditing Considerations in Audits of Governmental Entities and Other Recipients of Governmental Financial Assistance,* provides guidance for compliance auditing of entities (e.g., state and local governments and not-for-profit organizations) that receive federal financial assistance. When performing these types of audits, the CPA may be required to determine and report on whether the entity has complied with laws, regulations, and the provisions of contracts or grant agreements that may have a direct and material effect on each major federal assistance program.[5] As with other compliance auditing engagements, this evidential matter is obtained by performing tests of internal controls over compliance with laws and regulations and by performing substantive tests of compliance.

Special considerations are involved in defining the population when using audit sampling to test controls over compliance with laws, regulations, and provisions that may have a direct and material effect on the major federal assistance programs. The CPA may define the population in one of two ways. Because a particular internal control procedure often is applicable to the items of more than one major program, the CPA may (1) define the items from each major program as a separate population, or (2) define all items to which the control is applicable as a single population. Since the size of the population has little or no effect on sample size, it usually is more efficient to select one sample from all the items to which the control is applicable.

As an example, assume that a CPA is performing a compliance audit of the federal financial assistance of the city of Mystic.[6] Mystic has six major federal financial assistance programs. One of its control procedures consists of a transaction review that is designed to ensure that only legally allowable costs are charged to each program. The CPA could decide to select separate attribute samples to test the operating effectiveness of the transaction review for each of the six major programs. However, it would be more efficient to select one attribute sample from the population of all transactions that are subject to the control procedure. Assuming that based on the CPA's planned assessed level of control risk, he or she has specified the risk of assessing control risk too low at 5 percent and the tolerable rate at 5 percent, and he or she expects the population deviation rate to be 1 percent. As indicated in Table 3.2 on page 58, the required sample size from the entire population would be 93 transactions, with 1 allowable deviation. Providing that no more than 1 deviation from performance of the procedure is found in the sample, the CPA would be able to assess control risk at the planned level for all six major federal financial assistance programs.

GLOSSARY

Adjusted precision, A″   The precision amount calculated to yield the same beta risk as expressed by planned precision, *A*.

---

[5]A major financial assistance program is determined based on a risk-based approach. This risk-based approach is defined in OMB Circular A-133, *Audits of States, Local Governments, and Non-Profit Organizations,* and includes consideration of current and prior audit experience, oversight by federal agencies and pass-through, and inherent risk of the federal program.

[6]This example assumes that the CPA is engaged to perform an audit in accordance with the Single Audit Act (Act.).

Alpha risk The chance that the sample evidence erroneously fails to support the material correctness of a client's account balance when the same audit procedures, if applied to the total population, would support the material correctness of the account balance. Referred to as risk of incorrect rejection in SAS No. 39, *Audit Sampling*.

Audit risk The chance that material misstatement will occur in the accounting process and will not be detected by the auditor's examination. Audit risk is the *product* of (1) the risk that internal control allows a material misstatement to go undetected, (2) the risk that other audit procedures fail to detect a material misstatement, and (3) the beta risk. In practice, risks (1) and (2) are quantified before the auditor applies statistical sampling in a substantive test. Likewise, audit risk is usually predefined to equal no more than 5 percent. Consequently, the auditor solves for beta risk as follows:

$$\text{Beta risk} = \frac{\text{audit risk}}{(\text{control risk})(\text{other audit procedure risk})}$$

Beta risk The chance that the sample evidence erroneously supports the material correctness of the client's account balance when the same audit procedures, if applied to the total population, would reveal a material misstatement. Referred to as risk of incorrect acceptance in SAS No. 39, *Audit Sampling*.

Decision interval The range from the recorded client book value (adjusted for systematic misstatements) plus and minus the precision.

Materiality (at the financial statement level) The maximum amount of misstatement in a set of financial statements that may exist without affecting the decision of an informed user.

Normal curve area table A table that shows the relative area under a normal curve from one standard deviation to another. The table is used to determine the beta risk coefficient and can be used to determine the reliability coefficient.

Precision interval The range described by the estimated audit value plus and minus the precision.

Risk of incorrect acceptance The risk that the sample supports the conclusion that the recorded account balance is not imaterially misstated when it is. (An aspect of sampling risk for substantive test; in statisties, the equivalent term is beta risk.)

Risk of incorrect rejection The risk that the sample supports the conclusion that the recorded account balance is materially misstated when it is not. (An aspect of sampling risk for substantive test; in statisties, the equivalent term is alpha risk.)

Systematic misstatement A recurring misstatement that is not random. The term "random misstatement" is used to mean accidental, unintentional, or not occurring in any pattern. An example of a systematic misstatement is a pricing error on invoices prepared by a particular employee.

Tolerable misstatement   The maximum monetary misstatement for an account balance or class of transactions that may exist without causing the financial statements to be materially misstated.

REVIEW QUESTIONS

5-1. Indicate whether each one of the following statements is true (T) or false (F).

   a. The greater the tolerable misstatement (amount considered material), the smaller the sample size.

   b. One minus audit risk is equal to the confidence level.

   c. A graph of most accounting populations generally will resemble a normal distribution.

   d. Audit hypothesis testing cannot be used unless the actual value of the universe standard deviation is known.

   e. The assessed level of control risk varies inversely with beta risk.

   f. A decision interval is constructed based on estimated audited value plus and minus precision.

   g. One minus reliability is alpha risk.

   h. If a client account balance is overstated by an amount less than tolerable misstatement, beta risk for the smaller amount is greater than beta risk for tolerable misstatement.

   i. Beta risk is usually measured in terms of a material misstatement.

   j. A'' is always smaller than A' and A.

   k. Any combination of CR and AP whose product equals 0.50 permits a tolerable beta risk of 0.10 for an audit risk of 0.05.

5-2. Define alpha risk and beta risk. Relate these terms to the risk of incorrect rejection and the risk of incorrect acceptance.

5-3. Explain how alpha risk and beta risk are controlled.

5-4. Why is beta risk not encountered if an accounting estimation approach is used instead of an audit hypothesis testing approach?

5-5. In an audit context, why is beta risk of greater concern to the auditor than alpha risk?

5-6. Identify each lettered item in the following illustration. For example, f = tolerable misstatement.

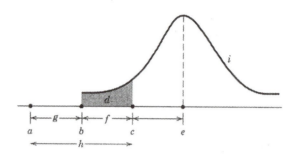

5-7. How does an auditor determine the amount of the desired beta risk?

5-8. In the beta risk equation, $\beta = AR/CR \times AP$, which factors are determined by professional judgment and which are guided by authoritative auditing literature?

5-9. What is a decision interval and how is it constructed?

5-10. Define audit risk. Define detection risk.

5-11. What is the relationship between audit risk and audit assurance?

5-12. What are other audit procedures in an audit sampling context?

5-13. What does it mean to say that control risk is 20 percent?

5-14. Identify the acceptable ranges (percentages) within which (a) control risk, (b) other audit procedure risk, (c) audit risk, and (d) beta risk should fall.

5-15. Calculate beta for each of the following situations:

	AR	**CR**	**AP**
a.	5%	100%	100%
b.	5%	50%	70%
c.	5%	10%	50%
d.	5%	20%	50%
e.	5%	10%	80%

5-16. Using the normal curve area table (Table 5.2), determine U_R for each of the following reliability levels:

a. 92%

b. 98%

c. 95%

5-17. How does beta affect the sample size equation?

5-18. Criticise the following statement: "Throughout the audit for all purposes the auditor is going to use $1,000,000 as a material amount."

5-19. Assume that you have decided to use a percentage of net income as preliminary materiality for an audit. List three qualitative factors that you might consider in deciding what is material.

5-20. Explain why the total amount of materiality allocated to individual accounts (tolerable misstatement) sums to more than the amount considered material to the financial statements as a whole.

5-21. If tolerable misstatement is $100,000, $U_R = 1.96$ (95 percent), calculate acceptable precision based on the following beta risks (use the normal curve area table, Table 5.1).

    a. Beta equals 20%

    b. Beta equals 50%

    c. Beta equals 5%

5-22. What is A'' and when should it be calculated?

5-23. If A' is greater than A, will A'' be larger or smaller than A'?

5-24. Misstatement analysis is not as useful in variable sampling as it is in attribute sampling. Do you agree? Explain.

5-25. If a systematic misstatement is discovered by an auditor in sampling from an accounts receivable population, should the decision interval be constructed around the original book value or the book value be adjusted for the discovered systematic misstatement?

5-26. After a decision interval is constructed, how is it used to ascertain whether the client's book value is or is not materially misstated?

5-27. What should the auditor do if EAV does not fall within book value $\pm A''$?

5-28. Given the following facts, could you conclude that the sample evidence supports material correctness of the client's book value based on planned beta risk?

Book value	$500.000
EAV	470,000
A	20,000
A'	17,000
U_R	1.96
Tolerable misstatement	25,000

MULTIPLE-CHOICE QUESTIONS FROM PROFESSIONAL EXAMINATIONS

5-29. In an application of mean-per-unit sampling, the following information has been obtained:

Reported book value	$600,000
Point estimate (estimated total value)	591,000
Allowance for sampling risk (precision)	±22,000
Tolerable misstatement	±45,000

The appropriate conclusion would be that the reported book value is:

a. Acceptable only if the risk of incorrect rejection is at least twice the risk of incorrect acceptance.

b. Acceptable

c. Not acceptable.

d. Acceptable only if the risk of incorrect acceptance is at least twice the risk of incorrect rejection.

5-30. An auditor selects a preliminary sample of 100 items out of a population of 1000 items. The sample statistics generate an arithmetic mean of $120, a standard deviation of $12, and a standard error of the mean of $1.20. If the sample was adequate for the auditor's purposes and the auditor's achieved precision was plus or minus $2000, the minimum acceptable dollar value of the population would be:

a. $122,000.

b. $120,000.

c. $118,000.

d. $117,600.

5-31. In which of the following cases would the auditor be most likely to conclude that all of the items in an account under consideration should be examined rather than tested on a sample basis?

	The Measure of Tolerable Misstatement Is	Misstatements Are Expected to Be
a.	Large	Low
b.	Small	High
c.	Large	High
d.	Small	Low

5-32. Which of the following models expresses the general relationship of risks associated with the auditor's assessment of control risk *(CR)*, analytical procedures and other relevant substantive tests, *(AP)*, and audit risk *(AR)* that would lead the auditor to conclude that additional substantive tests of details of an account balance are not necessary?

	AP	*CR*	*AR*
a.	20%	40%	10%
b.	20%	60%	5%
c.	10%	70%	$4^{1/2}$
d.	30%	40%	$5^{1/2}$

5-33. How would increases in tolerable misstatement and assessed level of control risk affect the sample size in a substantive test of details?

	Increase in Tolerable Misstatement	*Increase in Assessed Level of Control Risk*
a.	Increase sample size	Increase sample size
b.	Increase sample size	Decrease sample size
c.	Decrease sample size	Increase sample size
d.	Decrease sample size	Decrease sample size

5-34. While performing a substantive test of details during an audit, the auditor determined that the sample results supported the conclusion that the recorded account balance was materially misstated. It was, in fact, not materially misstated. This situation illustrates the risk of:

a. Incorrect rejection.

b. Incorrect acceptance.

c. Assessing control risk too low.

d. Assessing control risk too high.

5-35. A number of factors influence the sample size for a substantive test of details of an account balance. All other factors being equal, which of the following would lead to a larger sample size?

a. A lower assessed level of control risk.

b. Increased use of analytical procedures to obtain evidence about particular assertions.

c. Smaller expected frequency of deviations.

d. Smaller measure of tolerable misstatement.

5-36. Using the following results from a variables sample, compute the standard error of the mean.

Population size = 10,000
Sample size = 144
Sample standard deviation = $24.00
Confidence level = 90% (U_R = 1.65)
Mean = $84.00

a. $60.00.

b. $7.00.

c. $2.30.

d. $2.00.

5-37. The auditors of Smith Electronics wish to limit the overall risk of material misstatement in the audit of accounts receivable to 5 percent. They believe that inherent risk is 100 percent, control risk is 50 percent, and the risk that other procedures will fail to detect a material misstatement is 40 percent. What is the maximum beta risk the auditors should specify in their substantive test of details of accounts receivable?

a. 5 percent

b. 10 percent

c. 20 percent

d. 25 percent

5-38. An auditor randomly selects 100 items of finished goods perpetual inventory, physically counts them, and computes an "audited value" for each (calculated as quantity times unit cost per production reports). The auditor then compares the audited value with the "book value" (inventory cost per perpetual inventory records) and uses difference estimation to estimate the correct total for the finished goods inventory. Results of the 100-item sample are as follows:

Total audited value	$605,000
Total book value (of these 100 items)	$630,000
Number of items incorrectly stated (out of 100)	17

The total book value of the entire finished goods inventory (1100 items) is $6,988,000. On the basis of difference estimation, the auditor's estimate as to the correct total is:

a. $6,655,000.

b. $6,713,000.

c. $6,963,000.

d. $7,263,000.

CASES

Case 5-1   Blumenthal, Inc.

(Estimated time to complete: 20 minutes)

Assume that your CPA firm is auditing Blumenthal, Incorporated, and that, as senior accountant on the job, one of your first tasks is to supervise confirmation of accounts receivable. There are 1000 accounts, with no extreme values, and the control account balance is $225,000. You decide to choose the accounts to be confirmed by statistical sampling methods, and your objective is to obtain reasonable assurance of the validity of the dollar amount of receivables. A pilot sample indicates an estimated population standard deviation of $15. In your judgment a 95 percent confidence level (5 percent alpha risk) is appropriate.

    a. If you specify a required precision of ± $1500, what would be the required sample size?

    b. If you specify a required precision of ± $2250, what would be the required sample size?

    c. The staff accountant assisting you on the job does not understand the relationship between the required sample sizes in (a) and (b) above. How would you explain the magnitude and direction of the differences in required sample size to her?

    d. What factors would you consider in specifying precision? In this situation, what do you think would be an appropriate precision figure?

    e. If you specified a precision of ± $1500 and a confidence level of 99 percent rather than 95 percent, what would be the required sample size?

    f. What criteria would you use for deciding whether a confidence level of 95 percent or 99 percent was more appropriate?

    g. How would you explain to the inquiring staff accountant the magnitude and direction of the differences in the required sample size in (e) as compared with (a)?

Case 5-2   Statistical, Inc.

(Estimated time to complete: 25 minutes)

During the course of an audit engagement, a CPA attempts to obtain satisfaction that there are no material misstatements in the accounts receivable of a client. Statistical sampling is a tool that the auditor often uses to obtain representative evidence to achieve the desired satisfaction. On a particular engagement an auditor determined that a material misstatement in a population of accounts would be $35,000. The auditor specified a 95 percent confidence level (5% alpha risk). The auditor decided to use unrestricted random sampling with replacement* and took a preliminary random sample of 100 items *(n)* from a population of 1000 items *(N)*. The sample produced the following data:

Arithmetic mean of sample items, $\bar{x}$	$4000
Standard deviation of sample items, *SD*	$ 200

The auditor also has available the following information:

Standard error of the mean, $SE = SD/\sqrt{n}$

Population precision $A' = N \cdot U_R \cdot SE$

Partial List of Reliability Coefficients	
If Reliability Coefficient (U_R) Is	**The Reliability Is**
1.70	91.086%
1.75	91.988
1.80	92.814
1.85	93.568
1.90	94.256
1.95	94.882
1.96	95.000
2.00	95.450
2.05	95.964
2.10	96.428
2.15	96.844

a. Define the statistical terms "reliability" and "precision" as applied to auditing.

b. If all necessary audit work is performed on the preliminary sample items and no misstatements are detected,

(1) What can the auditor say about the total amount of accounts receivable at the 95 percent reliability level?

(2) At what confidence level can the auditor say that the population is not misstated by $35,000?

c. Assume that the pilot sample was sufficient.

(1) Compute the auditor's estimate of the population total.

(2) Indicate how the auditor should relate this estimate to the client's recorded amount.

(AICPA adapted)

---

* This problem is taken from the Uniform CPA Examination and uses sampling with replacement. Consequently, the finite population correction factor adjustment $[\sqrt{1 - (n/N)}]$ to achieved precision can be ignored.

Case 5-3   Draper, Inc.

(Estimated time to complete: 25 minutes)

You desire to evaluate the reasonableness of the book value of the inventory of your client, Draper, Inc. You satisfied yourself as to inventory quantities. During the examination of the pricing and extension of the inventory, the following data were gathered using appropriate unrestricted random sampling with replacement procedures.*

Total items in the inventory, N	12,700
Total items in the sample, n	400
Total audited value of items in the sample	$38,400
$\sum\limits_{j=1}^{400} (x_j - \bar{x})^2$	$312,816
Equation for estimated population standard deviation	$SD = \sqrt{\dfrac{\sum\limits_{j=1}^{n} x_j - \bar{x})^2}{n-1}}$
Equation for estimated standard error of the mean	$SE = \dfrac{SD}{\sqrt{n}}$
Confidence level coefficient of the standard error of the mean at a 95 percent confidence (reliability) level (5 percent alpha risk)	± 1.96

a. Based on the sample results, what is the estimate of the total value of the inventory?

b. What statistical conclusion can be reached regarding the estimated total inventory value calculated in (a) at the confidence level of 95 percent? Present computations in good form where appropriate.

c. Independent of your answers to (a) and (b), assume that the book value of Draper's inventory is $1,700,000 and based on the sample results the estimated total value of the inventory is $1,690,000. The auditor desires a confidence (reliability) level of 95 percent. Discuss the audit and the statistical considerations the auditor must evaluate before deciding whether the sampling results support acceptance of the book value of Draper's inventory.

(AICPA adapted)

---

* This problem is taken from the Uniform CPA Examination and uses sampling with replacement. Consequently, the finite population correction factor adjustment $[\sqrt{1 - (n/N)}]$ to achieved precision can be ignored.

Case 5-4   Fairview Publishing Company

(Estimated time to complete: 45 minutes)

Fairview Publishing Company has 1000 royalty contracts: one with each textbook author. Royalty percentages vary from 3 to 8 percent of net sales, and royalties are accrued semiannually at December 31 and June 30. The company does not accumulate sales, returns, and so on, by titles. However, this information is necessary to make an accurate accrual for royalties payable on each textbook. Semiannually, the company makes an *educated guess* of royalties payable on each textbook. Subsequently, by analyzing sales invoices, return reports, and so on, it determines net sales by textbook and applies the contract royalty rate to determine actual royalties for each textbook. Adjustments resulting from this calculation are made at the time of the next semiannual accrual. The amount of the adjustment for each textbook will not necessarily be proportional to the educated guess.

The previous accountants selected a sample of 125 textbooks on a judgment basis, and by analyzing sales invoices, return reports, and so forth, determined the actual royalties payable on those textbooks. They then compared the audited values for the textbooks to the company's estimate of royalties payable for those textbooks. If the company's estimate for royalties payable was reasonably close to the audited values for the textbooks sampled, they accepted the book value as stated.

We would like to test this year's accrual of $1,405,165 by statistical sampling. Use the sample of 80 royalties selected to *estimate the royalty accrual using difference estimation.* Then, *determine the precision* achieved at 90 percent reliability.

    a. What is the mean (average) difference?

    b. What is the estimated total difference?

    c. What is the estimated audit value?

    d. What is A' at 90 percent reliability?

    e. If tolerable misstatement is preset at $27,000 and control risk and risk of other audit procedures is assessed at 100 percent, what is acceptable precision? Given acceptable precision, is your sample size of 80 adequate?

    f. Does the statistical evidence support material correctness of the $1,405,165 liability?

Sample of 80 Items from Royalty Contracts (Difference Method)

Item Number	Population Number	Book Value	Audited Value	Difference	Difference Squared
1	113	$2,030	$2,030.00	$ 0	0
2	420	1,979	2,137.32	158.32	25,065.22
3	347	219	238.71	19.71	388.48
4	541	985	1,053.95	68.95	4,754.10
5	964	679	679.00	0	0

Sample of 80 Items from Royalty Contracts (Difference Method) (Continued)

Item Number	Population Number	Book Value	Audited Value	Difference	Difference Squared
6	377	2,233	2,233.00	0	0
7	607	1,760	1,760.00	0	0
8	319	1,657	1,657.00	0	0
9	71	340	323.00	(17.00)	289.00
10	254	426	426.00	0	0
11	221	872	810.96	(61.04)	3,725.88
12	886	1,362	1,266.66	(95.34)	9,089.72
13	84	1,256	1,256.00	0	0
14	998	1,558	1,558.00	0	0
15	520	1,001	1,001.00	0	0
16	226	2,083	2,083.00	0	0
17	690	1,778	1,778.00	0	0
18	265	1,523	1,523.00	0	0
19	837	1,293	1,422.30	129.30	16,718.49
20	624	2,116	1,946.72	(169.28)	28,655.72
21	401	2,075	2,261.75	186.75	34,875.56
22	775	201	201.00	0	0
23	125	32	32.00	0	0
24	76	697	766.70	69.70	4,858.09
25	175	168	168.00	0	0
26	636	984	984.00	0	0
27	463	1,317	1,317.00	0	0
28	458	633	689.97	56.97	3,245.58
29	958	1,438	1,438.00	0	0
30	793	1,794	1,686.36	(107.64)	11,586.37
31	711	425	463.25	38.25	1,463.06
32	324	2,081	2,205.86	124.86	15,590.02
33	869	520	520.00	0	0
34	891	1,485	1,603.80	118.80	14,113.44
35	807	1,912	1,797.28	(114.72)	13,160.68
36	785	369	369.00	0	0
37	345	1,435	1,435.00	0	0
38	965	1,538	1,538.00	0	0
39	259	1,961	1,961.00	0	0
40	237	1,449	1,449.00	0	0
41	523	1,831	1,831.00	0	0
42	782	1,132	1,052.76	(79.24)	6,278.98
43	856	580	580.00	0	0

Sample of 80 Items from Royalty Contracts (Difference Method) (Continued)

Item Number	Population Number	Book Value	Audited Value	Difference	Difference Squared
44	819	1,477	1,550.85	73.85	5,453.82
45	102	1,704	1,601.76	(102.24)	10,453.02
46	217	1,498	1,348.20	(149.80)	22,440.04
47	658	1,238	1,238.00	0	0
48	655	1,154	1,084.76	(69.24)	4,794.18
49	591	2,041	2,041.00	0	0
50	285	2,411	2,652.10	241.10	58,129.21
51	38	577	577.00	0	0
52	590	1,291	1,291.00	0	0
53	540	1,915	1,915.00	0	0
54	471	1,489	1,489.00	0	0
55	350	828	770.04	(57.96)	3,359.36
56	264	2,080	1,934.40	(145.60)	21,199.36
57	665	855	855.00	0	0
58	473	1,475	1,548.76	73.75	5,439.06
59	483	2,147	2,254.35	107.35	11,524.02
60	475	1,369	1,369.00	0	0
61	786	419	419.00	0	0
62	847	1,726	1,726.00	0	0
63	176	448	416.64	(31.36)	983.45
64	920	1,365	1,365.00	0	0
65	133	2,403	2,403.00	0	0
66	943	1,752	1,752.00	0	0
67	616	1,797	1,940.76	143.76	20,666.94
68	912	750	750.00	0	0
69	550	1,156	1,156.00	0	0
70	368	1,005	1,075.35	0	4,949.12
71	416	2,409	2,409.00	0	0
72	668	2,063	2,063.00	0	0
73	138	881	969.10	88.10	7,761.61
74	393	907	907.00	0	0
75	234	972	972.00	0	0
76	799	1,531	1,531.00	0	0
77	495	1,359	1,494.90	135.90	18,468.81
78	161	1,544	1,544.00	0	0
79	921	1,885	2,054.65	169.65	28,781.12
80	349	818	818.00	0	0
TOTALS		$105,946	$106,820.96	$ 874.96	418,261.51

Case 5-5   Accounts Receivable, Inc.

(Estimated time to complete: 20 minutes)

Audit hypothesis testing is applied to an accounts receivable total consisting of 1000 accounts. The sample size is 100. The client's book total is $850,000. A 95 percent reliability is needed (U_R of 1.96). The desired precision and tolerable misstatement is $6000. The audit total of the sample is $80,000. The sum of the squared deviations is $89,100.

Answer the following questions:

a. Achieved precision A' is $_____

b. Estimated audit value is $_____

c. Assume that $A' = A$; show whether the client's book total is acceptable.

d. In planning sample size, what beta risk was used? _____

e. What actions would you recommend if the sample evidence indicates that the book value is *not* materially correct?

Case 5-6   AHT, Inc.

(Estimated time to complete: 35 minutes)

(Audit Hypothesis Testing) Fill in the following blanks assuming sampling *without* replacement:

Book value (believed to be correct)	$2,820,000
Tolerable misstatement	$ 60,000
Estimate of standard deviation	$ 150
Population elements	$ 1000
Desired risk of incorrect rejection	5%
Desired risk of incorrect acceptance	5%
Sample standard deviation	$ 140
Sample mean	$ 2,800
Risk of incorrect rejection coefficient	_____
Desired precision	_____
Sample size	_____
Dollar-value estimate of population total	_____
Achieved precision	_____
What is the maximum potential overstatement?	_____
What is the maximum potential understatement?	_____
Assuming the following book values and achieved precisions, should you accept or reject the book value?	_____

	Book Value	*Achieved Precision*	
(1)	$2,820,000	$15,000	
(2)	2,820,000	35,000	_____
(3)	2,820,000	45,000	_____
(4)	2,840,000	15,000	_____
(5)	2,840,000	25,000	_____

Case 5-7   Smith, Inc.

(Estimated time to complete: 30 minutes)

The auditors wish to use mean-per-unit sampling to evaluate the reasonableness of the book value of the accounts receivable of Smith, Inc. Smith has 10,000 receivable accounts with a total book value of $1,500,000. The auditors estimate the population's standard deviation to be equal to $25. After examining the overall audit plan, the auditors believe that the account's tolerable misstatement is $60,000, and that a risk of incorrect rejection of 5 percent and a risk of incorrect acceptance of 10 percent are appropriate.

a. Calculate the required sample size.

b. Assuming the following results:

Average audited value	= $146
Standard deviation of sample	= $28

Use the mean-per-unit method to:

(1) Calculate the point estimate of the account's audited value.

(2) Calculate the projected misstatement for the population.

(3) Calculate the adjusted precision, A''.

(4) State the auditors' conclusion in this situation.

Case 5-8   Microtext Corporation and Industrial Supply Company

(Estimated time to complete: 20 minutes)

You are in the process of planning the audit of Microtext Corporation and Industrial Supply Company for the year ended December 31, 200X. Presented on the following page is selected financial information for the two companies.

	Microtext Corporation	Industrial Supply
Total assets	$24,000,000	$5,400,000
Total revenue	64,000,000	8,900,000
Equity	10,500,000	2,800,000
Net income before taxes	1,000,000	1,000,000

a. Develop an estimate of the appropriate amount of planning materiality at the overall financial statement level for each company.

b. Assume that you are allocating the amount of overall materiality for Microtext Corporation to seven individual accounts. Describe how this might be done.

c. Describe three characteristics of a small misstatement that might render it qualitatively material.

SUPPLEMENTARY TOPIC: REVIEW QUESTIONS

S-1. Describe the audit sampling techniques that would typically be used by a CPA for the following purposes:

    a. Tests of controls over compliance with laws, regulations, and provisions.

    b. Substantive tests of compliance in an audit of an entity's financial statements.

S-2. Describe how attribute sampling may be used in an attestation engagement designed to provide an opinion on management's assertion of compliance with specified requirements.

S-3. When engaged to attest to an entity's compliance with laws, regulations, and provisions that have a material effect on major federal assistance programs under SAS No. 74, the CPA obtains evidence of compliance by performing both tests of controls and substantive tests of compliance. If the entity has several major programs, the CPA may define the population for tests of controls in one of two ways.

    a. Describe the two ways that the population may be defined for the tests of controls over compliance with laws and regulations.

    b. Indicate which way of defining the population is more efficient and explain your answer.

6 PROBABILITY-PROPORTIONAL-TO-SIZE SAMPLING

LEARNING OBJECTIVES

After a careful study and discussion of this chapter, you will be able to:

1. Define the objective and assumptions of probability-proportional-to-size sampling (PPS sampling).
2. List advantages and disadvantages of using PPS sampling.
3. Identify when PPS sampling is appropriate.
4. Apply PPS sampling in an auditing context.
5. Define PPS sampling concepts such as "upper bound," "most likely overstatement (or understatement) misstatements," and "tainting."

Several statistical sampling plans are available to the auditor. Most of the plans we have discussed are derivations of two classical statistical sampling methods—attribute sampling, which is used primarily for testing controls, and variable sampling, which is used primarily for substantive testing. **Probability-proportional-to-size sampling (PPS sampling)** is a modified form of attribute sampling that can be used for both proportional tests of controls and substantive testing. The discussion in this chapter is limited primarily to substantive testing. This chapter explains the application and evaluation technique of the basic PPS plan and the circumstances under which the use of PPS sampling is appropriate.[1]

OBJECTIVES AND ASSUMPTIONS OF PPS SAMPLING

The selection of a particular statistical sampling plan requires that: (1) conclusions that can be drawn from the sample meet the test objectives of the auditor, and (2) assumptions of the plan match the characteristics of the population being sampled. PPS sampling is designed to allow the auditor to make a statement about the dollar amount of misstatement (both overstatement and understatement misstatements) in the audited population. Substantive testing using PPS sampling is a popular alternative to the variable sampling methods explained in Chapter 5. PPS sampling is designed to generate a conclusion similar to the following:

Based on the sample's evidence, I am *X*% confident that the dollar amount of misstatement in the account does not exceed $*Y* (where $*Y* depends on the sampling results).

The auditor will then compare the value obtained for $*Y* with the tolerable misstatement to make a decision about the acceptability of the reported book value of the account.

Before the auditor decides to use the PPS sampling plan, he or she should ascertain whether the assumptions of the plan are valid for the population being tested. Two assumptions inherent in PPS sampling are:

1. The misstatement rate in the population should be small (less than 10 percent) and the population should contain 2000 or more items. (Use of the Poisson probability distribution for evaluation of the sample requires this feature.)[2]
2. amount of misstatement in any item of the population cannot be more than the reported book value of the item. That is, if the book value of a customer's balance is $100, the amount of misstatement in the balance cannot exceed $100.

[1]Probability-proportional-to-size sampling is frequently referred to as dollar-unit sampling. In the United States PPS sampling was first applied in an auditing context by K. Stringer of Deloitte. Haskins & Sells (now Deloitte & Touche). The Stringer method is referred to as cumulative monetary sampling.

[2]Roberts presents a PPS sampling plan useful for high misstatement rate population situations. See Donald M. Roberts. *Statistical Auditing* (New York: AICPA, 1978), pp. 116–119.

If the assumptions of the PPS sampling plan are valid for the population being tested and the conclusions derived from using the plan coincide with the audit test objectives, the auditor should consider applying PPS sampling.

ADVANTAGES AND DISADVANTAGES OF USING PPS SAMPLING

PPS sampling has several attractive features aside from the general advantages of using statistical sampling. A discussion of the advantages and disadvantages of PPS sampling should allow the auditor to determine the applicability of the plan for a particular test. Some of the advantages of PPS sampling are:

1. PPS sampling satisfies the objectives of SAS No. 39 (AU 350) and can easily be used within the conceptual framework of audit sampling.
2. PPS sampling solves the problem of detecting a very small number of large misstatements (needles in the haystack) by giving the big items a much greater chance of being included in the audit sample. This is achieved by breaking up the big but infrequent physical units into small but frequent monetary units.
3. PPS sampling is generally easier to use than classical variables sampling. The calculations in a classical variables application are more tedious.
4. PPS sampling can be applied to a combination of several account balances. Accounts can be tested together because the sampling units (dollars) are homogeneous.
5. PPS sampling allows use of the overall materiality amount as tolerable misstatement without the need for allocation.
6. PPS sampling will usually result in a smaller sample size relative to classical variables sampling, if no or few misstatements are expected.
7. PPS sampling does not depend on the sampling distribution being closely approximated by the normal distribution.
8. PPS sampling provides an alternative to using variable sampling to stratify a population. (Both PPS sampling and stratified sampling give greater weight to items with large book values.)

Some of the disadvantages of PPS sampling are:

1. The PPS sampling evaluation technique requires the amount of misstatement in each physical unit of the population not to exceed the book value of the unit.
2. Physical units that are understated have a lower probability of selection because they contain a smaller number of dollars to be selected for sampling. Furthermore, PPS sampling cannot find misstatements in physical units with a book value of zero; however, many sampling plans suffer from this problem.

3. It is not appropriate for use in testing for understatements of accounts.
4. As the number of misstatements increases, sample size increases, and sample size may be larger than the sample size computed under a classical variable sampling application.
5. It may overstate the allowance for sampling risk when misstatements are found and cause the auditor to reject a correct client book value.

BASIC DESCRIPTION OF PPS SAMPLING

PPS sampling is a modified form of attribute sampling that permits dollar conclusions about the total dollar amount of misstatement in the population. Unlike classical attribute sampling techniques, which focus on the physical units (e.g., invoices and vouchers) of the population, PPS sampling focuses on the dollar units of the population. Suppose the auditor is sampling a population of $100,000 accounts receivable that contain 5000 individual customer balances. Instead of viewing the population as 5000 different physical units from which to draw a sample, the auditor would think of the population as 100,000 individual dollar units from which to draw a sample.

When an individual dollar is selected for examination, the dollar is not tested by itself. Instead, it acts as a hook and drags a whole item (physical unit) with it. As we discussed in Chapter 2, to find the item associated with the particular dollar unit being sampled, the auditor must add progressively through the population. For an illustration of this method, consider the following partial listing of accounts:

Item Number	Book Value	Cumulative Total	Associated Dollar Units
1	$ 50	$ 50	1–5
2	100	150	51–150
3	80	230	151–230
4	200	430	231–430
5	300	730	431–730
.	.	.	.
.	.	.	.
.	.	.	.

If dollar unit 250 were selected, for example, the auditor would pull for examination account number 4, because 250 falls in the range 231-430. This method of selection results in selecting items with a probability directly proportional to their size. That is, a $100 item has a 10 times greater chance of being selected than a $10 item because it contains 10 times as many dollar units that could be selected for sampling. Ultimately, samples will contain a higher percentage of large items than small items. In this respect, PPS sampling is similar to stratified sampling in that both give greater weight to items with larger recorded amounts.

Once the physical units have been found that correspond to the selected dollar units, the auditor examines the physical units for misstatement. If a misstatement is found in a physical unit, the unit is said to be tainted. **Tainting** t (or relative misstatement) is the amount of misstatement in the unit divided by the reported book value of the unit.

$$t = \frac{\text{amount of misstatement}}{\text{reported book value of unit}}$$

The value for t tells the auditor the amount of misstatement in each dollar unit contained in the physical unit. Specifically, t gives the auditor a value for the misstatement in the dollar unit selected for sampling. For example, if a customer's account balance is reported at $100 and is overstated by $50 (audited value = $50):

$$t = \frac{\$500}{\$100} = .50$$

The auditor can state that each dollar unit in the customer's balance is misstated by $0.50. Tainting t for each dollar unit found in misstatement in the sample is used to determine the test results. Misstatements are classified as either understatement or overstatement misstatements, and, within each group, tainting values are ranked in descending order. For example, if two misstatements produce taintings of 0.37 and 0.42, then regardless of the dollar amounts of the misstatements, 0.42 is designated t_1 and 0.37 is designated t_2.

After the ranking procedure is completed, the Poisson probability distribution is used to evaluate the results of the dollar units sampled at a specified risk level, SR. The evaluation produces an estimate of the maximum amount of dollar misstatement in the population for both understatement and overstatement possibilities with a given degree of reliability. (The calculations involved are presented in the next section.) The auditor can then decide whether the population should be accepted as not materially misstated or rejected as being misstated by a material amount.

EVALUATION BASED ON THE POISSON PROBABILITY DISTRIBUTION

Poisson probabilities are obtained from an equation that represents an idealized mathematical process generating occasional random events. Applied to an accounting population, the events are misstatements and the process is the internal control system. The Poisson distribution allows the auditor to state with a specified risk (SR), the upper misstatement limit UML_x per sample size n of the population, given the sample contains x misstatements. When the auditor specifies a risk level for the test, he or she determines which UML_x to use for evaluation. Values for UML_x are found in Table 3.6 (see Chapter 3). At a specified risk *(SR)*, UML_x divided by sample size n gives the maximum misstatement rate that is projected to the population.

Maximum misstatement rate for the population at the specified risk of incorrect acceptance (beta risk) is[3]

$$\frac{UML_x}{n}$$

A portion of Table 3.6, which is used to determine UML_x values, is reproduced below. UML_x's are read from the body of the table.

Number of *Occurrences*	*Risk Levels*		
	10%	*5%*	*2.5%*
0	2.4	3.0	3.7
1	3.9	4.8	5.6
2	5.4	6.3	7.3
3	6.7	7.8	8.8

The following table contains examples of maximum misstatement rates at different *SR* levels and a sample size of 50 with a defined number of misstatements.

Number of *Misstatements* *Found*	*Risk Level, SR*	*Maximum* *Misstatement Rate* *$UML_x/50$*
0	5%	6.0% (3.0 ÷ 50)
0	10	4.8 (2.4 ÷ 50)
1	5	9.6 (4.8 ÷ 50)
1	10	7.8 (3.9 ÷ 50)

The maximum misstatement rate does not generate information concerning the dollar magnitude of possible misstatement in the population. The PPS sampling approach in auditing was developed to convert misstatement rates into dollars. Goodfellow, Loebbecke, and Neter outline the method for PPS sampling evaluation of the maximum misstatement rates found with the Poisson distribution.[4] The fol-

---

[3]Note that with PPS sampling the specified risk level is the risk of incorrect acceptance (SAS No. 39; AU 350) or, statistically, the *beta* risk. As is explained later in this chapter, the auditor does not consider alpha risk in estimating the sample size, but may incorporate an adjustment to control alpha risk in the evaluation of the sample results.

[4]James L. Goodfellow, James K. Loebbecke, and John Neter, "Some Perspectives on CAV Sampling Plans." *CA Magazine* (October and November 1974). The notation CAV refers to combined attribute and variable sampling.

lowing discussion is an elaboration of this method. The evaluation technique is first developed when overstatement misstatements are found. Then, an example is presented illustrating both understatement and overstatement misstatements.

Consider a population that contains N physical units with total book value of the population equal to BV. The maximum misstatement rate from a sample of size n at a specified risk level SR is UML_x/n when x overstatement misstatements are found. The projection of the maximum number of physical units that are misstated for the population is

$$\text{Maximum number of overstated physical units} = N \cdot \frac{UML_x}{n}$$

If the maximum amount of overstatement of each of these units is X, then an estimate of the *maximum dollar amount of overstatement* in the population is

$$\text{Maximum dollar amount of overstatement} = N \cdot \frac{UML_x}{n} \cdot X$$

If a PPS sample were taken, BV is the total number of units (dollars) in the population, and the maximum dollar amount of overstatement each dollar may contain is $1 (recall assumption number 2 of PPS sampling). Since $BV = N$ and $X = 1$, the estimate of the maximum dollar overstatement in the population *Max* equals

$$\text{Maximum dollar amount of overstatement, } Max = BV \cdot \frac{UML_x}{n} \cdot 1$$

This estimate of the maximum amount of overstatement in the population can be refined by using additional information found in the sample and by recognizing the cumulative nature of the Poisson *UML* values.

First, if no misstatements are found in a sample, the auditor will estimate the maximum dollar amount of overstatement (referred to as the **basic bound** when there are no misstatements) as

$$\text{Basic bound} = BV \cdot \frac{UML_0}{n} \cdot 1$$

The "basic bound" tells the auditor that no matter what the results of the sample are, he or she will always estimate the maximum dollar amount of overstatement to be at least the basic bound for the given risk level. When one misstatement is found in the sample, the estimate of the maximum dollar amount of overstatement will be larger than the basic bound. In fact, the increase in the estimate caused by finding a misstatement is

$$\text{Addition to basic bound of one misstatement found} = BV \cdot \frac{UML_1 - UML_0}{n} \cdot 1$$

Then the estimate of maximum dollar amount of overstatement in the population is equivalent to basic bound plus the additional effect of finding one overstatement misstatement in the sample. That is,

$$Max = BV \cdot \frac{UML_1}{n} \cdot 1$$

$$= \left(BV \cdot \frac{UML_0}{n} \cdot 1 \right) + \left(BV \cdot \frac{UML_1 - UML_0}{n} \cdot 1 \right)$$

If two overstatement misstatements were observed, the estimate of the maximum dollar amount of overstatement would be equivalent to basic bound plus the additional effect of finding the first misstatement and the additional effect of finding the second misstatement. That is,

$$Max = BV \cdot \frac{UML_2}{n} \cdot 1 = \left(BV \cdot \frac{UML_0}{n} \cdot 1 \right)$$

$$+ \left(BV \cdot \frac{UML_1 - UML_0}{n} \cdot 1 \right) + \left(BV \cdot \frac{UML_2 - UML_1}{n} \cdot 1 \right)$$

In general, the cumulative nature of the Poisson *UML* values can be broken down into parts to be used to find the estimate of the maximum dollar amount of overstatement. These parts then can be used to find the basic bound and the effect of finding each additional overstatement misstatement.

The cumulative nature of the Poisson *UML* values is not important when the maximum dollar amount of overstatement is considered to be $1 for each addition to the basic bound. However, the cumulative property is very useful if *additional information found in the PPS sample is also used*. The tainting values of overstatement misstatement along with their relative rankings can be used to make an estimate of the maximum dollar amount of overstatement in the population. The basic bound will remain the same as before because the amount of overstatement misstatement is considered to be maximal ($1). However, if one misstatement is found with tainting *t*, then the additional effect of finding this misstatement in the sample will be

$$\text{Addition to basic bound of one misstatement} = BV \cdot \frac{UML_1 - UML_0}{n} \cdot t_1$$

If two overstatement misstatements are found, their rankings will determine their additional effect on the estimate of the maximum dollar amount of overstatement in the population. Let t_1 represent the misstatement ranking number 1 and t_2 represent the misstatement ranking number 2, then

$$\text{Effect of finding the first misstatement} = BV \cdot \frac{UML_1 - UML_0}{n} \cdot t_1$$

and

$$\text{Effect of finding the second misstatement} = BV \cdot \frac{UML_2 - UML_1}{n} \cdot t_2$$

The resulting value for the estimate of the maximum dollar amount of overstatement in the population at the specified reliability will be the most conservative (pessimistic) estimate when tainting values are used.

To illustrate the evaluation technique, consider an accounts receivable of $100,000. If a sample of size 100 contains two overstatement misstatements with $t_1 = 0.8$ and $t_2 = 0.5$, the estimate of the maximum dollar amount of overstatement at 5 percent risk of incorrect acceptance (using Table 3.6) is

$$Max = \left(\$100,000 \cdot \frac{3.0}{100} \cdot 1 \right) + \left(\$100,000 \cdot \frac{4.8 - 3.0}{100} \cdot 0.8 \right)$$
$$+ \left(\$100,000 \cdot \frac{6.3 - 4.8}{100} \cdot 0.5 \right) = \$5,190$$

The calculation for the effect of finding the first misstatement for t_1 is ($100,000 · 1.8/ 100 · .8). Likewise, the effect of finding the second misstatement for t_2 is ($100,000 · 1.5/100 · 0.5).

The projected misstatement is calculated as follows:

Misstatement	Tainting %	Sampling Interval	Projected Misstatement
1	0.8	$1000	$ 800
2	0.5	1000	500
	Total Projected Misstatement		$1300

The estimate of the maximum dollar amount of overstatement includes the projected misstatement.

PPS SAMPLING FOR OVERSTATEMENTS

The steps of PPS sampling used for overstatements are outlined here. Following the outline, a typical application is presented.

Step Number	Action
1	State the objectives of the test and establish the parameters of the particular test.

Define:

$$BV = \text{book value of the population}$$
$$TM = \text{tolerable misstatement}$$
$$SR = \text{risk level}$$
$$N = \text{number of physical units in the population}$$

2   Select the sample.
Use: **Systematic PPS sampling** if the population is in random order with respect to the audited characteristic.

$$n = \text{sample size} = \frac{UML_0 \cdot BV}{TM}$$

$$I = \text{sampling interval} = \frac{BV}{n}$$

RS = random start between 0 and I

UML_0 = value from Table 3.6, based on zero expected misstatements

Dollar units selected will be RS, $RS + I$, $RS + 2I$, $RS + 3I$, . . . , $RS + (n + 1)I$.

3   Audit the physical units associated with the selected dollar units.
4   Evaluate the sample and determine tainting t for each physical unit in error.
Let
t_1 = tainting of largest relative misstatement
t_2 = tainting of second largest relative misstatement, and so on.
5   Determine the basic bound and additions to the basic bound as discussed earlier (*Max*).
6   Make a decision about the acceptability of reported book value by comparing *Max* with *TM*.

Instead of using systematic PPS sampling as illustrated in step 2, the sample could be selected by using a random-number table or a random-number generator. Also, systematic sampling with multiple starts, the sampling interval from step 2 would be multiplied by the desired number of starts. Recall that this was illustrated in Chapter 2.

To illustrate steps 1 to 6, assume that the auditor is trying to determine if a client's inventory balance of $3,000,000 is not materially misstated in terms of price and quantity. Figure 6.1 presents an illustrative application.

Parameters

$$BV = \$3,000,000$$

$$N = 50,000 \text{ perpetual inventory records}$$

$$TM = \$60,000$$

$$SR = 5 \text{ percent}$$

Sample-Size Equation

$$n = \frac{3.0 \cdot 3,000,000}{60,000} = 150$$

Sampling Interval and Sample Selection

$$I = \frac{3,000,000}{150} = 20,000$$

$$RS = 1795 \text{ (from a random - number table)}$$

Select dollar units: 1795; 21,795; 41,795; etc. All inventory records in the population are less than $20,000 and greater than zero.

Sample Evaluation

Two misstatements observed. No. 1 had a book value of $1000 with overstatement of $500, and No. 2 had a book value of $2000 with overstatement of $1600. (Remember: t_1 is the highest relative misstatement, not the highest dollar misstatement.)

$$t_1 = \frac{1600}{2000} = 0.8 \qquad t_2 = \frac{500}{1000} = 0.5$$

$$Max = \left(\$3,000,000 \cdot \frac{3.0}{150} \cdot 1 \right) +$$

$$\left(\$3,000,000 \cdot \frac{1.8}{150} \cdot 0.8 \right) +$$

$$\left(\$3,000,000 \cdot \frac{1.5}{150} \cdot 0.5 \right) = \$103,800^{*}$$

Auditor's Conclusion

Based on the sample evidence, the auditor is 95 percent confident that the dollar amount of overstatement in the inventory account does not exceed $103,800. Because $103,800 is greater than tolerable misstatement ($60,000), the auditor may decide to reject the book value of the population and increase the sample size.

FIGURE 6.1   Illustrative PPS Sampling Application—Overstatements

*Includes $26,000 (0.8 × 20,000 + 0.5 × 20,000) of projected misstatement.

One of the facts stated in Figure 6.1 is that all inventory records ($N = 50,000$ physical units) are less than \$20,000; that is, no physical unit exceeded the sampling interval. In instances where physical units in the population are greater than the sampling interval, they are examined 100 percent. Consequently, the sample size is equal to *n* minus all 100 percent-examined units. This is important because in calculating *Max the reduced sample size and the reduced book value should be used.*

Another very important point also is illustrated in Figure 6.1. When a monetary overstatement is observed, the maximum dollar amount of overstatement exceeds the tolerable misstatement. When this happens, Roberts states:

As a result the auditor must obtain additional information to be able to decide whether or not there is a material amount of misstatement. When, in fact, there is not a material amount of misstatement, the result is overauditing. Stringer and others have recognized this and suggest determining the sample size so that the upper bound [max] with no observed misstatements is below the material amount [tolerable misstatement][5].

This can be accomplished by first estimating tolerable misstatement *(TM)* and then calculating an adjusted tolerable misstatement *(TM')* as a fraction of tolerable misstatement. In practice, several different approaches are used to estimate adjusted tolerable misstatement *(TM')*. One conservative approach is to make *TM'* one-half of *TM*. This is the approach adopted in this chapter. A more mathematical approach is explained and illustrated below. A similar approach to the mathematical approach is illustrated in the explanation of nonstatistical sampling in Chapter 7.

SAMPLING RISK AND PPS SAMPLING

Statistical sampling plans are designed to give the auditor a method for making quantitative statements about the risks that result from conclusions based on a sample rather than application of an audit procedure to all items in a population. As in variable-sampling audit hypothesis testing, two types of sampling risks are inherent in PPS sampling when sample results are projected to the population—alpha risk and beta risk.

Recall from Chapter 5 that beta risk is the chance that the auditor will accept a population as materially correct when, in fact, it is materially misstated. In PPS sampling, the auditor controls beta risk when he or she specifies the risk level *SR* for the sampling plan. Beta risk is the risk level specified for PPS sampling.

The auditor establishes the desired beta risk for PPS sampling in the same manner as that used in Chapter 5 for variable sampling. The audit risk model for establishing beta risk is

$$TD \text{ (beta)} = \frac{AR}{CR \times AP}$$

---

[5]Roberts, *Statistical Auditing*, p. 122. For additional discussion of how to handle this problem, see R. Kaplan, "Sample Size Computations for Dollar-unit Sampling," *Studies on Statistical Methodology in Auditing: Journal of Accounting Research* (Supplement, 1975), pp. 126–133.

TABLE 6.1   Probability-Proportionate-to-Size Sampling Table (for Overstatements)

Number of Overstatement Misstatements	Risk of Incorrect Acceptance (Beta Risk)								
	1%	*5%*	*10%*	*15%*	*20%*	*25%*	*30%*	*37%*	*50%*
0	4.61	3.00	2.31	1.90	1.61	1.39	1.21	1.00	.70
1	6.64	4.75	3.89	3.38	3.00	2.70	2.44	2.14	1.68
2	8.41	6.30	5.33	4.72	4.28	3.93	3.62	3.25	2.68
3	10.05	7.76	6.69	6.02	5.52	5.11	4.77	4.34	3.68
4	11.61	9.16	8.00	7.27	6.73	6.28	5.90	5.43	4.68
5	13.11	10.52	9.28	8.50	7.91	7.43	7.01	6.49	5.68
6	14.57	11.85	10.54	9.71	9.08	8.56	8.12	7.56	6.67
7	16.00	13.15	11.78	10.90	10.24	9.69	9.21	8.63	7.67
8	17.41	14.44	13.00	12.08	11.38	10.81	10.31	9.68	8.67
9	18.79	15.71	14.21	13.25	12.52	11.92	11.39	10.74	9.67
10	20.15	16.97	15.41	14.42	13.66	13.02	12.47	11.79	10.67

Source: Used with permission of the AICPA.

However, for convenience, this chapter uses beta risk levels of 5 or 10 percent for illustrations of PPS sampling. Other risk levels are found in Table 6.1.

DETERMINING TOLERABLE MISSTATEMENT USING PPS SAMPLING

As discussed in Chapter 5, the auditor determines tolerable misstatement for a particular account by first making a preliminary judgment about materiality for the financial statements as a whole. A unique advantage of PPS sampling is that this overall materiality amount does not have to be allocated to individual accounts. The overall amount of materiality may be used as tolerable misstatement for all of the accounts tested using PPS sampling. As an example, assume that the auditor makes a judgment that overall material misstatement is $500,000; this total amount may be used for a PPS sampling test of the inventory account and a PPS sampling test of property, plant, and equipment.

DETERMINING THE PPS SAMPLE SIZE

To calculate sample size in a PPS application, the auditor predefines (1) book value, (2) a reliability factor for the risk of incorrect acceptance, (3) tolerable misstatement, (4) expected misstatement, and (5) an expansion factor. The book value is the recorded amount of the population. As described on the preceding page, tolerable misstatement is the maximum dollar misstatement that may exist in the population without causing the financial statements to be materially misstated. Expected misstatement is the auditor's estimate of the dollar amount of misstatement in the population. It is estimated based on prior experience and knowledge of the client. The reliability factor for the risk of misstatement is always determined from the "zero errors" row of Table 6.1. If a 10 percent risk of incorrect acceptance is desired, the auditor uses a reliability factor of 2.31 from Table 6.1. The expansion factor comes from Table 6.2. For a 20 percent risk of incorrect acceptance, the expansion factor is 1.3.

The equation for sample size is

$$n = \frac{\text{book value} \times \text{reliability factor}}{\text{tolerable misstatement} - (\text{expected misstatement} \times \text{expansion factor})}$$

The auditor determines the risk of incorrect acceptance based on the extent of evidence required from the sample—the same approach that is used for classical sampling. The risk of incorrect rejection is indirectly controlled by the auditor's estimate of expected misstatement. If the auditor underestimates expected misstatement, the sample size will be too small and additional testing will be necessary.

If book value is $500,000, the risk of incorrect acceptance is 5 percent, tolerable misstatement is $25,000, and expected misstatement is $6250, sample size is

$$n = \frac{\$500,000 \times 3.00}{\$25,000 - (6250 \times 1.6)}$$
$$= 100$$

Recall, also, that alpha risk is the chance of concluding that the population is materially misstated when, in fact, it is materially correct. When PPS sampling is used, the auditor does not specifically control alpha risk. However, simulation studies have helped to establish a revision of the evaluation technique used in PPS sam-

TABLE 6.2   Expansion Factors for Expected Misstatement

	\multicolumn{9}{c}{*Risk of Incorrect Acceptance*}
	1%	*5%*	*10%*	*15%*	*20%*	*25%*	*30%*	*37%*	*50%*
Factor	1.9	1.6	1.5	1.4	1.3	1.25	1.2	1.15	1.0

Source: Used with permission of the AICPA.

pling that confines alpha risk to 5 percent. To limit alpha risk to 5 percent, the auditor determines both the **most likely estimate for overstatement and understatement misstatements.** That is

$$MLM_{o/s} = \text{most likely misstatement for overstatements}$$

$$= \frac{sum\ of\ overstatement\ taintings}{n} \cdot BV$$

$$MLM_{u/s} = \text{most likely misstatement for understatements}$$

$$= \frac{sum\ of\ understatement\ taintings}{n} \cdot BV$$

The $MLM_{o/s}$ and the $MLM_{u/s}$ are the auditor's best estimates of the actual misstatements of understatement and overstatement in the population. These two values can be netted to give an adjusting entry for the population if the auditor believes the sample is sufficiently large.

When both overstatements and understatements are found, the risk of material misstatement of the account may be determined by calculating *Net Max$_{o/s}$*, as follows:

$$Net\ Max_{o/s} = Max - MLM_{u/s}$$

The auditor can be confident, at the specified level, that the account is not misstated by more than *Net Max$_{o/s}$*. Thus, if *Net Max$_{o/s}$* is \$50,000 and the risk of incorrect acceptance for the test is 10 percent, the auditor is 90 percent confident that the misstatement in the account does not exceed \$50,000. If \$50,000 is less than tolerable misstatement, the auditor can be 90% confident that the account balance is not materially misstated.

PPS SAMPLING FOR OVERSTATEMENTS AND UNDERSTATEMENTS

PPS sampling is used by some auditors to test for material understatements as well as overstatements. In evaluating the results, these auditors calculate a *Net Max$_{u/s}$* and a *Net Max$_{o/s}$*, and the book value of the population is accepted if these amounts are less than tolerable misstatement for the account. However, we believe that using PPS sampling to test for understatements is *inappropriate*. Because the auditor selects sample items based on their book values, there is a bias against selecting understated items. Therefore, the auditors' estimate of the maximum understatement in the population is likely to be too low.

PPS SAMPLING FOR ATTRIBUTES

If the auditor selects a test of controls sample using PPS sampling, the incidence of control deviations may be related to an upper bound of monetary misstatement. Assume that a PPS sample is selected from a population of sales invoices to ascertain whether credit was properly authorized. The population of sales invoices for the entire year has a recorded value of $789,000. Based on a preliminary review of the credit sales controls and past experience, the auditor believes that the internal control is very good. By using a risk level of 5 percent and a predefined upper precision limit of 5 percent, the auditor selected a sample of 60 sales invoices.

Using Table 3.6 to evaluate the sample observation, if zero control deviations are noted, the auditor may conclude that unauthorized sales dollars do not exceed $39,450 at a 5 percent risk level. The upper bound of monetary (dollar) control deviation is calculated as follows:

Upper bound of monetary control deviation

$$= \frac{3.0 \text{ from Table 6.1 (5\% risk)}}{60 \text{ sample size}} \times \$789,000 \, BV$$

$$= \$39.450$$

Similarly, if one control deviation is discovered, the auditor may conclude: I am 95 percent confident that no more than $63,120 of the sales invoice dollars were not properly approved.

$$\$63,120 = \frac{4.8}{60} \times \$789,000$$

As shown above, adapting PPS sampling to test controls is easily accomplished. The auditor defines the attribute just as he or she would when attribute sampling is used (see Chapter 3). The primary difference between the PPS sampling and attribute sampling concerns sample selection. Attribute sampling is based on physical unit sampling, but PPS sampling is based on dollar sampling units.

SUMMARY

PPS sampling is a statistical sampling plan that can be used for substantive or test of controls sampling. When the auditor wishes to estimate the maximum amount of monetary misstatement contained in a population, he or she should consider using PPS sampling. To determine if PPS sampling is appropriate for a particular circumstance, the assumptions of the plan are very important.

The PPS sampling plan is based on the Poisson probability distribution. The chapter explains and illustrates evaluation techniques by using the Poisson distribution. Advantages and disadvantages of the plan are discussed to allow an enlightened decision by the auditor contemplating use of PPS sampling.

GLOSSARY

Basic bound   The maximum dollar amount of misstatement in a population, given that no misstatements were observed. The calculation of the basic bound is dependent on the risk of incorrect acceptance and the sample size.

Maximum dollar amount of overstatement, Max   The basic bound plus the additional effects of finding misstatements in a sample, if any. It is also referred to as upper bound.

Most likely misstatement for overstatements and understatements misstatements, MLM   The sum of overstatement (or understatement) taintings times the book value divided by sample size.

PPS sampling   A plan used for both substantive and tests of controls sampling. In the PPS sampling plan, each sampling unit has a probability of being selected that is approximately proportionate to its reported book value.

Systematic PPS sampling   A PPS sampling method in which selected sample items are based on every *BV/n*th item and a defined random start(s).

Tainting   An account balance or other physical unit containing a misstatement. Tainting *t* is the amount of misstatement in the physical unit divided by the reported book value of the unit.

REVIEW QUESTIONS

6-1. Indicate whether each of the following is true (T) or false (F).

    a. Sampling units with zero or negative book values must be treated separately when PPS sampling is used.

    b. In a PPS substantive sampling application, the risk level specified is beta risk.

    c. PPS sampling is a modified form of discovery sampling.

    d. A PPS sample may be selected via a random-number table (unrestricted random sampling) or systematic sampling.

    e. Physical units (account items) that are overstated have a lower probability of selection in a PPS sampling application.

f. To use PPS sampling for testing controls, the auditor defines attributes just as he or she would when using attribute sampling.

g. PPS sampling is actually a form of stratified sampling.

h. If a PPS sample indicates that the proportion of dollar transactions associated with a control deviation is greater than was planned, internal control can be assessed as planned.

i. When systematic PPS sampling is used, all accounts exceeding the total book value divided by the sample size are examined on a 100 percent basis.

6-2. What is the general form of conclusion that is generated by a PPS sampling application?

6-3. List the two underlying assumptions of the PPS sampling model.

6-4. Contrast sample selection by using classical sampling with sample selection using PPS selection.

6-5. PPS sampling is similar to stratified sampling in some respects. Do you agree?

6-6. What are the primary advantages of PPS sampling relative to variable sampling plans presented in Chapter 5? What are the primary disadvantages?

6-7. What is tainting and how is it calculated?

6-8. Calculate the maximum misstatement *rate* at 97.5 percent reliability for a sample size of 100 assuming 0 misstatements, 2 misstatements, and 3 misstatements.

6-9. Calculate the basic bound, tainting, addition to basic bound, and the maximum dollar amount of overstatement in the population for the following situations:

Situation A

$$N = \$250{,}000$$
$$n = 100$$
Overstatement misstatement $= \$5000$ book and $\$4000$ audit
$$SR = 5 \text{ percent}$$

Situation B

$$N = \$250{,}000$$
$$n = 100$$
First overstatement misstatement $= \$5000$ book and $\$4000$ audit
Second overstatement misstatement $= \$2000$ book and $\$1000$ audit
$$SR = 10 \text{ percent}$$

6-10. What is the PPS sample size equation?

6-11. Describe how a PPS sample would be selected by using systematic sampling (use random start) and by using a random-number table.

6-12. How is beta risk controlled in a PPS sampling application? Contrast your response with controlling beta risk in a variable sampling application as presented in Chapter 5.

6-13. How is alpha risk controlled in a PPS sampling application?

6-14. Calculate the most likely misstatement (overstatement and understatement) for the following situation.

$$BV = \$100,000$$
$$n = 100$$
$$\text{Overstatement taintings} = 0.20, 0.30, 0.40$$
$$\text{Understatement taintings} = 0.60, 0.22, 0.08$$

6-15. Determine the PPS sample size for the audit of an accounts receivable balance of $175,000. Use a 10 percent beta risk and assume tolerable misstatement is set equal to $5000. The receivable balance contains $2000 of credit balance accounts.

6-16. Contrast PPS substantive sampling with PPS tests of controls sampling.

MULTIPLE-CHOICE QUESTIONS FROM PROFESSIONAL EXAMINATIONS

6-17. When an internal auditor uses probability-proportional-to-size sampling to examine the total value of invoices, each invoice:

  a. Has an equal probability of being selected.

  b. Can be represented by no more than one dollar unit.

  c. Has an unknown probability of being selected.

  d. Has a probability proportional to its dollar value of being selected.

6-18. An auditor may use either of two statistical sampling approaches in substantive testing, probability-proportional-to-size (PPS) sampling, and classical variables sampling. PPS sampling is primarily applicable in testing for:

  a. The number of misstatements in year-end sales cutoff.

  b. An overstatement of accounts receivable.

  c. A credit balance in accounts receivable.

  d. Proper segregation of duties in accounts receivable collections.

6-19. Which of the following would be an improper technique when using probability-proportional-to-size sampling in an audit of accounts receivable?

    a. Combining negative and positive dollar error item amounts in the appraisal of a sample.

    b. Using a sampling technique in which the same account balance could be selected more than once.

    c. Selecting a random starting point and then sampling every nth dollar unit (systematic sampling).

    d. Defining the sampling unit in the population as an individual dollar and not as an individual account balance.

6-20. In selecting a sample using probability-proportional-to-size sampling, the dollar is the sampling unit. Thus, if the 300th dollar of invoices is selected:

    a. Only that dollar is audited.

    b. Only an invoice with exactly $300 is audited.

    c. An invoice of less than $300 cannot be selected.

    d. The invoice containing the 300th dollar is audited.

6-21. An internal auditor has been assigned to take a probability-proportional-to-size sample of a population of vouchers in the purchasing department. The population has a total book value of $300,000. The internal auditor believes that a maximum misstatement of $900 is acceptable and would like to have 95 percent confidence in the results. (The reliability factor at 95 percent and zero misstatements = 3.00). Additional information is provided below.

Table of First 10 Vouchers in Population		
Voucher #	**Balance**	**Cumulative Balance**
1	$100	$ 100
2	150	250
3	40	290
4	200	490
5	10	500
6	290	790
7	50	840
8	190	1,030
9	20	1,050
10	180	1,230

Given a random start of $50 as the first dollar amount, what is the number of the fourth voucher to be selected, assuming that the sample size will be 1000?

a. 4.

b. 6.

c. 7.

d. 8.

6-22. Which of the following statements is true concerning probability-proportional-to-size (PPS) sampling, also known as dollar-unit sampling?

a. The sampling distribution should approximate the normal distribution.

b. Overstated units have a lower probability of sample selection than units that are understated.

c. The auditor controls the risk of incorrect acceptance by specifying that risk level for the sampling plan.

d. The sampling interval is calculated by dividing the number of physical units in the population by the sample size.

6-23. A sampling plan is needed to test for overstatement of a $3 million accounts payable book balance. The auditor determines that a $100,000 misstatement is material and that a 95 percent confidence level is appropriate. Based on these determinations, the sample of size 90 is needed. The sampling plan *most* likely used is:

a. Stop and go.

b. Cluster sampling.

c. Probability-proportional-to-size sampling.

d. Attribute sampling.

6-24. In a *probability-proportional-to-size* sample with a sampling interval of $15,000, an auditor discovered that a sampled accounts receivable with a recorded amount of $20,000 was overstated by $4,000. The projected misstatement of this sample was:

a. $3,000.

b. $3,750.

c. $4,000.

d. $12,000.

6-25. An auditor is considering the use of probability-proportional-to-size sampling. This technique is likely to be especially beneficial if:

a. The auditor is interested in testing the proper valuation of accounts payable.

b. The auditor believes that the items to be tested are just as likely to be overstated as understated.

c. The auditor is interested in testing the accuracy and valuation of accounts receivable.

d. The error rate in the population is believed to be quite large.

CASES

Case 6-1   Clip Joint, Inc.

(Estimated time to complete: 45 minutes)

Donna Marsh, senior internal auditor of Clip Joint, Inc., is concerned about the accuracy of the firm's inventory balance for the June 30 fiscal year-end. The inventory was counted without internal audit supervision. Donna wants to design a PPS sampling application that will give her 5 percent risk that inventory overstatement does not exceed $50,000. Clip Joint's final inventory summary shows a balance of $1,000,000. Because she expects a few misstatements in her recount work, Donna sets the adjusted tolerable misstatement for sample-size determination at $25,000.

    a. What is the needed sample size?

    b. Calculate $Max_{o/s}$ given that she observed the following misstatements:

	Book	**Audit**
No. 1	$2000	$500
No. 2	1000	900
No. 3	3000	3350

    c. Calculate the most likely overstatement and the most likely understatement misstatements.

    d. Calculate *Net Max$_{o/s}$*.

    e. Write a suitable conclusion for Donna's workpapers.

Case 6-2   Roll Tide*

(Estimated time to complete: 30 minutes)

Mike Edwards has decided to use PPS sampling, sometimes called dollar-unit sampling, in the audit of Roll Tide's accounts receivable balance. Few, if any, misstatements of account balance overstatement are expected.

Edwards plans to use the PPS sampling test (see Table 6.1).

    a. Identify the advantages of probability-proportional-to-size sampling over classical variables sampling.

    b. Calculate the sampling interval and the sample size Edwards should use given the following information:

Tolerable misstatement $15,000
Risk of incorrect acceptance 5%

*AICPA adapted, except requirements D-F

Number of misstatements allowed 0
Recorded amount of accounts receivable $300,000
Note: Requirements (b) and (c) are *not* related.

c. Calculate the total projected misstatement if the following three misstatements were discovered in a probability-proportional-to-size sample:

	Recorded Amount	*Audit Amount*	*Sampling Interval*
1st error	$400	$320	$5,000
2nd error	500	0	5,000
3rd error	3,000	2,500	5,000

d. If no misstatements were found, what could the auditor conclude?

e. Calculate the upper limit on misstatements (*Max*) based on the results in (c), above, assuming that the specifications in (b) apply.

f. Calculate (b) and (c), from previous page, assuming that a 15 percent risk of incorrect acceptance was appropriate.

Case 6-3   Wagner's Appliance Company

(Estimated time to complete: 30 minutes)

An internal auditor for Wagner's Appliance Company used dollar-unit sampling in an audit of a perpetual inventory balance. The book value of the inventory was $20,000,000.

The internal auditor tested the account balance at a 5 percent risk of incorrect acceptance.

a. List three advantages and three disadvantages of using dollar-unit sampling techniques.

b. Determine the appropriate sample size and sampling interval for a tolerable misstatement of $1,500,000 assuming zero misstatements are expected.

c. Assuming a sample size of 50, calculate the projected total misstatement if the following errors were found:

Inventory Amount	*Audited Amount*	*Error ÷ Inventory amount*
$ 800	$ 400	0.5
$2,200	$1,760	0.2

Case 6-4   Bell & Tyler, Inc.

(Estimated time to complete: 35 minutes)

Howard March has decided to use probability-proportional-to-size sampling to test the valuation of accounts receivable Bell & Tyler, Inc. The receivables consist of 850 accounts with a total recorded value of $500,000. Howard has determined the following:

Tolerable misstatement $25,000
Risk of incorrect acceptance 5%
Expected misstatement $2,000

a. Calculate the required sample size.

b. Calculate the sampling interval.

Assume that after testing accounts, Howard encountered the following results:

Recorded Amount	Audited Amount
$ 50	$ 47
800	760
8,500	8,100

c. Calculate projected misstatement.

d. Calculate the upper limit on misstatements *(Max)*.

e. Explain how Howard should consider the results calculated in *d*, above.

Case 6-5   Carter & Warren, Inc.

(Estimated time to complete: 35 minutes)

You are planning the audit of Carter & Warren, Inc., for the year ended December 31, 200X. You are using probability-proportional-to-size sampling for the confirmation of accounts receivable and price testing of inventory, and you have assessed materiality at the financial statement level as $500,000. The book balances of the two accounts are presented below:

Accounts receivable	$12,500,000
Inventory	18,300,000

a. Determine the sample size for the test of accounts receivable, assuming that you have specified a risk of incorrect acceptance of 5%, and estimate the amount of misstatement in the account to be $20,000.

b. Determine the sample size for the test of inventory, assuming that you have specified a risk of incorrect acceptance of 10%, and estimate the amount of misstatement in the account to be $30,000.

c. Assume that in your confirmation of accounts receivable you find the following misstatements:

	Book Value	Audited Value
1st error	$12,500	$10,500
2nd error	500	0

Calculate the projected misstatement and the upper limit on misstatements (*MAX*).

7 NONSTATISTICAL AUDIT SAMPLING

LEARNING OBJECTIVES

After a careful study and discussion of this chapter, you will be able to:

1. Identify the requirements that apply to all audit samples, statistical or nonstatistical.
2. Describe the primary differences between statistical and nonstatistical audit sampling.
3. List the relative advantages of nonstatistical audit sampling.
4. Distinguish formal from informal nonstatistical audit sampling plans.
5. List the relative advantages of a formal over an informal nonstatistical audit sampling plan.
6. Use a formal approach to the planning and evaluation of a nonstatistical audit sample.

This chapter explains nonstatistical sampling. Statistical and nonstatistical sampling are not entirely separate subjects. SAS No. 39 (AU 350), *Audit Sampling,* applies equally to statistical and nonstatistical sampling. SAS No. 39 takes the viewpoint that there is an underlying rationale for sampling in auditing that is applicable whether the sampling approach is statistical or nonstatistical.

All audit samples, statistical or nonstatistical, must meet the following requirements:

- Selection of a sample that is expected to be representative.
- Determination of sample size based on a consideration of tolerable misstatement or rate, sampling risk, and population characteristics.
- Projection of sample results and consideration of sampling risk.

In other words, the same basic requirements for sample selection, planning, and evaluation apply whether the approach to audit sampling is statistical or nonstatistical.

HOW DOES STATISTICAL SAMPLING DIFFER FROM NONSTATISTICAL SAMPLING?

Nonstatistical sampling does not have the same level of mathematical rigor as statistical sampling. It uses approximations and rules of thumb rather than the stricter requirements of statistical plans. However, the objectives and requirements of audit sampling remain the same whether a statistical or nonstatistical approach is taken so there are many similarities between the two approaches.

Statistical sampling, as explained in Chapter 1, has the following essential features:

- Sample items should have a known probability of selection (e.g., selected randomly).
- Sample results should be evaluated mathematically, that is, in accordance with probability theory.

When a nonstatistical sampling approach is followed, adherence to these two essential features may be relaxed but must still meet the requirements of SAS No. 39 concerning sample selection, planning, and evaluation. Figure 7.1 summarizes the key differences between statistical and nonstatistical sampling.

Selecting a Nonstatistical Sample

For *selection* of an audit sample, SAS No. 39 (AU 350.24) requires that "sample items should be selected in such a way that the sample can be expected to be representative of the population." The random-based selection methods explained in Chapter 2 are one means of obtaining representative samples. When using statistical

	Selection	*Evaluation*
Statistical	Random-Based Method Only	Mathematical Consideration of Sampling Risk
Nonstatistical	Haphazard, Random-Based, or Approximation of Random-Based	Judgmental Consideration of Sampling Risk

FIGURE 7.1　**Distinctions between Statistical and Nonstatistical Sampling**

sampling, use of one of these random-based methods is required. When nonstatistical sampling is used, it is not essential to use one of the random-based methods, but use of a random-based method is permissible. In other words, use of a random-based method is a necessary but not sufficient condition for statistical sampling. Thus, using a random-based selection method does not by itself make an audit sampling application a statistical sample.

The key point is that for a nonstatistical sample, it is also permissible to use a less rigorous selection method. One of these methods, called *haphazard* selection, was explained in Chapter 2. Using haphazard selection, the user selects sampling units without any conscious bias, that is, without any special reason for including or omitting items from the sample. The haphazard selection method does not mean careless selection. In fact, due care must be exercised to avoid bias in selection. The difference from statistical sampling is that the sampling units need not have a known probability of selection. The auditor avoids bias judgmentally by avoiding selection according to some obvious characteristic such as nature, size, appearance, or location.

For example, selecting all items above a certain dollar amount (say, all plant and equipment asset additions over $5000) does not meet the requirements for representative selection. This audit approach is *not* sampling. When the auditor takes this approach, he or she is in effect dividing additions to plant and equipment assets into two populations and selecting 100 percent of one of those populations. This approach is common in auditing practice, but it should not be confused with sampling.

When using a nonstatistical sampling selection method, it is advisable to increase the sample size to compensate for the less rigorous selection method. In practice, auditors increase sample size anywhere from 20 to 100 percent to compensate for the potential bias that may be introduced by using an approach other than random-based selection.

Evaluation of a Nonstatistical Sample

For *evaluation* of audit sample results, SAS No. 39 (AU 350) requires that the auditor project sample results to the items from which the sample was selected and give appropriate consideration to sampling risk. The requirement to project sample results has to be met by some form of quantitative analysis *whether a statistical or a nonstatistical approach is used.* The key difference between statistical and nonstatistical sampling is the way in which sampling risk is considered. When statistical sampling is used, the consideration of sampling risk is accomplished by quantitative analysis. The auditor, for example, computes an upper limit on the dollar amount of overstatement or the rate of deviations at the specified level of sampling risk. In contrast, when nonstatistical sampling is used, consideration of sampling risk is judgmental.

WHY USE NONSTATISTICAL AUDIT SAMPLING?

Because nonstatistical sampling is less rigorous than statistical sampling, the question naturally arises: "Why would an auditor use a less rigorous method?" SAS No. 31 (AU 326.21), *Evidential Matter,* notes that "an auditor typically works within economic limits; his or her opinion, to be economically useful, must be formed within a reasonable length of time and at a reasonable cost." It goes on to point out that "there should be a rational relationship between the cost of obtaining evidence and the usefulness of the information obtained." Thus, nonstatistical sampling is used because it is often less costly and time-consuming to apply than statistical sampling, but can be as effective in achieving audit objectives. Reasons cited for this are as follows:

- *Lower Training Costs.* It usually takes less time to learn to apply nonstatistical sampling approaches, and this results in lower training costs.
- *Ease of Implementation.* Because nonstatistical approaches are less complex, they are generally easier and quicker to apply in the field. Also, the reduced complexity makes it less likely that the methods will be misapplied by audit staff.
- *Impracticality of Random-Based Selection.* In some cases it is not practical or not economically feasible to apply random-based selection. A population of source documents may be large and unnumbered. Inventory items on the plant floor may have to be selected for counting before a price list is available.
- *Proposed Adjustment Based on Qualitative Analysis.* The increased precision of a statistical estimate is often not needed because the proposed audit adjustment is based on the auditor's qualitative analysis of sample results rather than a mathematical calculation.

SAS No. 39 (AU 350) requires that in addition to the evaluation of the frequency and amounts of monetary misstatements and the frequency of deviations from pertinent control procedures, the auditor should consider the qualitative aspects of sample results. By considering the nature and cause of misstatements or deviations and the possible relationships to other phases of the audit, the auditor is often able to identify additional misstatements. The auditor uses qualitative analysis to identify the items likely to be misstated and then applies procedures specifically to those items. In some cases, the procedures may be performed by client personnel with the auditor's supervision and review. For example, the auditor's qualitative analysis of misstatements in plant and equipment asset additions may indicate mistakes in the allocation of indirect costs for self-constructed assets. Instead of proposing an adjustment for all plant and equipment asset additions based on sample results, the auditor takes the approach of testing more of the additions that are self-constructed assets. As a result, the auditor detects more known misstatements that are corrected.

This use of qualitative analysis rather than quantification of sample results to propose an adjustment is often the most efficient and effective approach. Even when statistical sampling is used, in the interest of audit efficiency, the auditor may use sample sizes that are not large enough to reliably estimate the amount of misstatement. The sample results are used to identify situations in which the risk of material misstatement is unacceptably large. Once the situation is identified, the auditor relies on qualitative analysis to determine a proposed adjustment. Also, as explained at the end of Chapter 5 in the section "Proposing a Statistical Adjustment," when sample results are used to calculate an adjustment, the statistical method only produces a range of acceptable book adjustments. For these reasons, the ability to quantitatively evaluate sampling risk provided by statistical sampling may not be a cost-beneficial advantage in many audit sampling applications.

WHAT IS A "FORMAL" NONSTATISTICAL SAMPLING PLAN?

Nonstatistical sampling plans can be formal or informal. A **formal nonstatistical sampling plan** uses a structured approach to calculate sample size and evaluate sample results. The methods of sample-size calculation and sample results evaluation are based on the underlying mathematics of a statistical plan, but the selection of sample items and consideration of sampling risk are normally less rigorous than the statistical plan.

Many formal nonstatistical sampling plans use the underlying mathematics of sequential sampling for attribute sampling plans and probability-proportional-to-size (PPS) sampling for variables sampling plans. Recall that these plans use the same underlying sampling distribution (sampling table) as depicted in Table 3.6. These plans are not based on normal distribution theory, and, thus, the mathematics are simpler. A formal nonstatistical plan based on these statistical plans uses the same equation to compute sample size as the statistical plans. Differences from the statistical plans are largely confined to a relaxation of the requirements for sample selection and evaluation. Use of a formal nonstatistical sampling plan is illustrated later in this chapter.

An **informal nonstatistical sampling plan** is essentially an unstructured approach to determination of sample size and evaluation of sample results. The auditor must meet the same requirements of SAS No. 39 (AU 350), but the approach is entirely qualitative. For example, an auditor determining the sample size for a substantive test must consider tolerable misstatement, sampling risk, and population characteristics. An auditor using a statistical plan or formal nonstatistical plan explicitly considers these factors in a computation of sample size. An auditor using an informal nonstatistical approach considers these factors qualitatively. The auditor knows that a decrease in tolerable misstatement increases sample size, but has to determine the amount of the increase without the quantitative aid of an equation or table.

WHY USE A FORMAL NONSTATISTICAL SAMPLING APPROACH?

SAS No. 39 (AU 350) mandates use of neither statistical sampling nor a formal nonstatistical sampling plan. Why would an auditor decide to adopt a formal rather than an informal approach to audit sampling? The following disadvantages are typically suggested for an informal approach:

- *Training Difficulties.* There is essentially no systematic way to train staff in the informal approach. Only through experience can an auditor gain some sense of the qualitative relationships among sample size and the factors that SAS No. 39 (AU 350) requires to be considered.

- *Absence of Consistency and Uniformity.* An auditor using an equation to determine sample size, given the same tolerable misstatement and sampling risk, will determine the same sample size as another auditor. Professional judgments about tolerable misstatement may differ, but there will be no difference in the effect of tolerable misstatement on sample size. In contrast, use of an informal approach means that auditors faced with the same, or very similar, circumstances may reach significantly different judgments about the scope of audit work that is necessary. Greater consistency and uniformity results in more reliable audit time budget and fee estimates.

- *Peer Review Exceptions.* When one CPA firm makes a peer review of another firm to assess compliance with quality control policies and procedures, a lack of documentation of compliance with SASs can result in an exception. When an informal sampling approach is used, the workpapers may not contain sufficient information to demonstrate compliance with SAS No. 39 (AU 350) requirements that apply to all audit samples.

- *Misevaluation of Sampling Risk.* Because the approach to sample results evaluation is unstructured, there is a greater likelihood that the informal approach will result in failing to recognize unacceptable sampling risk.

In practice, some auditors using an informal approach to audit sampling still use sample sizes of 5 to 10 without considering the enormous sampling risk associated with samples of that size. For example, with a sample size of 5, the sample results may indicate no misstatements or deviations, but the upper limit on the rate of misstatement or deviation at a 5 percent sampling risk would be 60 percent. In other words, up to 60 percent of the untested items in the population may be misstated or contain deviations.

ILLUSTRATION OF A FORMAL APPROACH TO NONSTATISTICAL SAMPLING[1]

The following discussion provides a comprehensive illustration of the use of a formal approach to nonstatistical sampling in planning and performing a substantive test.

Preliminary Judgment about Materiality

As described in Chapter 5, an essential first step in planning substantive tests is to make a preliminary judgment about the amount that will be considered material to the financial statements taken as a whole.

Developing a Rule of Thumb

In using a formal approach to nonstatistical sampling, the auditor will often use a rule of thumb to determine materiality. As discussed in Chapter 5, a usable rule of thumb for making a preliminary judgment about materiality requires specification of a base and a related percentage. Common bases used in practice are income before taxes, total revenue, and total assets. Total revenue and total assets generally are considered more stable and predictable. Obtaining the base amount from the financial statements is, of course, preferable, but if these amounts are unavailable or if significant audit adjustments are expected, estimating annual data from interim information or historical averages may be appropriate.

Common percentages applied to these bases are 5 to 10 percent of income before taxes and 0.5 to 2 of total revenue or total assets. Factors that influence the choice of the percentage include, but are not limited to, the size of the company (generally, the smaller the company, the larger the percentage) and the use that will be made of the financial statements. For example, 15 or 20 percent of income before taxes may be an appropriate measure of materiality of a small nonpublic company that is closely held and has no outstanding debt.

Illustration of Planning Materiality

The auditor is planning the audit of the financial statements of EZS Company with the following selected financial data:

Total revenue	$11,675,000
Total assets	9,850,000
Income before taxes	910,000

---

[1]Adapted from W. Wade Gafford and D. R. C., Michael, "Materiality, Audit Risk and Sumpling: A Nuts-and-Bolts Approach." *Journal of Accountancy* (October 1984 and November 1984).

The auditor is using a flexible rule of thumb that permits choice of a base dependent on the auditor's judgment in the circumstances. Total revenue is selected as the base, and the auditor uses approximately 1 percent of that base. In this instance, the auditor's judgment about materiality for planning purposes is $115,000.

Relating the Preliminary Judgment to Specific Substantive Tests

Once the auditor has made a preliminary judgment about the amount considered material to the financial statements taken as a whole (planning materiality), that amount needs to be related to specific substantive tests. The amount to be used in planning audit procedures for sampling applications is the basic allowance for potential undetected misstatement. It is obtained by making initial and additional reductions from planning materiality.

Initial Reduction from Planning Materiality

Planning materiality should be reduced for an estimate of misstatements that the auditor (1) expects to detect through audit procedures other than sampling applications, and (2) anticipates the client will not correct. If the auditor knows that, at the conclusion of the engagement, the financial statements will be affected by detected misstatements that the client will not agree to correct, this reduces the allowance available for undetected misstatements. Planning materiality reduced by this amount may be called adjusted planning materiality.

Additional Reductions from Planning Materiality

This sampling approach requires additional reductions from adjusted planning materiality. The auditor's objective is to estimate an amount that will be the basic allowance for potential undetected misstatement that stems from an imprecision resulting from sampling. This basic allowance is essentially the equivalent of the basic bound—that is, the upper limit on monetary misstatement achieved when no misstatements are detected—in a statistical PPS sampling plan. In Chapter 6, the basic allowance is referred to as adjusted tolerable misstatement.

To estimate this basic allowance, adjusted planning materiality is reduced by

- Projected misstatements in all populations expected to be sampled.
- The anticipated increase in imprecision.

Some auditors introduce additional conservatism by also reducing adjusted planning materiality for a judgmentally determined cushion to allow for the fact that reductions made in the planning stage are estimates.

Often, projected misstatements in sampled populations are not corrected; only the actual misstatements detected in sampled items are adjusted. Thus, to determine the basic allowance, adjusted planning materiality should be reduced by the projected misstatement that is anticipated for all populations sampled.

Also, when misstatements are detected in sample items, part of the adjusted planning materiality is, in effect, used up by the additional imprecision. Detected misstatements are extrapolated to the population to determine projected misstatement; however, because the projection is based on a sample, it cannot be a precise estimate of the amount of misstatement. Thus, when determining the basic allowance, an allowance for additional imprecision is estimated and deducted from adjusted planning materiality.

Illustration of Allowance for Undetected Misstatement

Based on knowledge of the nature and amount of misstatements detected in previous audits of EZS Company, the auditor anticipates $15,000 of known misstatement to be detected in the current audit that the client will resist correcting. (The auditor expects $10,000 of misstatement in accounting estimates and $5000 of misstatement in items that will be examined 100 percent.) Adjusted planning materiality is, thus, $100,000 ($115,000 − $15,000).

The auditor has concluded that sampling will be used in two areas in the current audit: inventories, and property and equipment. The recorded amounts of the relevant accounting populations are:

Inventories	$1,440,000
Additions to property and equipment	$1,030,000

Based on past experience, the auditor expects a projected misstatement of $10,000 of overstatement in the two accounting populations. The additional reduction for imprecision is estimated at an additional $10,000. The auditor decides to allow for an additional cushion of $5000 because of the difficulty of estimating misstatements. The auditor next establishes a basic allowance of $75,000, computed as follows:

Planning materiality	$115,000
Reduction for anticipated uncorrected known misstatement from nonsampling tests	(15,000)
Adjusted planning materiality	$100,000
Reduction for expected projected misstatement in sampling applications	(10,000)
Reduction for additional imprecision	(10,000)
Cushion for above estimates	(5,000)
Basic allowance (basic bound)	$75,000

Using the Basic Allowance

The basic allowance is used in essentially two ways in planning the extent of substantive tests:

1. To determine a dollar-amount cut-off for items that are individually significant because of their size.
2. To calculate sample size for sampling applications.

Individually Significant Amounts

In examining a specific population, the auditor will want to apply the planned audit procedure to all items that are individually significant. The auditor is unwilling to accept any risk of failing to detect misstatement for these items. An item may be individually significant because of its nature or its amount. Examples of items that may be individually significant because of their nature are unusual or unexpected names of suppliers or customers for items recorded in a particular account.

To determine the cut-off amount for individually significant items, the general rule of thumb is to divide the basic allowance by 3. All items equal to or larger than this amount are examined. Dividing by 3 is based on the sampling theory of a PPS statistical plan. Essentially, if all items in the financial statements equal to this amount are considered a single population, use of the PPS sample size formula (at a 5 percent sampling risk level) indicates a sample size equal to the number of items in that population.

Illustration of Individually Significant Amounts

The auditor uses the $75,000 basic allowance to establish a cut-off amount of $25,000 ($75,000/3) for individually significant amounts. The auditor will examine all inventory items (price testing and extensions) and all property additions that are $25,000 or more.

Scanning the lists for these two populations, the auditor selects items that are greater than the $25,000 cut-off. These items total $140,000 for inventory and $130,000 for property and equipment. All selected items will be examined. The remaining populations, computed below, will be sampled.

Inventories	$1,440,000
Individually significant items	(140,000)
Remaining population	$1,300,000
Property and equipment additions	$1,030,000
Individually significant items	(130,000)
Remaining population	$ 900,000

Calculating Sample Size

The basic allowance is used to calculate sample size in all sampling applications. It should be noted that the basic allowance does not have to be allocated to account balances. The only time allocation is required is when a classical statistical sampling plan is used; these are the variable sampling methods explained in Chapter 5.[2] A PPS statistical plan or a nonstatistical plan based on PPS theory allows use of the same basic allowance for all sampling applications. The financial statements may be viewed as one population, and the basic allowance for undetected misstatement applies to the financial statements taken as a whole.

Sample size for a specific substantive test is calculated as follows:

$$\frac{\text{Sample}}{\text{size}} = \frac{\text{Remaining population recorded amount}}{\text{Basic allowance}} \cdot \frac{\text{Risk}}{\text{factor}}$$

Illustration of Sample-Size Determination

The basic allowance is $75,000, and the remaining population recorded amount for inventory is $1,300,000. Solely for the purpose of illustration, a risk factor of 3 is used to determine sample size. Determining the appropriate risk factor is explained in the next section. Risk factors is in the approach under discussion may vary from 3 to 1, depending on the auditor's assessment of matters explained in the next section. Sample size for inventory, assuming a maximum risk factor of 3, is determined as follows:[3]

$$\frac{\text{Sample}}{\text{size}} = \frac{\$1,300,000}{\$75,000} \cdot 3 = 52$$

Establishing Detection Risk for a Specific Substantive Test

For specific substantive test, detection risk is the risk of failing to detect an amount of misstatement that would be material to the financial statements for that test. As discussed in Chapter 5, detection risk may be established by assessing the following risks:

1. *Inherent risk*—the risk of material misstatement occurring considered independent of controls.

---

[2]For an explanation of the way in which materiality is allocated to accounts when using variable sampling methods, see G. R. Zuber, R. K. Elliott, W. R. Kinney, Jr., and James J. Leisenring, "Using Materiality in Audit Planning," *Journal of Accountancy* (March 1983), pp. 42–54.

[3]This is the same equation used for a PPS plan explained in Chapter 6. In symbols, it is

$$n = \frac{BV \cdot M_0}{TE'}$$

2. *Control risk*—the risk that control policies and procedures will fail to prevent or detect material misstatement.

3. *Detection risk for related procedures*—the risk that other related audit procedures such as analytical procedures will fail to detect material misstatement.

Objective of Risk Assessment

The auditor's objective in assessing these risks is to establish a detection risk for a specific substantive test that will hold the audit, or overall, risk for reaching a conclusion that the population is not materially misstated when it is materially misstated, at a relatively low level. Audit risk is the result of combining inherent, control, and detection risk. Quantified, the desired audit risk may be 5 percent.

One approach to determining the detection risk for a substantive sample is introduced in the appendix to Statement on Auditing Standards No. 39 (AU 350), *Audit Sampling*, as is explained in Chapter 5. Another approach to the audit risk model is presented here in a table that relates qualitative categories for component risks to a factor used in the sample-size equation. For example, the auditor may decide that control risk is assessed as maximum, slightly below maximum, moderate, or low.

After similar qualitative categories are established for the other risks. the appropriate risk factors are assigned to these qualitative assessments. For example, if inherent risk and control risk are at the maximum and no other relevant auditing procedures are applied, the appropriate risk factor is 3. This means that the auditor's sole source of evidence for reaching a conclusion on the account balance is the substantive test being applied using sampling. Of course, the detection risk in this case is the sole determinant of audit risk and should be relatively low or, in quantitative terms, say, 5 percent.

The risk factors to be used in determining sample size appear in the rows and columns of the body of the table:

Assessment of Control Risk (and Inherent Risk)	*Reliance on Other Relevant Auditing Procedures[a]*			
	None	*Little*	*Moderate*	*Substantial*
Maximum	3.0	2.7	2.3	2.0
Slightly below maximum	2.7	2.4	2.0	1.6
Moderate	2.3	2.1	1.6	1.2
Low	2.0	1.6	1.2	1.0

[a]Other relevant auditing procedures include analytical procedures or other tests of details directed to the same audit objective as the substantive test being applied using sampling.

Based on this table, for example, if moderate reliance is placed on other relevant procedures and control risk is assessed as moderate, the sample-size factor to be used in the equation is 1.6. If little reliance is placed on other procedures and control risk is assessed as moderate, the table indicates a factor of 2.1.

Illustration of Risk Assessment

The auditor assesses control risk as moderate for inventory pricing and extension, and believes that other relevant auditing procedures, including comparison of gross margin by product and location on a month-by-month basis, are moderately effective. Using the preceding table, the auditor identifies a risk factor of 1.6 to determine sample size for the inventory sampling application as follows:

$$\text{Sample size} = \frac{\$1,300,000}{\$75,000} \cdot 1.6 = 28$$

The auditor concludes that substantial reliance is possible on other relevant audit procedures for property and equipment additions and assesses control risk as low. Thus, the appropriate risk factor is 1.0, and sample size is determined as follows:

$$\text{Sample size} = \frac{\$900,000}{\$75,000} \cdot 1.0 = 12$$

Sample Selection

Because sample-size determination is based on PPS sampling theory, the auditor may use the PPS selection method explained in Chapters 2 and 6 or a method that approximates PPS selection. If a less rigorous selection technique is used, the auditor should compensate by increasing the sample size computed. There is no specific percentage of increase that can be considered "correct." As mentioned earlier, practice among accounting firms varies from 20 to 100 percent. We believe that 20 percent normally is adequate, but the auditor may choose to vary the increase according to the circumstances.

Evaluating Sample Results

When the auditor detects misstatements in selected items, two separate evaluations should be made: qualitative and quantitative. The qualitative evaluation involves investigating the cause of misstatements. Investigation of the cause of misstatements may lead the auditor to (1) apply additional procedures; (2) revise his or her judgments about internal control or the effectiveness of analytical procedures; or (3) take other actions as the circumstances dictate.

The quantitative evaluation involves projecting the misstatements to determine how much misstatement the remaining population is likely to contain. The projection method recommended here is based on PPS sampling theory and recognizes that larger items are selected more often than smaller items. Each misstatement is evaluated using the percentage of misstatement occurring—the so-called misstatement proportion.

The misstatement proportion is calculated by dividing the misstatement amount by the recorded amount. For example, if a $100 item (recorded amount) is misstated by $10 (audit value $90), the misstatement proportion is 10 percent. The projected misstatement is calculated by summing the misstatement proportions, multiplying by the dollar amount of the remaining population, and dividing by the sample size, as shown in the following formula:

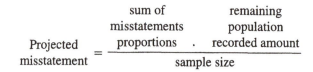

$$
\frac{\text{Projected}}{\text{misstatement}} = \frac{\begin{array}{c}\text{sum of}\\ \text{misstatements}\\ \text{proportions}\end{array} \cdot \begin{array}{c}\text{remaining}\\ \text{population}\\ \text{recorded amount}\end{array}}{\text{sample size}}
$$

After the auditor has determined the projected misstatement for the remaining population, it is compared to the estimate of projected misstatement for the entire engagement. If this amount exceeds the projected misstatement used in planning or is a greater portion of it than the auditor will be able to tolerate when the results of all audit tests are combined, an alternative strategy should be developed.

Illustration of Misstatement Evaluation

In testing inventory prices and extensions, the auditor detects the following misstatements and computes the sum of proportions as follows:

Sample Items That Contain Misstatements			
Recorded Amount	*Audited Amount*	*Misstatement Amount*	*Misstatement Proportion*
10,530	10,310	220	.02
5,740	4,018	1,722	.30
3,114	3,425	(311)	(.10)
			.22

Using the previously stated equation, the auditor calculates projected misstatement for inventory pricing as follows:

$$\begin{array}{c}\text{Projected}\\\text{misstatement}\end{array} = \frac{0.22 \times \$1,300,000}{28} = \$10,214$$

The auditor finds no misstatements in testing the property and equipment additions. (If misstatements had been detected, the auditor would need to project the misstatement, make a qualitative assessment of its nature and cause, and reevaluate whether the planned control risk assessment and reliance on other procedures were appropriate.) A qualitative assessment of inventory pricing misstatements was made that did not cause the auditor to reevaluate the risk assessments made in planning.

The auditor should consider the sample results in combination with the other information obtained in the remainder of the audit and combine the results of all audit tests.

USE OF NONSTATISTICAL SAMPLING FOR TESTS OF CONTROLS

As mentioned earlier, formal nonstatistical sampling plans for tests of controls are often based on the sequential sampling statistical plan. There is generally some relaxation of the requirements for sample selection and evaluation as there is for nonstatistical substantive audit sampling.

A common approach is to select a convenient sample size such as 25 and use it for all tests of controls that involve audit sampling. Usually, the decision to follow this approach is made as a matter of CPA firm policy. Use of the same sample size for all tests-of-controls sampling applications avoids the use of tables and other complexities.

A sample size of 25 for a test of controls assumes a risk of assessing control risk too low of approximately 10 percent and no expected deviations. When deviations are detected in sample results, control risk is assessed at the maximum and a primarily substantive approach is taken to substantive testing.

SUMMARY

This chapter explains nonstatistical sampling. SAS No. 39 (AU 350) imposes the same basic requirements for sample selection, planning, and evaluation whether the approach to audit sampling is statistical or nonstatistical. Nonstatistical sampling does not have the same level of mathematical rigor as statistical sampling. The primary differences between statistical sampling and nonstatistical sampling are related to the fact that nonstatistical sampling relaxes the requirements for sample selection and evaluation. Sample selection does not require the use of a random-based selection method as long as the method results in a sample that the auditor believes is representative. Sample evaluation does not require a quantification of sampling risk as long as sample results are projected and sampling risk is considered qualitatively. Nonstatistical sampling is used rather than statistical sampling because it is often less costly and time consuming, but can be as effective in achieving audit objectives.

Nonstatistical sampling plans can be formal or informal. A formal nonstatistical plan uses a structured approach to calculate sample size and evaluate sample results. Many formal nonstatistical sampling plans use the underlying mathematics of sequential sampling for tests of controls and PPS sampling for substantive tests. A formal nonstatistical approach to audit sampling has several advantages over an informal approach, including greater uniformity in practice and less chance of misevaluation of sampling risk.

GLOSSARY

Formal nonstatistical sampling plan   An approach to audit sampling that is based on the underlying mathematics of statistical sampling, but relaxes the requirements for random selection and mathematical evaluation of sampling risk.

Informal nonstatistical sampling plan   An approach to audit sampling that uses an unstructured approach to determination of sample size and evaluation of sample results.

REVIEW QUESTIONS

7-1. Indicate whether each of the following is true (T) or false (F).

    a. SAS No. 39 (AU 350) requires that all audit samples—statistical or nonstatistical—must be selected using a random-based selection method.

    b. Using a nonstatistical sampling approach, the auditor does not have to project sample results to the population.

    c. The key difference between statistical and nonstatistical sampling is that an auditor using the nonstatistical approach considers sampling risk qualitatively.

    d. The increased precision of a statistical estimate is often not needed to propose an audit adjustment based on sample results.

    e. When a formal approach to nonstatistical audit sampling is used, the determination of sample size is usually made using the same equation as a statistical sample.

    f. A qualitative analysis of sample results is not important when a statistical sampling plan is used.

    g. An informal nonstatistical audit sampling approach is less likely to result in peer review comments about deficiencies because the calculation of sample size cannot be miscomputed.

7-2. Compare and contrast the formal approach to nonstatistical sampling explained in this chapter with statistical PPS sampling. How do the approaches differ? In what respects are they the same?

7-3. An auditor has analyzed additions to property and equipment for the year as follows:

Number of Additions	Range	Dollar Amount
5	Above $20,000	$190,000
20	1000 to 19,999	60,000
25		$250,000

The auditor plans to substantiate all the additions above $20,000 and rely on analytical procedures for the remaining amount.

    a. Is this audit approach acceptable?

    b. Is any detection risk associated with this approach?

    c. Is any sampling risk associated with this approach?

7-4. You are planning an audit sample for confirmation of accounts receivable. The aged trial balance of receivables after removal of individually significant items has a remaining population of $1,000,000.

    Assume that you have concluded that a tolerable misstatement of $50,000* is appropriate in the circumstances and that you believe moderate reliance on analytical procedures is appropriate and control risk should be assessed as moderate.

    a. What sample size would you use for confirmation of accounts receivable?

    b. How would you decide the degree of reliance that was appropriate for other relevant auditing procedures such as analytical procedures and the assessed level of control risk?

7-5. Explain the differences between statistical and nonstatistical sampling.

7-6. Why would an auditor decide to use nonstatistical sampling rather than statistical sampling?

7-7. How does a formal nonstatistical sampling plan differ from an informal one?

---

*For convenience and ease of computation, assume that tolerable misstatement and the basic allowance are equal.

7-8. Why would an auditor decide to use a formal nonstatistical sampling plan rather than an informal one?

7-9. What sample selection methods may be used when performing a nonstatistical audit sampling application?

CASES

Case 7-1 Nonstatistical, Inc.

(Estimated time to complete: 25 minutes)

You are examining additions to property and equipment for the year using a formal nonstatistical approximation of the PPS statistical method. The population recorded amount is $1,000,000, and you believe a tolerable misstatement of $25,000* is appropriate. You have concluded that "moderate" reliance on other related substantive procedures is justified and that control risk should be assessed as slightly below maximum.

a. In determining the remaining population recorded amount, what dollar cut-off would be a reasonable amount for identifying individually significant additions?

b. Assume that there are ten additions above the cut-off amount that total $200,000. What sample size is appropriate?

c. Assume that after vouching the additions, you found misstatements in two items as follows:

Recorded Amount	Audited Amount
$5000	$4000
2000	3000

What is the projected monetary misstatement based on your sample?

Case 7-2 Landi Corporation

(Estimated time to complete: 25 minutes)

The auditors of Landi Corporation wish to use a structured approach to nonstatistical sampling to evaluate the reasonableness of the accounts receivable. Landi has

---

*For convenience and ease of computation, assume that tolerable misstatement and the basic allowance are equal.

15,000 receivable accounts with a total book value of $2,500,000. The auditors have assessed the combined level of inherent and control risk at a moderate level, and believe that their other substantive procedures are so limited as to require a "maximum" risk assessment. After considering the overall audit plan, the auditors believe that the account's tolerable misstatement is $57,500.*

a. Calculate the required sample size.

b. Assuming the following results:

Number of items in sample		100

Two misstatements:	*Recorded Amount*	*Audited Amount*
	$8,000	6,000
	$5,000	4,000

Calculate the projected misstatements.

c. Use the results in (b) to arrive at a conclusion as to whether or not to accept the account as being materially correct. Assume that in determining the tolerable misstatement the auditors estimated the projected misstatement of accounts receivable to be $20,000.

Case 7-3   Ryan Corporation

(Estimated time to complete: 25 minutes)

Assume you are testing the valuation of accounts receivable in the audit of Ryan Corporation. The client has $1,000,000 of total recorded receivables, composed of 2,000 accounts. You have decided to use structured nonstatistical sampling and have determined the following:

Tolerable misstatement	$50.000
Assessment of inherent and control risk	Moderate
Risk related to other substantive procedures	Moderate

a. Calculate the required sample size.

b. Assume that you have tested the sample and discovered three misstatements:

---

*For convenience and ease of computation, assume that tolerable misstatement and the basic allowance are equal.

Book Value	Audited Value
$100	$ 90
512	600
900	520

The remainder of the sample had an average value (book and audited) of $501.00. Calculate the projected misstatement of the population.

c. Use the results obtained in *b* to come to a conclusion as to whether to "accept" or "reject" the population

A APPENDIX A: CALCULATION WORKSHEETS

Worksheet No.	*Purpose*
1	Calculation of the estimated standard deviation
2	Stratified MPU—determination of sample size by the optimal allocation method
3	Stratified MPU—determination of achieved precision
4	Calculation of estimated standard deviation of differences

WORKSHEET 1   CALCULATION OF THE ESTIMATED STANDARD DEVIATION

$$\text{Standard deviation} = \sqrt{\frac{\sum\limits_{j=1}^{n} x_j^2 - n\bar{x}^2}{n-1}}$$

Step No.	Operation	Computation
1	Sample size	
2	Sum of each sample value	
3	Sum of squares of each sample value	
4	② ÷ ①	
5	① × ④ × ④	
6	③ − ⑤	
7	① − 1.0	
8	⑥ ÷ ⑦	
9	$\sqrt{⑧}$ (standard deviation)	

WORKSHEET 2   STRATIFIED MPU—DETERMINATION OF SAMPLE SIZE BY THE OPTIMAL ALLOCATION METHOD

$$n_1 = \frac{(N_i SD_i)(\Sigma N_i SD_1)}{(A/U_R)^2 + \Sigma N_i SD_i^2}$$

Step No.	Operation	Computation			
		Stratum 1	*Stratum 2*	*Stratum 3*	*Total*
1	Size of stratum				
2	Estimated standard deviation of each stratum (see Worksheet 1)				
3	Acceptable precision				
4	Reliability				
5	U_R based on ④				
6	③ ÷ ⑤				
7	⑥ × ⑥				
8	① × ②				
9	Crossfoot step ⑧				
10	⑨ × ⑧				
11	② × ⑧				
12	Crossfoot step ⑪				
13	⑦ + ⑫				
14	⑩ ÷ ⑬				

Caution:

If any stratum sample size (step 14) is greater than the size of stratum (step 1), set that stratum sample size equal to step 1 and recalculate the sample sizes for the remaining strata using this worksheet, after eliminating the "saturated" stratum. The saturated stratum is audited 100 percent.

WORKSHEET 3   STRATIFIED MPU—DETERMINATION OF ACHIEVED PRECISION

$$A' = U_R \sqrt{\Sigma \frac{N_i SD_i^2 (N_i - n_i)}{n_i}}$$

		Computation			
Step No.	*Operation*	*Stratum 1*	*Stratum 2*	*Stratum 3*	*Total*
1	Stratum size				
2	Stratum sample size				
3	Reliability				
4	Reliability factor (U_R)				
5	Stratum standard deviation (see Worksheet 1)				
6	① × ⑤				
7	⑤ × ⑥				
8	Crossfoot step ⑦				
9	⑦ ÷ ②				
10	⑨ × ①				
11	Crossfoot step ⑩				
12	⑪ − ⑧				
13	√ ⑫				
14	Achieved precision ④ × ⑬				

WORKSHEET 4   CALCULATION OF THE ESTIMATED STANDARD DEVIATION OF DIFFERENCES

$$SD_d = \sqrt{\frac{\Sigma d_i^2 - n\overline{d}}{n - 1}}$$

Step No.	Operation	Computation
1	Sample size	
2	Sum of differences	
3	Sum of squares of each difference	
4	② ÷ ①	
5	① × ④ × ④	
6	③ − ⑤	
7	① − 1.0	
8	⑥ ÷ ⑦	
9	$\sqrt{⑧}$	

B APPENDIX B: LIST OF EQUATIONS

1. Mean of a sample (see page 93)

$$\bar{x} = \frac{\Sigma x_j}{n}$$

2. Standard deviation of a sample (see page 94)

$$SD = \sqrt{\frac{\Sigma(x_j - \bar{x})^2}{n-1}} \quad \text{or} \quad SD = \sqrt{\frac{\Sigma x_j^2 - n\bar{x})^2}{n-1}}$$

3. Achieved precision—stratified MPU (see page 103)

$$A' = U_R \cdot SE \cdot N\sqrt{1 - (n/N)}$$

4. Achieved precision—stratified (MPU) (see page 108)

$$A' = U_R\sqrt{\Sigma \frac{N_i SD_i^2 (N_i - n_i)}{n_i}}$$

5. Acceptable precision for audit hypothesis test (see page 162)

$$A = TM \cdot \frac{U_R}{U_R + Z_{\text{beta}}}$$

6. Adjusted precision (A") (see page 159)

$$A'' = A' + TM\left(1 - \frac{A'}{A}\right)$$

7. Precision for proposing an adjustment (see page 170)

$$A''' = A'/U_R \times (1.96)$$

8. Standard error of the mean (see page 97)

$$SE = \frac{SD}{\sqrt{n}}$$

9. Unstratified MPU sample size with replacement (see page 100)

$$n' = \left(\frac{U_R \cdot SD \cdot N}{A} \right)^2$$

10. Unstratified MPU sample size without replacement (see page 100)

$$n = \frac{n'}{1 + (n'/N)}$$

11. Stratified MPU sample size (see page 108)

$$n_i = \frac{(N_i SD_i)(\Sigma N_i SD_i)}{(A/U_R)^2 + \Sigma N_i SD_i^2}$$

12. Estimated audit value (see page 103)

$$EV = \bar{x} \cdot N$$

13. Mean of sample differences (see page 110)

$$\bar{d} = \frac{\Sigma d_i}{n}$$

14. Estimated population differences (see page 111)

$$\hat{D} = N \cdot \bar{d}$$

15. Standard deviation of differences (see page 112)

$$SD_d = \sqrt{\frac{\Sigma d_i^2 - n\bar{d}^2}{n - 1}}$$

16. Audit risk (see page 150)

$$AR = IR \times CR \times AP \times TD_{\text{beta}}$$

17. Beta risk (see page 151)

$$TD \text{ (beta)} = \frac{AR}{CR \times AP}$$

18. PPS sample size (see page 206)

$$n = \frac{UML_0 \cdot BV}{TM - (\text{expected misstatement} \times \text{expansion factor})}$$

19. Tainting (see page 197)

$$t = \frac{\text{amount of misstatement}}{\text{reported book value of unit}}$$

20. Basic bound (see page 199)

$$\text{Basic bound} = BV \cdot \frac{UML_0}{n} \cdot 1$$

21. Most likely misstatement for overstatements (see page 207)

$$MLM_{o/s} = \frac{\text{sum of overstatement taintings}}{n} \cdot BV$$

22. Most likely misstatement for understatements (see page 207)

$$MLM_{u/s} = \frac{\text{sum of understatement taintings}}{n} \cdot BV$$

23. Net max overstatement (see page 207)

$$\text{Net Max}_{o/s} = \text{Max} - MLM_{u/s}$$

C APPENDIX C: SAS NO. 39— AUDIT SAMPLING (AU 350 AS AMENDED)

.01 Audit sampling is the application of an audit procedure to less than 100 percent of the items within an account balance or class of transactions for the purpose of evaluating some characteristic of the balance or class.[1] This section provides guidance for planning, performing, and evaluating audit samples.

.02 The auditor often is aware of account balances and transactions that may be more likely to contain misstatements.[2] He considers this knowledge in planning his procedures, including audit sampling. The auditor usually will have no special knowledge about other account balances and transactions that, in his judgment, will need to be tested to fulfill his audit objectives. Audit sampling is especially useful in these cases.

.03 There are two general approaches to audit sampling: nonstatistical and statistical. Both approaches require that the auditor use professional judgment in planning, performing, and evaluating a sample and in relating the evidential matter produced by the sample to other evidential matter when forming a conclusion about the related account balance or class of transactions. The guidance in this section applies equally to nonstatistical and statistical sampling.

---

[1]There may be other reasons for an auditor to examine less than 100 percent of the items comprising an account balance or class of transactions. For example, an auditor may examine only a few transactions from an account balance or class of transactions to (a) gain an understanding of the nature of an entity's operations or (b) clarify his understanding of the entity's internal control. In such cases, the guidance in this statement is not applicable.

[2]For purposes of this section the use of the term misstatement can include both those due to errors and fraud as appropriate for the design of the sampling application.

.04   The third standard of field work states, "Sufficient competent evidential matter is to be obtained through inspection, observation, inquiries, and confirmations to afford a reasonable basis for an opinion regarding the financial statements under audit." Either approach to audit sampling, when properly applied, can provide sufficient evidential matter.

.05   The sufficiency of evidential matter is related to the design and size of an audit sample, among other factors. The size of a sample necessary to provide sufficient evidential matter depends on both the objectives and the efficiency of the sample. For a given objective, the efficiency of the sample relates to its design; one sample is more efficient than another if it can achieve the same objectives with a smaller sample size. In general, careful design can produce more efficient samples.

.06   Evaluating the competence of evidential matter is solely a matter of auditing judgment and is not determined by the design and evaluation of an audit sample. In a strict sense, the sample evaluation relates only to the likelihood that existing monetary misstatements or deviations from prescribed controls are proportionately included in the sample, not to the auditor's treatment of such items. Thus, the choice of nonstatistical or statistical sampling does not directly affect the auditor's decisions about the auditing procedures to be applied, the competence of the evidential matter obtained with respect to individual items in the sample, or the actions that might be taken in light of the nature and cause of particular misstatements.

UNCERTAINTY AND AUDIT SAMPLING

.07   Some degree of uncertainty is implicit in the concept of "a reasonable basis for an opinion" referred to in the third standard of field work. The justification for accepting some uncertainty arises from the relationship between such factors as the cost and time required to examine all of the data and the adverse consequences of possible erroneous decisions based on the conclusions resulting from examining only a sample of the data. If these factors do not justify the acceptance of some uncertainty, the only alternative is to examine all of the data. Since this is seldom the case, the basic concept of sampling is well established in auditing practice.

.08   The uncertainty inherent in applying audit procedures is referred to as audit risk. Audit risk consists of (a) the risk (consisting of inherent risk and control risk) that the balance or class and related assertions contain misstatements that could be material to the financial statements when aggregated with misstatements in other balances or classes, and (b) the risk (detection risk) that the auditor will not detect such misstatement. The risk of these adverse events occurring jointly can be viewed as a function of the respective individual risks. Using professional judgment, the auditor evaluates numerous factors to assess inherent risk and control risk (assessing control risk at less than the maximum level involves performing tests of controls), and performs substantive tests (analytical procedures and test of details of account balances or classes of transactions) to restrict detection risk.

.09   Audit risk includes both uncertainties due to sampling and uncertainties due to factors other than sampling. These aspects of audit risk are sampling risk and nonsampling risk, respectively. [As amended August, 1983, by Statement on Auditing Standards No. 45.] (See section 313.)

.10   Sampling risk arises from the possibility that, when a test of controls or a substantive test is restricted to a sample, the auditor's conclusions may be different from the conclusions he would reach if the test were applied in the same way to all items in the account balance or class of transactions. That is, a particular sample may contain proportionately more or less monetary misstatements or deviations from prescribed controls than exist in the balance or class as a whole. For a sample of a specific design, sampling risk varies inversely with sample size: the smaller the sample size, the greater the sampling risk.

.11   Nonsampling risk includes all the aspects of audit risk that are not due to sampling. An auditor may apply a procedure to all transactions or balances and still fail to detect a material misstatement. Nonsampling risk includes the possibility of selecting audit procedures that are not appropriate to achieve the specific objective. For example, confirming recorded receivables cannot be relied on to reveal unrecorded receivables. Nonsampling risk also arises because the auditor may fail to recognize misstatements included in documents that he examines, which would make that procedure ineffective even if he were to examine all items. Nonsampling risk can be reduced to a negligible level through such factors as adequate planning and supervision (see section 311, *Planning and Supervision*) and proper conduct of a firm's audit practice (see section 161, *The Relationship of Generally Accepted Auditing Standards to Quality Control Standards*). [As amended August, 1983, by Statement on Auditing Standards No. 45.] (See section 313.)

Sampling Risk

.12   The auditor should apply professional judgment in assessing sampling risk. In performing substantive tests of details the auditor is concerned with two aspects of sampling risk:

- *The risk of incorrect acceptance* is the risk that the sample supports the conclusion that the recorded account balance is not materially misstated when it is materially misstated.

- *The risk of incorrect rejection* is the risk that the sample supports the conclusion that the recorded account balance is materially misstated when it is not materially misstated.

The auditor is also concerned with two aspects of sampling risk in performing tests of controls when sampling is used:

- *The risk of assessing control risk too low* is the risk that the assessed level of control risk based on the sample is less than the true operating effectiveness of the control.

- *The risk of assessing control risk too high* is the risk that the assessed level of control risk based on the sample is greater than the true operating effectiveness of the control.

.13   The risk of incorrect rejection and the risk of assessing control risk too high relate to the efficiency of the audit. For example, if the auditor's evaluation of an audit sample leads him to the initial erroneous conclusion that a balance is materially misstated when it is not, the application of additional audit procedures and consideration of other audit evidence would ordinarily lead the auditor to the correct conclusion. Similarly, if the auditor's evaluation of a sample leads him to unnecessarily assess control risk too high for an assertion, he would ordinarily increase the scope of substantive tests to compensation for the perceived ineffectiveness of the control. Although the audit may be less efficient in these circumstances, the audit is, nevertheless, effective.

.14   The risk of incorrect acceptance and the risk of assessing control risk too low relate to the effectiveness of an audit in detecting an existing material misstatement. These risks are discussed in the following paragraphs.

SAMPLING IN SUBSTANTIVE TESTS OF DETAILS

Planning Samples

.15   Planning involves developing a strategy for conducting an audit of financial statements. For general guidance on planning, see section 311, *Planning and Supervision*.

.16   When planning a particular sample for a substantive test of details, the auditor should consider

- The relationship of the sample to the relevant audit objective (see section 326, *Evidential Matter*).
- Preliminary judgments about materiality levels.
- The auditor's allowable risk of incorrect acceptance.
- Characteristics of the population, that is, the items comprising the account balance or class of transactions of interest.

.17   When planning a particular sample, the auditor should consider the specific audit objective to be achieved and should determine that the audit procedure, or combination of procedures, to be applied will achieve that objective. The auditor should determine that the population from which he draws the sample is appropriate for the specific audit objective. For example, an auditor would not be able to detect understatements of an account due to omitted items by sampling the recorded items. An appropriate sampling plan for detecting such understatements would involve selecting from a source in which the omitted items are included. To illustrate, subsequent cash disbursements might be sampled to test recorded accounts payable for understatement because of omitted purchases, or shipping documents might be sampled for understatement of sales due to shipments made but not recorded as sales.

.18   Evaluation in monetary terms of the results of a sample for a substantive test of details contributes directly to the auditor's purpose, since such an evaluation can be related to his judgment of the monetary amount of misstatements that would be material. When planning a sample for a substantive test of details, the auditor should consider how much monetary misstatement in the related account balance or class of transactions may exist without causing the financial statements to be materially misstated. This maximum monetary misstatement for the balance or class is called *tolerable misstatement* for the sample. Tolerable misstatement is a planning concept and is related to the auditor's preliminary judgments about materiality levels in such a way that tolerable misstatement, combined for the entire audit plan, does not exceed those estimates.

.19   The second standard of field work states, "A sufficient understanding of internal control is to be obtained to plan the audit and to determine the nature, timing, and extent of tests to be performed." After assessing and considering the levels of inherent and control risks, the auditor performs substantive tests to restrict detection risk to an acceptable level. As the assessed levels of inherent risk, control risk, and detection risk for other substantive procedures directed toward the same specific audit objective decrease, the auditor's allowable risk of incorrect acceptance for the substantive tests of details increases and, thus, the smaller the required sample size for the substantive tests of details. For example, if inherent and control risks are assessed at the maximum, and no other substantive tests directed toward the same specific audit objectives are performed, the auditor should allow for a low risk of incorrect acceptance for the substantive tests of details.[3] Thus, the auditor would select a larger sample size for the tests of details than if he allowed a higher risk of incorrect acceptance.

.20   The Appendix illustrates how the auditor may relate the risk of incorrect acceptance for a particular substantive test of details to his assessments of inherent risk, control risk, and the risk that analytical procedures and other relevant substantive tests would fail to detect material misstatement.

.21   As discussed in section 326, the sufficiency of tests of details for a particular account balance or class of transactions is related to the individual importance of the items examined as well as to the potential for material misstatement. When planning a sample for a substantive test of details, the auditor uses his judgment to determine which items, if any, in an account balance or class of transactions should be individually examined and which items, if any, should be subject to sampling. The auditor should examine those items for which, in his judgment, acceptance of some sampling risk is not justified. For example, these may include items for which

---

[3]Some auditors prefer to think of risk levels in quantitative terms. For example, in the circumstances described, an auditor might think in terms of a 5 percent risk of incorrect acceptance for the substantive tests of details. Risk levels used in sampling applications in other fields are not necessarily relevant to determining appropriate levels for applications in auditing because an audit includes many interrelated tests and sources of evidence.

potential misstatements could individually equal or exceed the tolerable misstatement. Any items that the auditor has decided to examine 100 percent are not part of the items subject to sampling. Other items that, in the auditor's judgment, need to be tested to fulfill the audit objective but need not be examined 100 percent, would be subject to sampling.

.22   The auditor may be able to reduce the required sample size by separating items subject to sampling into relatively homogeneous groups on the basis of some characteristic related to the specific audit objective. For example, common bases for such groupings are the recorded or book value of the items, the nature of internal control structure policies or procedures related to processing the items, and special considerations associated with certain items. An appropriate number of items is then selected from each group.

.23   To determine the number of items to be selected in a sample for a particular substantive test of details, the auditor should consider the tolerable misstatement, the allowable risk of incorrect acceptance, and the characteristics of the population. An auditor applies professional judgment to relate these factors in determining the appropriate sample size. The Appendix illustrates the effect these factors may have on sample size.

Sample Selection

.24   Sample items should be selected in such a way that the sample can be expected to be representative of the population. Therefore, all items in the population should have an opportunity to be selected. For example, haphazard and random-based selection of items represent two means of obtaining such samples.[4]

Performance and Evaluation

.25   Auditing procedures that are appropriate to the particular audit objective should be applied to each sample item. In some circumstances the auditor may not be able to apply the planned audit procedures to selected sample items because, for example, supporting documentation may be missing. The auditor's treatment of unexamined items will depend on their effect on his evaluation of the sample. If the auditor's evaluation of the sample results would not be altered by considering those unexamined items to be misstated, it is not necessary to examine the items. However, if considering those unexamined items to be misstated would lead to a conclusion that the balance or class contains material misstatement, the auditor should consider alternative procedures that would provide him with sufficient evidence to form a conclusion. The auditor should also consider whether the reasons for his

[4]Random-based selection includes, for example, random sampling, stratified random sampling, sampling with probability-proportional-to-size, and systematic sampling (for example, every hundredth item) with one or more random starts.

inability to examine the items have implications in relation to his planned assessed level of control risk or his degree of reliance on management representations.

.26   The auditor should project the misstatement results of the sample to the items from which the sample was selected.[5,6] There are several acceptable ways to project misstatements from a sample. For example, an auditor may have selected a sample of every twentieth item (50 items) from a population containing one thousand items. If he discovered overstatements of $3,000 in that sample, the auditor could project a $60,000 overstatement by dividing the amount of misstatement in the sample by the fraction of total items from the population included in the sample. The auditor should add that projection to the misstatements discovered in any items examined 100 percent. This total projected misstatement should be compared with the tolerable misstatement for the account balance or class of transactions, and appropriate consideration should be given to sampling risk. If the total projected misstatement is less than tolerable misstatement for the account balance or class of transactions, the auditor should consider the risk that such a result might be obtained even though the true monetary misstatement for the population exceeds tolerable misstatement. For example, if the tolerable misstatement in an account balance of $1 million is $50,000 and the total projected misstatement based on an appropriate sample (see paragraph .23) is $10,000, he may be reasonably assured that there is an acceptably low sampling risk that the true monetary misstatement for the population exceeds tolerable misstatement. On the other hand, if the total projected misstatement is close to the tolerable misstatement, the auditor may conclude that there is an unacceptably high risk that the actual misstatements in the population exceed the tolerable misstatement. An auditor uses professional judgment in making such evaluations.

.27   In addition to the evaluation of the frequency and amounts of monetary misstatements, consideration should be given to the qualitative aspects of the misstatements. These include (a) the nature and cause of misstatements, such as whether they are differences in principle or in application, are due to errors or fraud, or are due to misunderstanding of instructions or to carelessness, and (b) the possible relationship of the misstatements to other phases of the audit. The discovery of fraud ordinarily requires a broader consideration of possible implications than does the discovery of an error.

.28   If the sample results suggest that the auditor's planning assumptions were incorrect, he should take appropriate action. For example, if monetary misstatements are discovered in a substantive test of details in amounts or frequency that are greater than is consistent with the assessed levels of inherent and control risk, the auditor should alter his risk assessments. The auditor should also consider whether

---

[5]If the auditor has separated the items subject to sampling into relatively homogeneous groups (see paragraph .22), he separately projects the misstatement results of each group and sums them.

[6]See section 316, *Consideration of Fraud in a Financial Statement Audit,* paragraph .34, for a further discussion of the auditor's consideration of differences between the accounting records and the underlying facts and circumstances. This section provides specific guidance on the auditor's consideration of an audit adjustment that is, or may be, due to fraud.

to modify the other audit tests that were designed based upon the inherent and control risk assessments. For example, a large number of misstatements discovered in confirmation of receivables may indicate the need to reconsider the control risk assessment related to the assertions that impacted the design of substantive tests of sales or cash receipts.

.29 The auditor should relate the evaluation of the sample to other relevant audit evidence when forming a conclusion about the related account balance or class of transactions.

.30 Projected misstatement results for all audit sampling applications and all known misstatements from nonsampling applications should be considered in the aggregate along with other relevant audit evidence when the auditor evaluates whether the financial statements taken as a whole may be materially misstated.

SAMPLING IN TESTS OF CONTROLS

Planning Samples

.31 When planning a particular audit sample for a test of controls, the auditor should consider:

- The relationship of the sample to the objective of the test of controls.
- The maximum rate of deviations from prescribed controls that would support his planned assessed level of control risk.
- The auditor's allowable risk of assessing control risk too low.
- Characteristics of the population, that is, the items comprising the account balance or class of transactions of interest.

.32 For many tests of controls, sampling does not apply. Procedures performed to obtain an understanding of internal control sufficient to plan an audit do not involve sampling.[7] Sampling generally is not applicable to tests of controls that depend primarily on appropriate segregation of duties or that otherwise provide no documentary evidence of performance. In addition, sampling may not apply to tests of certain documented controls. Sampling may not apply to tests directed toward obtaining evidence about the design or operation of the control environment or the accounting system. For example, inquiry or observation of explanation of variances from budgets when the auditor does not desire to estimate the rate of deviation from the prescribed control.

---

[7]The auditor often plans to perform tests of controls concurrently with obtaining an understanding of internal control (see section 319.59) for the purpose of estimating the rate of deviation from the prescribed control, as to either the rate of such deviations or monetary amount of the related transactions. Sampling, as defined in this section, applies to such tests of controls.

.33 When designing samples for tests of controls the auditor ordinarily should plan to evaluate operating effectiveness in terms of deviations from prescribed controls, as to either the rate of such deviations or the monetary amount of the related transactions.[8] In this context, pertinent controls are ones that, had they not been included in the design of internal control would have adversely affected the auditor's planned assessed level of control risk. The auditor's overall assessment of control risk for a particular assertion involves combining judgments about the prescribed controls, the deviations from prescribed controls, and the degree of assurance provided by the sample and other tests of controls.

.34 The auditor should determine the maximum rate of deviations from the prescribed control that he would be willing to accept without altering his planned assessed level of control risk. This is the *tolerable rate*. In determining the tolerable rate, the auditor should consider (a) the planned assessed level of control risk, and (b) the degree of assurance desired by the evidential matter in the sample. For example, if the auditor plans to assess control risk at a low level, and he desires a high degree of assurance from the evidential matter provided by the sample for tests of controls (i.e., not perform other tests of controls for the assertion), he might decide that a tolerable rate of 5 percent or possibly less would be reasonable. If the auditor either plans to assess control risk at a higher level, or he desires assurance from other tests of controls along with that provided by the sample (such as inquiries of appropriate entity personnel or observation of the application of the policy or procedure), the auditor might decide that a tolerable rate of 10 percent or more is reasonable.

.35 In assessing the tolerable rate of deviations, the auditor should consider that, while deviations from pertinent controls increase the risk of material misstatements in the accounting records, such deviations do not necessarily result in misstatements. For example, a recorded disbursement that does not show evidence of required approval may nevertheless be a transaction that is properly authorized and recorded. Deviations would result in misstatements in the accounting records only if the deviations and the misstatements occurred on the same transactions. Deviations from pertinent control procedures at a given rate ordinarily would be expected to result in misstatements at a lower rate.

.36 In some situations, the risk of material misstatement for an assertion may be related to a combination of controls. If a combination of two or more controls is necessary to affect the risk of material misstatement for an assertion, those controls should be regarded as a single control, and deviations from any controls in combination should be evaluated on that basis.

.37 Samples taken to test the operating effectiveness of controls are intended to provide a basis for the auditor to conclude whether the controls are being applied as prescribed.

---

[8]For simplicity the remainder of this section will refer to only the rate of deviations.

When the degree of assurance desired by the evidential matter in the sample is high, the auditor should allow for a low level of sampling risk (that is, the risk of assessing control risk too low).[9]

.38   To determine the number of items to be selected for a particular sample for a test of controls, the auditor should consider the tolerable rate of deviation from the controls being tested, the likely rate of deviations, and the allowable risk of assessing control risk too low. An auditor applies professional judgment to relate these factors in determining the appropriate sample size.

Sample Selection

.39   Sample items should be selected in such a way that the sample can be expected to be representative of the population. Therefore, all items in the population should have an opportunity to be selected. Random-based selection of items represents one means of obtaining such samples. Ideally, the auditor should use a selection method that has the potential for selecting items from the entire period under audit. Section 319A.55 provides guidance applicable to the auditor's use of sampling during interim and remaining periods.

Performance and Evaluation

.40   Auditing procedures that are appropriate to achieve the objective of the test of controls should be applied to each sample item. If the auditor is not able to apply the planned audit procedures or appropriate alternative procedures to selected items, he should consider the reasons for this limitation, and he should ordinarily consider those selected items to be deviations from the prescribed control for the purpose of evaluating the sample.

.41   The deviation rate in the sample is the auditor's best estimate of the deviation rate in the population from which it was selected. If the estimated deviation rate is less than the tolerable rate for the population, the auditor should consider the risk that such a result might be obtained even though the true deviation rate for the population exceeds the tolerable rate for the population. For example, if the tolerable rate for a population is 5 percent and no deviations are found in a sample of 60 items, the auditor may conclude that there is an acceptably low sampling risk that the true deviation rate in the population exceeds the tolerable rate of 5 percent. On the other hand, if the sample includes, for example, two or more deviations, the auditor may conclude that there is an unacceptably high sampling risk that the rate of deviations in the population exceeds the tolerable rate of 5 percent. An auditor applies professional judgment in making such an evaluation.

---

[9]The auditor who prefers to think of risk levels in quantitative terms might consider, for example, a 5 percent to 10 percent risk of assessing control risk too low.

.42   In addition to the evaluation of the frequency of deviations from pertinent controls, consideration should be given to the qualitative aspects of the deviations. These include (a) the nature and cause of the deviations, such as whether they are due to errors or fraud or are due to misunderstanding of instructions or to careless-ness, and (b) the possible relationship of the deviations to other phases of the audit. The discovery of fraud ordinarily requires a broader consideration of possible impli-cations than does the discovery of an error.

.43   If the auditor concludes that the sample results do not support the planned assessed level of control risk for an assertion, he should reevaluate the nature, tim-ing, and extent of substantive procedures based on a revised consideration of the assessed level of control risk for the relevant financial statement assertions.

DUAL-PURPOSE SAMPLES

.44   In some circumstances the auditor may design a sample that will be used for dual purposes: assessing control risk and testing whether the recorded monetary amount of transactions is correct. In general, an auditor planning to use a dual-pur-pose sample would have made a preliminary assessment that there is an acceptably low risk that the rate of deviations from the prescribed control in the population exceeds the tolerable rate. For example, an auditor designing a test of a control over entries in the voucher register may plan a related substantive test at a risk level that anticipates an assessment level of control risk below the maximum. The size of a sample designed for dual purposes should be the larger of the samples that would otherwise have been designed for the two separate purposes. In evaluating such tests, deviations from pertinent procedures and monetary misstatements should be evaluated separately using the risk levels applicable for the respective purposes.

SELECTING A SAMPLING APPROACH

.45   As discussed in paragraph .04, either a nonstatistical or statistical approach to audit sampling, when properly applied, can provide sufficient evidential matter.

.46   Statistical sampling helps the auditor (a) to design an efficient sample, (b) to measure the sufficiency of the evidential matter obtained, and (c) to evaluate the sample results. By using statistical theory, the auditor can quantify sampling risk to assist himself in limiting it to a level he considers acceptable. However, statistical sampling involves additional costs of training auditors, designing individual sam-ples to meet the statistical requirements, and selecting the items to be examined. Because either nonstatistical or statistical sampling can provide sufficient evidential matter, the auditor chooses between them after considering their relative cost and effectiveness in the circumstances.

EFFECTIVE DATE

.47 This section is effective for audits of financial statements for periods ended on or after June 25, 1983. Earlier application is encouraged. [As amended, effective retroactively to June 25, 1982, by Statement on Auditing Standards No. 43.]

APPENDIX

Relating the Risk of Incorrect Acceptance for a Substantive Test of Details to Other Sources of Audit Assurance

1. Audit risk, with respect to a particular account balance or class of transactions, is the risk that there is a monetary misstatement greater than tolerable misstatement affecting an assertion in an account balance or class of transactions that the auditor fails to detect. The auditor uses professional judgment in determining the allowable risk for a particular audit after he considers such factors as the risk of material misstatement in the financial statements, the cost to reduce the risk, and the effect of the potential misstatements on the use and understanding of the financial statements.

2. An auditor assesses inherent and control risk, and plans and performs substantive tests (analytical procedures and substantive tests of details) in whatever combination to reduce audit risk to an appropriate level. However, the second standard of field work contemplates that ordinarily the assessed level of control risk cannot be sufficiently low to eliminate the need to perform any substantive tests to restrict detection risk for all of the assertions relevant to significant account balances or transactions classes.

3. The sufficiency of audit sample sizes, whether nonstatistical or statistical, is influenced by several factors. Table 1 illustrates how several of these factors may affect sample sizes for a substantive test of details. Factors a, b, and c in Table 1 should be considered together (see paragraph .08). For example, high inherent risk, the lack of effective controls, and the absence of other substantive tests related to the same audit objective ordinarily require larger sample sizes for related substantive tests of details than if there were other sources to provide the basis for assessing inherent or control risks below the maximum, or if other substantive tests related to the same objective were performed. Alternatively, low inherent risk, effective controls, or effective analytical procedures and other relevant substantive tests may lead the auditor to conclude that the sample, if any, needed for an additional test of details can be small.

Table 1   Factors Influencing Sample Sizes for a Substantive Test of Details in Sample Planning

| Factor | Conditions leading to | | Related factor for substantive sample planning |
	Smaller sample size	Larger sample size	
a. Assessment of inherent risk.	Low assessed level of inherent risk.	High assessed level of inherent risk.	Allowable risk of incorrect acceptance.
b. Assessment of control risk.	Low assessed level of control risk.	High assessed level of control risk.	Allowable risk of incorrect acceptance.
c. Assessment of risk for other substantive tests related to the same assertion (including analytical procedures and other relevant substantive tests).	Low assessment of risk associated with other relevant substantive tests.	High assessment of risk associated with other relevant substantive tests.	Allowable risk of incorrect acceptance.
d. Measure of tolerable misstatement for a specific account.	Larger measure of tolerable misstatement.	Smaller measure of tolerable misstatement.	Tolerable misstatement.
e. Expected size and frequency of misstatements.	Smaller misstatements or lower frequency.	Larger misstatements or higher frequency.	Assessment of population characteristics.
f. Number of items in the population.	Virtually no effect on sample size unless population is very small.		

4. The following model expresses the general relationship of the risks associated with the auditor's assessment of inherent and control risks, and the effectiveness of analytical procedures (including other relevant substantive tests) and substantive tests of details. The model is not intended to be a mathematical formula including all factors that may influence the determination of individual risk components; however, some auditors find such a model to be useful when planning appropriate risk levels for audit procedures to achieve the auditor's desired audit risk.

$$AR = IR \times CR \times AP \times TD$$

An auditor might use this model to obtain an understanding of an appropriate risk of incorrect acceptance for a substantive test of details as follows:

$$TD = AR/(IR \times CR \times AP)$$

AR = The allowable audit risk that monetary misstatements equal to tolerable misstatement might remain undetected for the account balance or class of transactions and related assertions after the auditor has completed all audit procedures deemed necessary.[10] The auditor uses his professional judgment to determine the allowable audit risk after considering factors such as those discussed in paragraph 1 of this Appendix.

IR = Inherent risk is the susceptibility of an assertion to a material misstatement assuming there are no related controls.

CR = Control risk is the risk that a material misstatement that could occur in an assertion will not be prevented or detected on a timely basis by the entity's controls. The auditor may assess control risk at the maximum, or assess control risk below the maximum based on the sufficiency of evidential matter obtained to support the effectiveness of controls. The quantification for this model relates to the auditor's evaluation of the overall effectiveness of those controls that would prevent or detect material misstatements equal to tolerable misstatement in the related account balance or class of transactions. For example, if the auditor believes that pertinent controls would prevent or detect misstatements equal to tolerable misstatement about half the time, he would assess this risk as 50 percent. (CR is not the same as the risk of assessing control risk too low.)

AP = The auditor's assessment of the risk that analytical procedures and other relevant substantive tests would fail to detect misstatements that could occur in an assertion equal to tolerable misstatement, given that such misstatements occur and are not detected by internal control.

TD = The allowable risk of incorrect acceptance for the substantive test of details, given that misstatements equal to tolerable misstatement occur in an assertion and are not detected by internal control or analytical procedures and other relevant substantive tests.

5. The auditor planning a statistical sample can use the relationship in paragraph 4 of this Appendix to assist in planning his allowable risk of incorrect accept-

---

[10]For purposes of this Appendix, the nonsampling risk aspect of audit risk is assumed to be negligible, based on the level of quality controls in effect. [Footnote amended August, 1983, by Statement on Auditing Standards No. 45.] (See section 313.)

ance for a specific substantive test of details. To do so, he selects an acceptable audit risk (AR), and substantively quantifies his judgment of risks IR, CR, and AP. Some levels of these risks are implicit in evaluating audit evidence and reaching conclusions. Auditors using the relationship prefer to evaluate these judgment risks explicitly.

6. The relationships between these independent risks are illustrated in Table 2. In Table 2 it is assumed, for illustrative purposes, that the auditor has chosen an audit risk of 5 percent for an assertion where inherent risk has been assessed at the maximum. Table 2 incorporates the premise that no internal control system can be expected to be completely effective in detecting aggregate misstatements equal to tolerable misstatement that might occur. The table also illustrates the fact that the risk level for substantive tests for particular assertions is not an isolated decision. Rather, it is a direct consequence of the auditor's assessments of inherent and control risks, and judgments about the effectiveness of analytical procedures and other relevant substantive tests, and it cannot be properly considered out of this context. [As amended August, 1983, by Statement on Auditing Standards No. 45.] (See section 313.)

Table 2   Allowable Risk of Incorrect Acceptance (TD) for Various Assessments of CR and AP; for AR - .05 and IR - 5 1.0

Auditor's subjective assessment of control risk.		Auditor's subjective assessment of risk that analytical procedures and other relevant substantive tests might fail to detect aggregate misstatements equal to tolerable misstatement.			
		AP			
		10%	30%	50%	100%
		TD			
CR					
		*	*	*	50%
10%		*	55%	33%	16%
30%					
50%		*	33%	20%	10%
100%		50%	16%	10%	5%

*The allowable level of AR of 5 percent exceeds the product of IR, CR, and AP, and thus, the planned substantive test of details may not be necessary.

NOTE: The table entries for TD are computed from the illustrated model: TD equals $AR/(IR \times CR \times AP)$. For example, for IR = 1.0, CR = .50, AP = .30, TD = $.05/(1.0 \times .50 \times .30)$ or .33 (equals 33%).

D APPENDIX D: AUDIT SAMPLING: AUDITING INTERPRETATIONS OF SECTION 350

1. APPLICABILITY

.01 *Question*—Section 350, *Audit Sampling,* paragraph .01, footnote 1, states that there may be reasons other than sampling for an auditor to examine less than 100 percent of the items comprising an account balance or class of transactions. For what reasons might an auditor's examination of less than 100 percent of the items comprising an account balance or class of transactions *not* be considered audit sampling?

.02 *Interpretation*—The auditor's examination of less than 100 percent of the items comprising an account balance or class of transactions would not be considered to be an audit sampling application under the following circumstances.

a. *It is not the auditor's intent to extend the conclusion that he reaches by examining the items to the remainder of the items in the account balance or class.* Audit sampling is defined as the application of an audit procedure to less than 100 percent of the items within an account balance or class of transactions for the purpose of evaluating some characteristic of the balance or class. Thus, if the purpose of the auditor's application of an auditing procedure to less than 100 percent of the items in an account balance or class of transactions is something other than evaluating a trait of the entire balance or class, he is not using audit sampling.

For example, an auditor might trace several transactions through an entity's accounting system to gain an understanding of the nature of the entity's operations or clarify his understanding of the design of the entity's internal control. In such cases the auditor's intent is to gain a general understanding of the accounting system or other relevant parts of internal control, rather than the evaluation of a characteristic of all transactions processed. As a result, the auditor is not using audit sampling.

265

Occasionally auditors perform procedures such as checking arithmetical calculations or tracing journal entries into ledger accounts on a test basis. When such procedures are applied to less than 100 percent of the arithmetical calculations or ledger postings that affect the financial statements, audit sampling may not be involved if the procedure is not a test to evaluate a characteristic of an account balance or class of transactions, but is intended only to provide limited knowledge that supplements the auditor's other evidential matter regarding a financial statement assertion.

b. *Although he might not be examining all the items in an account balance or class of transactions, the auditor might be examining 100 percent of the items in a given population.* A "population" for audit sampling purposes does not necessarily need to be an entire account balance or class of transactions. For example, in some circumstances, an auditor might examine all of the items that comprise an account balance or class of transactions that exceed a given amount or that have an unusual characteristic and either apply other auditing procedures (e.g., analytical procedures) to those items that do not exceed the given amount or possess the unusual characteristic or apply no auditing procedures to them because of their insignificance. Again, the auditor is not using audit sampling. Rather, he has broken the account balance or class of transactions into two groups. One group is tested 100 percent, the other group is either tested by analytical procedures or considered insignificant. The auditor would be using audit sampling only if he applied an auditing procedure to less than all of the items in the second group to form a conclusion about that group. For the same reason, cutoff tests often do not involve audit sampling applications. In performing cutoff tests auditors often examine all significant transactions for a period surrounding the cut-off date and, as a result, such tests do not involve the application of audit sampling.

c. *The auditor is testing controls that are not documented.* Auditors choose from a variety of methods including inquiry, observation, and examination of documentary evidence in testing controls. For example, observation of a client's physical inventory count procedures is a test that is performed primarily through the auditor's observation of controls over such things as inventory movement, counting procedures and other procedures used by the client to control the count of the inventory. The procedures that the auditor uses to observe the client's physical inventory count generally do not require use of audit sampling. However, audit sampling may be used in certain tests of controls or substantive tests of details of inventory, for example, in tracing selected test counts into inventory records.

d. *The auditor is not performing a substantive test of details.* Substantive tests consist of tests of details of transactions and balances, analytical review and/or a combination of both. In performing substantive tests, audit sampling is generally used only in testing details of transactions and balances.

[Issue Date: January, 1985.]

INDEX